# SPIRITUALITY
# AND
# JUSTICE

## DONAL DORR

GILL AND MACMILLAN
Dublin

ORBIS BOOKS
Maryknoll, New Yo

Published in Ireland by
Gill and Macmillan Ltd
Goldenbridge
Dublin 8
with associated companies in Auckland, Dallas, Delhi,
Hong Kong, Johannesburg, Lagos, London, Manzini,
Melbourne, Nairobi, New York, Singapore, Tokyo, Washington

Published in the USA and Canada by
Orbis Books, Maryknoll
Maryknoll, New York 10545

7171 1376 0 (Gill and Macmillan)

0-88344-449-6 (Orbis Books)

Print origination in Ireland by Print Prep Ltd, Dublin
Printed in Hong Kong

# Contents

# Introduction

In this book I examine the relationship between spirituality and justice. These are the two topics on which, I believe, most religious and theological interest centres today. At present, the links between the two are rather strained. Many of those who are most concerned about social justice find themselves reacting against the traditional spirituality. They believe it lacks a social dimension: it seems to them to presume and promote a rather individualistic understanding of the faith. They also find it escapist at times — encouraging the Christian to look for salvation outside this world or in some interior, purely spiritual dimension of it. On the other hand, many of those who are most concerned with spirituality find themselves reacting against the social activists. While admiring those who dedicate their lives to working for justice, they perceive in many of them a lack of serenity, a restless activism, and at times a smouldering anger which can be destructive of themselves and others.

I believe that a lot of people on both sides of this divide are looking for a way to link spirituality with justice. Those who are exploring old and new forms of spirituality are well aware of the risk of individualism and complacency. They see the danger of forgetting that, for the Christian, salvation is not *from* the world but is salvation *of* the world; and the related danger of using prayer to escape from facing up to the massive injustice in society today. So they are deeply troubled as they ask themselves where they stand in relation to the poor and the oppressed.

People in this situation would like to be able to integrate into their spirituality an effective commitment to justice in society. However, they are rather intimidated by what this

1

seems to involve. They are mystified and threatened by such phrases as 'social analysis' and 'structural injustice'. When confronted with the jargon of economics many of them go blank. Yet they have the feeling that in order to get seriously involved in working for justice they would need to study economics and political philosophy. I believe they would welcome a fairly simple account of the meaning of structural injustice — especially if it could find a place for spirituality.

On the other hand, many of those who have persevered in the struggle for justice have become aware of the importance of a spirituality of justice. They feel an urgent need for a nourishment of the spirit that will enable them to continue their work in the face of apathy and opposition. Some have had the experience of becoming 'burned out', drained of life and hope. They have perhaps come to believe that they need not just a spirituality of justice but a wider spirituality. The commitment to justice would have a prominent place in it, but it would also include other aspects of the Christian faith.

The aim of this book is to respond to the needs of these two groups of people. I would like to help each group to see the importance of the values stressed by the other. But what I hope to do is something more than just mediate between the two groups. I believe that many on both sides are looking for some kind of synthesis. I would like this book to be of help to them in their search. I hope I can convey something of the integrated view I have been struggling to work out for myself.

The book links together the two main topics which have engaged my theological and pastoral attention over the past ten years. The topics are religious experience and social justice. Being interested in the two subjects at the same time, I was able to some extent to deal with both of them together in seminars and workshops. But, when it came to writing, the two seemed so far apart that I had to treat them separately.

In 1978 I published a book entitled *Remove the Heart of Stone*. In it I explored the religious experience of the Christian — and particularly the breakthrough into full consciousness of the reality symbolised by baptism. In that book my attention was focused on the personal aspects of Christian faith, with some consideration of the supportive role which can be played by a group. I did not attempt to examine in any

2

detail the more public aspects of faith — the call of the Christian to transform society. I felt just a little uneasy about the favourable reaction of some readers: they seemed to assume that I agreed with them that the personal and interpersonal aspects of faith are so fundamental that the public or 'political' aspects are of secondary importance.

In 1983 I published another book. It was entitled *Option for the Poor: A Hundred Years of Vatican Social Teaching.* As the title indicates, it is a study of the evolution of the teaching of the Catholic Church on a major theme of social justice. This book seemed to put me firmly into the camp of those whose attention is focused mainly on the public aspect of the faith. But in fact I had not swung from one extreme to the other. It was simply that this too is an important topic which seemed to me to require exploration.

During the writing of that study of Catholic social teaching I had to exercise a certain discipline. The material was sparking off various thoughts in me — ideas that I was tempted to incorporate into the book. I decided not to add to the Vatican teaching anything except the background material that I felt was needed to interpret and explain it. But I promised myself — and my publishers — to write another book, one that would be much more personal, giving my own views on the whole question of what it means to make an option for the poor.

This new book offered me the chance to bring together in writing the themes of social justice and religious experience. For some time I was not quite sure whether I could manage it successfully. I began writing chapters on the different topics, more or less at the same time, moving from one to the other as interest or inspiration led me. Gradually the outline of an overall framework emerged. But for quite a long time I was not sure how much to include in this book. As I explain at the beginning of Chapter 13, I was tempted to omit the treatment of prayer and providence — afraid that I might fail to communicate my sense of how this is related to social justice. After a good deal of re-writing I feel fairly satisfied with my attempt to present an integrated spirituality that takes account of the personal, interpersonal, and public aspects of the Christian faith.

I have covered a lot of material in the book; and I have

adapted the style of writing to suit the topic. In some places I have simply shared my own experience in the hope that it may strike a chord in some readers. Other parts of the book are rather more theological; for there are words like 'liberation' and 'evangelisation' which need to be explained. There are various sections in which I have treated matters of economics. I know from experience that many religious people are inclined to 'switch off' once anybody begins to deal with economics. So I have tried to give this material in fairly small doses and to illustrate it with topical or personal examples. In spite of this, I expect some readers may get 'bogged down' in places. I would encourage such readers to skip ahead. Even though the various chapters follow on from each other, I see no reason why people should not take the parts they want from a book like this.

In order to facilitate this choice of material I give here a brief indication of the content of each of the fourteen chapters:

— In the first chapter I give the overall framework for what I consider to be a balanced spirituality. It is one that is concerned with the three main spheres of life — the personal sphere, the interpersonal sphere, and that of the wider society.

— In the second chapter I develop this by examining more closely what is meant by spirituality, and how it relates to theology. I include examples of how people can mould their theology to justify their options in life.

— The third chapter develops this last point more fully by examining the claim of Third World theologians that Western theology is used to give respectability to the present unjust world order.

— In the fourth chapter I go on to explain what is meant by 'an unjust world order'. I try to clarify the distinction between personal injustice and structural injustice. Then I go on to explain how 'development', which was supposed to solve the problem of poverty, has actually given rise to structural injustice.

— In the fifth chapter I begin the task of seeing what can be done to overcome structural injustice; the first thing is to clarify what is meant by an option for the poor.

— In the sixth chapter I examine the basis in the Old and New Testaments for such an option.

— In the next six chapters I give an extended treatment of

4

what it would mean in practice to make an option for the poor. This is done by considering first the alternative values that one is opting for, and then seeing how these values can be embodied in an alternative kind of society. The seventh chapter is devoted first to clarification of the notion of 'Kingdom values', and then to an examination of five such values — unity, security, justice, work, and progress.

— In the eighth chapter I go on to look at four other Kingdom values, ones that are more generally thought of as being 'religious' in character. They are: relationships, rootedness, harmony, and hope.

— In the ninth chapter I move on to examine how these values are to be realised in the structures of society. I consider the alternatives open to us in the economic sphere — both at the 'macro' level of national or global policy, and at the 'micro' level of personal life-style.

— In the tenth chapter I examine alternative approaches in political life, in education, and in the structures and life of the Church.

— The eleventh chapter is devoted to a study of alternative theologies — mainly from the Third World, but also in the First World.

— In the second section of this chapter I take up the challenge of trying to do theology in the context of Ireland, a small country on the periphery of the First World. I give an extended treatment of the Irish situation and offer suggestions about an alternative approach.

— The twelfth chapter is devoted to clarifying the meaning of the terms 'evangelisation', 'development', 'liberation', and 'mission'. I suggest that the meaning given to these words depends on the 'mindset' of the person who uses them.

— In the thirteenth chapter I turn to the question of prayer. I study two moods in which one may pray — freedom of spirit and desperation; and I examine how prayer leads to a certain convergence of the two.

— In the fourteenth chapter, which is the final one, I examine the question of whether, or how, our prayers are answered. I consider whether the concept of providence encourages people to use prayer as an escape from action. I suggest ways in which we may help the poor to re-discover a truly biblical concept of providence, one that inspires them to work for human liberation.

I wrote the book over the past year in a very remote rural mission in tropical Africa. But many of the ideas in it were worked out over the previous four years. During those years I divided my time between study in Ireland and work with groups in Africa and at home. My study dealt with the theology of development and social justice — and the bits of economics and other sciences required to make this theology realistic. My work with groups consisted mainly of specialised workshops for people engaged in working for human development, liberation, and justice.

I hope and believe that these different experiences have all left their mark on the book. Trying to write a 'modern' book in a situation where I am cut off from many of the amenities I had taken for granted (libraries, bookshops, phones, electricity, a reliable and prompt postal service) has helped me to appreciate how handicapped the poor are in trying to compete with the rich. But this rural setting has also given me the opportunity to appreciate the values of traditional life, and to learn from the people who live it. Being cut off from the centres of power has also given me a certain distance and perspective from which to look at the global situation — and at my previous work.

I owe very much to the members of the teams and groups with whom I have worked over the past few years. What they gave me, above all, was their experience of working 'on the ground'. I hope that the effect has been to make this book a response to real issues, real questions. These friends also inspired and challenged me. Ideas were sparked off in our interaction; so much so that I would find it hard to know how much I have borrowed from others. But I know that they believe with me that ideas and insights are to be shared, not hoarded. In Kenya I learned very much from the 'Anne Hope and Sally Timmel team', which evolved into the CDES team coordinated by Ikalur — and by their partners throughout Kenya and in other parts of Africa. There are many people in Ireland, Nigeria and elsewhere whose names I would like to mention here; but I know it would only cause embarrassment or trouble to some of them; so I have decided to mention just three people. Berne Okure helps me to believe in the work I am doing at present. Michael Campbell-Johnston has nourished me with invaluable material sent at intervals

6

from Rome. Finally, I take this opportunity to say 'thank you' in print to my brother Frank for inspiration and support — and for some of what I consider to be the more interesting ideas in this book, particularly in Chapter 9. I am especially grateful to three friends who read most of the text at different stages of its composition. They seemed to sense how much of myself had gone into it; and I felt they were not just responding to the book but were offering to me the life-giving encouragement I needed.

I want to express here (as I did in my last book) my gratitude to the authorities and staffs of two institutions of the Irish Church. They are *Trocaire*: the Catholic Agency for World Development, and Maynooth College. They sponsored and supported me while I was doing research on social justice. I hope that nobody connected with these institutions will be embarrassed or hurt by anything I have said in this book about theology or the Church, or about the Irish situation.

Not that I expect every reader to agree with all that I am saying. The book is a very personal one — much more so than is common in religious or theological books. I decided to include personal experiences and impressions because I feel that a lot of today's theology is written in an academic desert. I am trying to find ways of bringing life into theology. This experiment leaves me rather vulnerable — but maybe that is a good thing. It may perhaps encourage others — especially those who may disagree with me — to respond rather than just react. My highest hope for the book is that it would lead to a dialogue. In such a dialogue we could perhaps speak God's word to each other — to challenge us in our complacency and to give us Good News in our weakness.

Donal Dorr, March 1984

Most biblical quotations are taken from *The Good News Bible* (the Bible Societies and Collins Fontana). In some cases, however, I have used the RSV translation (Collins Fontana). Occasionally I have combined or adapted these translations or made my own.

An earlier draft of Chapter 1 was published in *The Furrow*, December 1983. Excerpts from earlier drafts of Chapter 14 and Chapter 15 have appeared in the missionary periodical *Africa*.

# 1

# A Balanced Spirituality

There is a passage in the Book of Micah which is used as the chorus for a very beautiful hymn:
  This is what Yahweh asks of you, only this:
  That you act justly,
  That you love tenderly,
  That you walk humbly with your God (Micah 6:8).
The three demands made by the Lord in this text provide the basis for a balanced spirituality. Many of the distorted spiritualities one meets today can be explained in terms of an over-emphasis on one or other of these three demands, to the neglect of others. In speaking of a spirituality here I do not mean just a set of theological ideas. I am thinking more of the outlook and attitudes we have; our spirituality is revealed not so much by the theories we propose as by the way we act and react. It is an *implicit* theology which, if we are reflective and articulate, may eventually become explicit — and then it is very convincing because it represents a truth that is lived.

### 'Walk humbly with your God'
We can begin by looking at the demand that we 'walk humbly with God'. I take this to refer to my personal relationship with God. Each one of us is called to a deeply personal *religious conversion.* This may be sudden or gradual; more likely it will come in the form of a combination of slow growth with some rather dramatic breakthroughs. What really matters is not so much the process as the effect — namely, an awareness that God has carved my name on the palm of his hand, so that even if a woman should forget her baby at the breast, God will not forget me (Is 49:15-16).

8

This sense of the love and care of God is what changes the notion of providence from an abstract theological theory into a living experience. It is a consciousness that even the hairs of my head are numbered and that not even a sparrow falls to the ground without God's permission (Mt 10:29).

The sense of providence is both the cause and the effect of my conviction that it makes sense to speak of 'the plan of God'. God is acting in my life to carry out his will for me; and what God wills is my salvation. The Lord is leading me, shaping me through the events of my daily life, enabling me to overcome obstacles and to grow in the way he wants me, so that I can become fully human, fully healed, and therefore a person who is of the kingdom, as Jesus was.

In the final chapter of this book I shall try to give a theological explanation of the Christian concept of Providence. In this first chapter I want simply to insist that theologians must resist the temptation to explain away either of the key elements in it, namely, God's sovereignty and human freedom. It may be difficult for the theologian to find some overall framework in which both elements are given their full weight. But theology is built on faith; it must respect the data of the Christian faith as found both in the Bible and in the living experience of Christians. So, as a theologian I do not doubt that I am free — at least in some degree; that is part of my experience and of my faith. Neither do I doubt that my free human actions are somehow used by God as part of his loving plan; that too is part of my faith — and even, in a sense, of my experience.

The sense of providence may begin with an awareness of God's care for me personally; but it does not end there — for otherwise religious conversion and personal religion would be reduced to a purely private affair between God and myself. I see the hand of God not merely in my own life but also in the lives of my friends. I can be led on to believe that God's plan of salvation is all-embracing — it touches the lives of nations as well as individuals. My trials, my rescue, my being led into a more authentic pattern of living, my whole destiny — all these are fitted by God into the destiny of my people and of all peoples. The Old Testament constantly keeps this perspective before us; for instance, God's care for Judith and for Cyrus is an integral part of his saving plan for his people (Judith 9:5-14; 13:24-25; Is 45:1-6).

9

The awareness that I am in the hands of God is a gift, one of his greatest graces; but somebody who is over-anxious or frenetically active is not really able to accept this gift. In order to be open to it, I need a certain peace and tranquillity, as the psychological under-pinning for the sense of providence. This deep peace of mind and heart is nourished by regular extended periods of prayer. In prayer I learn to let the harassments of daily life flow away. Presumably this is what Jesus was doing when, having been besieged by crowds all day, he went off alone to pray in the hills at night (e.g. Mt 14:23). Prayer is even more necessary if I want to retain the sense of God's providence when everything goes wrong, when others reject me, and when evil shows its full power. In such situations one follows Jesus into the agony prayer, as he struggles to recognise God's hand in the failure and tragedy that envelop him (Mt 26:36-44).

In his parable about the Pharisee and the tax-collector at prayer in the Temple, Jesus expressed a central feature of what it means to 'walk humbly with God'. To find oneself converted religiously is to experience a sense of forgiveness. This is not merely pardon for past sin but, above all, the awareness of being loved and accepted in spite of, and even in a sense because of, my weakness, my faithlessness, my lack of single-mindedness, my inability to respond as I would wish (Rom 7:21). With the tax-collector I pray: 'O God, be merciful to me a sinner' (Lk 18:13) — knowing that I shall have to make the same prayer tomorrow; for God's acceptance of my prayer does not justify me in such a way that I can tomorrow pray the prayer of the Pharisee.

The sense of providence is so central to religious conversion that it would seem that it must be present, at least in some implicit way, in *any* authentic religion. One of the most distinctive features of the Christian faith, as compared with other religions, is that it gives a very explicit expression to this sense of the love and care of God: Jesus reveals the *Fatherhood* of God even more thoroughly than was done in the Old Testament. (And of course there is a motherly aspect to God's care as well — cf. Ps 131:2; Is 42:14; 49:15; Jer 31:20 — as there is to the concern of Jesus who compares himself to a mother hen, Mt 23:37.)

The issue of the explicitness of the Christian sense of providence is not, however, quite as simple as I have suggested so far. There are many fine Christians who have what Karl Rahner would call 'a winter experience' of faith. Their sense of God's care seldom reaches the degree of explicitness which I outlined above; and they can speak of God's 'plan' — and especially of God's 'intervention' in their lives — only with many reservations and hesitations. On the other hand there are enthusiastic Christians who speak of God as though he were constantly at their disposal, like a 'Mr Fixit'. Our Christian instinct may recognise an authenticity in the 'winter experience' of faith which contrasts sharply with the glibness and triviality of the other.

I am not saying that the genuine Christian must always remain somewhat agnostic in regard to providence; in fact I have been claiming that the Christian conception of providence is remarkably explicit; but I want now to add a corrective to that position. All the words we use to express our sense of providence — 'love', 'care', 'fatherhood/motherhood', 'plan of God', 'God's presence and interventions', etc. — all these are used *analogously*. We are trying to find human words to express aspects of our relationship to a God who remains transcendent, beyond human comprehension. If these words we use are not to distort the full depth of the Christian experience, they have to be balanced out and qualified in some way. This balancing can sometimes be done by using other words. But it is done more effectively by *silence* — by being struck dumb, by being confronted with the inexpressible, the mysterious. The mystery is so deep that it cannot be conveyed in simple, univocal words; yet to use complex and difficult words seems to distort it even further. It is better then to be childlike — to be willing to use the simple words as Jesus did, while retaining the child's sense of wonder and humility.

I have already given many references to the Old and New Testament to show that the Christian conception of providence is quite explicit. But there is also a solid biblical basis for a certain degree of 'agnosticism' about God's plans and about the divine action in our world. For instance, Judith says: 'If you cannot sound the depths of the human heart or penetrate even the human mind, how can you fathom the God who made all things, or sound his mind, or unravel his purposes?'

11

(Judith 8:14). Again, the climax of the Book of Job is reached when Job, having been confronted by the incomprehensible power of God, has to confess: 'My words have been frivolous . . . I have spoken once but I will not speak again. . . . I have been holding forth on matters that I cannot understand, on marvels beyond me . . .' (Job 40:45; 42:3). Even Jesus, the beloved Son of the Father, has to say, 'as for that day, only the Father knows it, nobody else — not even the Son' (Mt 24:36). So a spirituality of providence has to be expressed not only in words but also in meaningful silence.

The Christian sense of providence includes a sense of the Lordship of Jesus Christ — in my personal life and in human history as a whole. What does it mean to have Jesus as the Lord of my life? The way in which I understand it is that I feel called to allow Jesus to be the criterion of my plans and actions: I discern the consonance or discordance between my proposed line of action and the life of Jesus. To accept Jesus as the Lord of my life is to allow my hopes and projects and concerns to be judged by his 'Way', his pattern of living as it shows itself to me in the gospels when I savour them in prayer. As for the Lordship of Jesus in human history: at present I experience this mainly through my commitment to a transformation of the world in accordance with the Kingdom values proclaimed by Jesus — above all in the Sermon on the Mount (Mt ch. 5-7; cf. Lk 6:17-49). At this point the demand to 'walk humbly with God' overlaps with the demand to 'act justly', which I shall be looking at in the third section of this chapter.

*'Love tenderly'*

The second demand of the Lord as expressed by Micah, the call to 'love tenderly', can be taken to refer to a second major area of Christian spirituality, namely, the interpersonal aspect. Here we are concerned with face-to-face relationships with other people — including friendships, family life, community living and even our more casual relationships. There is of course a great variety in the way I have to relate to others: at one end of the spectrum are my deepest friendships and at the other end are my contacts with those I meet in a passing way. But I am called to love them all — even to love them 'tenderly'. This means treating everybody with respect and gentleness in a manner appropriate to the kind of relationship.

12

I have suggested in the previous section that to 'walk humbly' with God we need to be *religiously* converted; I want now to add that to 'love tenderly' we need to be *morally* converted. The person who is morally converted in a deep degree has been given the gift of being other-centred, genuinely interested in other people. This is something that can be sensed very quickly, even by people who meet this person for the first time. It establishes a *rapport* which can eliminate the need for the cautious small-talk and the reconnoitring and skirmishing that characterises many relationships.

A crucial element in moral conversion is the willingness to expose oneself, by trusting the other person. It is really a matter of *entrusting* myself to the other, allowing myself to be vulnerable. This is what 'openness' means — being willing to take the risk of leaving myself open to rejection or hurt.

Moral conversion, like religious conversion, is a gift, a grace. I cannot just decide to be trusting, open to others. But when the gift is offered I can refuse it, or accept it only grudgingly and partially. Alternatively, I can recognise what a great gift is being offered, welcome it with open arms, and push it as far as possible, trusting 'the reasons of the heart' to lead me between the extremes of a 'cagey' reserve and an off-putting brashness.

If I am to share myself with others in an openness that is not cloying, the precondition is an ability really to *listen*. Some people are naturally good listeners while others are too self-conscious, or too anxious, to be able to listen well. Both the good listeners and those who find it hard to give their undivided attention to others can benefit from some training in what we might call 'deep listening'. What I have in mind is the kind of short training courses offered by the 'Co-counselling International' movement. There we can learn to give to the other person our full 'free attention' without allowing our own concerns or distress to interfere with respectful listening.

Really to listen to a person is already to affirm that person in a deep way. It allows the person to 'feel heard' and accepted rather than judged. Mostly that is the kind of affirmation that people need and want. But where there is a deep or more intimate relationship it may on occasion be appropriate to show our love for the other either by a more explicit expres-

13

sion of affirmation or of sympathy, or by challenging the person respectfully.

The Lord's demand that we 'love tenderly' also includes a demand for *fidelity*. Spontaneous openness and patient listening must be offered not just in the first flowering of friendship; our love is to be modelled on the enduring faithful love that God shows us (e.g. Jer 31:13). Therefore moral conversion involves not merely the power to reach out to others but also the power to 'stay with' them, to be loyal even in the difficult times. The prophet Hosea shows the limitless extent of this tender love which endures even in the face of the unfaithfulness of the other person (Hos 3:1-2).

There is a close relationship between the ability to 'love tenderly' and the power to 'walk humbly', between moral conversion and religious conversion. In order to be able to relate deeply and enduringly to others I need to be in touch with, and able to cope with, the negative parts of my own personality especially my feelings of inadequacy and fear. Religious conversion helps me to accept myself in my weakness. This gives me the kind of sympathy I need to have with others who, willingly or unwillingly, reveal themselves to me in their inadequacies as well as their gifts.

*'Act justly'*

The third element in a balanced spirituality is expressed in the demand of the Lord that we 'act justly'. Like the request that we 'love tenderly', this is a moral matter. But it merits separate mention because now we are no longer in the sphere of interpersonal, face-to-face relationships but in the area of public life, the political sphere. Justice is to be understood primarily as concerned with how society is organised, how wealth, power, privileges, rights, and responsibilities are distributed to every level — local, national, and global. Commutative justice — the kind of justice that deals with how individuals relate to each other — should be fitted into the wider pattern established by social justice for society as a whole; the older text-book theology wrongly started from commutative justice and this gave rise to many of the difficulties we had in regard to obligations of social justice.

To 'act justly' means much more than paying our debts and not stealing from others. It means, above all, working

14

to build a society that is intrinsically just — a society in which the structures are just. It means, for instance, constructing a society in which minorities such as homeless people are not discriminated against either in law or in practice; and a society in which women are not second-class citizens. It means struggling against the bias in our present society, a bias which enables the better-off people to widen the gap between themselves and the poor. It is easy to give examples:
— The children of the wealthy get better educational services, leading on to better jobs.
— The value of property in privileged areas rises more rapidly than in poor areas.
— Those who have money to invest in property or in building sites see their investment paying off, while the poor have to pay ever higher rents.
— Even the law of the land often gives more protection to property rights than to the basic rights of the poor; and in deprived areas the police and 'the law' can be experienced as oppressive rather than as protectors of the people.

At the international level, the same kind of bias operates — and as a result the poor countries lag further and further behind the wealthy nations.

To struggle to bring justice into society means in practice making 'an option for the poor'. This is not a matter of being biased against the rich, or discriminating morally against them. It is simply a question of recognising that, as Leo XIII pointed out in *Rerum Novarum* over ninety years ago, the wealthy are well able to look after their own interests but the poor need special protection from society and those in authority. But it can be very difficult for people like us to recognise that we are privileged in many ways. It is not easy to break with the vested interests of our own class, our friends and associates, in order to work for effective social justice. Much of the spirituality in which we were brought up discourages us from making such an option.

There are 'escapist' elements in the older spirituality. Emphasis was laid on the assurance that people (especially the poor) will be rewarded in heaven if they patiently endure injustice in this life and thus people were encouraged not to challenge social injustice. There are also dualist elements in that older spirituality — suggestions that those who are 'holy'

15

or 'spiritual' are not deeply involved in earthly affairs, and especially not in political matters. Furthermore, the spirituality in which we were brought up tended to support the given order in society, an order in which there was a great deal of inequality in wealth, power, and status between different categories of people. It suggested that this order was God-given and should not be questioned. It was not a very prophetic spirituality, one that would encourage people to challenge the existing order and seek the kind of radical changes that social justice requires.

Obviously, there is need for a real change of outlook — a change of heart, a conversion — if one is to respond adequately to the call to 'act justly'. I think it can be useful to speak of this as a 'political conversion', corresponding to the two other conversions of which I spoke earlier (i.e. 'religious conversion' concerned with my relationship to God, and 'moral' conversion' concerned with my interpersonal relationships). To be 'politically converted' involves two things:

> We need some *understanding* of how our society works — and particularly how it is structured in ways that favour certain groups and give them an unfair advantage over others, even when the privileged ones do not intend to be unjust.
> We need a *commitment* to correcting injustices, not just on an *ad hoc* basis but by replacing the unjust structures with ones that are equitable.

The test of a genuine conversion at this public or 'political' level will be the extent to which we are working to protect the poor and the marginalised. The Bible leaves no room for doubt that in God's eyes to be just is to safeguard and respect the rights of the poor, the oppressed, and the vulnerable (e.g. Is 10:1-2; Amos 8:4-6; Lev 25:10-17; Mt 15:6; 20:13-16; 25:35-37; Lk 4:18; 16:19-31; 20:47; James 2:1-9). But it is not enough for me to feel called by *my* God to be concerned for the poor; I must enable the poor themselves to experience God as *their* God, the God who is on their side to protect them against oppression, the God who 'puts down the mighty and exalts the lowly, who fills the hungry with good things and sends the rich away empty' (Lk 1:52-53).

If I really accept that God is above all the God of the poor, this has major implications for my spirituality. It means I must look for God particularly in the lives of the poor. I must refuse to accept that the actions of 'the important people' are what really shape the history and progress of the country, the Church, and the world. Instead, I will set out to see as really significant the events that touch the lives of the poor, for better or worse. The Old Testament showed that what happened to a group of despised Jewish slaves in Egypt was of major importance in the eyes of God (Exodus 3:7-8, etc.). The New Testament similarly brings out the point that those who are most important are people who seem to be insignificant (e.g. Mt 13:55; I Cor 1:26-28). So the Christian today must attribute particular value to the initiatives taken by those who are poor and despised, however insignificant such actions may seem by the standards of society. This aspect of Christian spirituality calls me to re-define what I mean by 'success'. It challenges me to change my priorities, my hopes, and my concerns, and to allocate my time and energy according to standards that may seem foolish to others, and even at times to myself.

There is no way in which such a major change of approach can take place without notable changes in my life-style, my friends and my loyalties. To 'opt for the poor' it is not enough for me to be providing services for them; I must be in some way *with* them, sharing at least some of their experiences, suffering and hoping with them. Together we may be able to work for a more just and human society, starting from below rather than from above.

If such a 'political conversion' is to succeed it will need to be supported by the two other kinds of conversion. I cannot really be 'with' poor people, in real solidarity with them, unless I am 'morally converted' — able to relate to them on a person-to-person basis. And I need also to be 'religiously converted' — convinced of God's saving presence and power, aware that in the long run it is only by God's power that salvation comes; otherwise I would be quite daunted at the apparent hopelessness of the task of working with the poor and marginalised.

*Balance and integration*
Any one of the three kinds of conversion can be complete

17

only if it is linked to the other two. A proper balance and integration of all three is the basis for a truly Christian spirituality; and this is more important than ever in today's world. If I am not *religiously* converted, or if this aspect of my conversion is inadequate, then I am allowing false gods to rule my life — ambition, or greed, or anxiety. If my *moral* conversion is absent or inadequate then I remain distrustful and closed to others; or else I am unfaithful, unreliable, disloyal. If I am not properly converted in the *political* sphere then I will assume that religion is just a private or interpersonal affair and so I will condone the structural injustices of society.

Unfortunately, it frequently happens that different people concentrate almost exclusively on one, or at most two, of the three aspects of conversion. Many 'good' people wake up to a deep sense of God's providence and this leads them to a prayerful and enthusiastic spirituality; but they may remain quite insensitive in their human relations and may lack all sense of the 'political' dimensions of the Christian faith. Other people build their spirituality around openness to others; but they may be lacking in depth because they give little time to prayer and reflection; and they may imagine that the world can be changed without major structural changes in society. Finally, there are some deeply committed Christians who are so intent on changing the social, economic, and political order that they sacrifice their own peace of spirit and their human relationships in a frenzy of quasi-political activity.

Our spirituality must be rooted not in just one or two aspects of conversion but in all three — the 'religious', the 'moral' and the 'political'. It is a distortion of Christian faith to neglect any of them or to fail to work for a full integration of the three.

This is what Yahweh asks of you, only this:
That you act justly,
That you love tenderly,
That you walk humbly with your God.

# 2

# Spirituality and Theology

From a purely logical point of view this chapter should have come before the previous one. However, it seemed better to devote the first chapter to a general conspectus of the different areas of life which a spirituality ought to cover. Having tried to do that I can now go on to clarify what I understand by spirituality – and how it relates to theory (theology) and to practice.

## What is spirituality?

When I first began to study theology I was not given any very clear account of the meaning of the word 'spirituality' or of the relationship between theology and spirituality. The general impression I had was that spirituality was rather similar to pastoral theology. Both of them seemed to be concerned with the application of theology to daily life. Pastoral theology was the attempt to apply dogmatic and moral theology in the interpersonal sphere and in public life. Spirituality, on the other hand, was concerned mainly with the personal life of prayer and asceticism. There seems to have been a general assumption that theological theory came first; and the task of pastoral theologians and of spiritual writers and directors was to ensure as far as possible that the theory was applied in practice.

I have now come to understand spirituality and revelation in a much more personal sense than I did some years ago. It is not enough to think of God speaking to us first of all in the Bible and through Church authorities; and then to see theology as working on this material, helping us to assimilate it, and to apply it in practice, through pastoral theology and spiritual theology. Now I prefer to begin at the other end – to accept that the most privileged 'place' in which God speaks to me is in my own spirituality. This means that I can no longer think of a person's spirituality as something that comes from outside. Rather it is that which is most deeply personal. My spirituality is me. Not the 'me' that so often is distracted, scattered, and inauthentic; but the most genuine and profound 'me' that exists.

As an embodied spirit, I am moulded in a certain way. One might say that my spirit has taken a certain 'shape'. This 'shape' is partly the result of my genetic heritage, and of the environment in which I lived before and after birth — right up to the present time. It is also the result of my own choices — the cumulative effect of major options and little ones which I have made in the course of my life. When I think of my spirituality, what I have in mind is the outlook, the approach, and the set of attitudes and values which are the expression of this 'me' at my most authentic.

But my spirituality is more than what *shapes* me. It is also what *moves* me. The point is that even though I have been moulded in a certain way, nevertheless I am free. That freedom is even more important than the mould I have taken. Life would not be worth living if all my actions were determined completely by my past. As the poet Patrick Kavanagh says, 'no one loves you for what you have done but for what you might do'. ['To be Dead', in *Collected Poems*.] And the actions that really count are the ones I do in response to something that moves me deeply.

There is a centre in me, out of which I act. Of course I do not perform all my actions out of this centre; but my most authentic and significant acts are rooted in it. When I am touched and moved at that focal point my free response represents me — and it also shapes me for the future. I may call this centre my 'heart'. Or I might consider using the Japanese word 'harah', the belly, which is seen as the centre of the person's strength. This recalls the words of Jesus in John's Gospel — 'out of his belly shall flow streams of living water' (Jn 7:38).

I have come to think recently that the word 'gut' is quite appropriate to describe this centre, the deepest source of my most authentic actions. It is when something 'gets me in the gut' that I am really moved to action. I can even *feel* myself being touched there, for several of my deepest emotions seem to find a focal point in my abdomen or my guts. It is no accident that the word 'emotion' contains the word 'motion'; for emotion is what is most likely to move a person to action. Needless to say, my past has played a major role in determining what moves me to action. But my emotions and values, all the things that urge me to action, are not entirely determined by what has happened to me and what I have done in the past. There is also the possibility of the new, the unpredictable. That is why it is not enough to say that my spirituality is a function of what shapes me; one must add that it is also a function of what moves me.

### An experience of God?

Where does God come into my spirituality? Well, God has played a special role in giving me the 'shape' I have — and therefore in moulding my spirituality. I cannot say that God has played a 'part' in this; for God's action is not just another contribution to the whole, alongside that of my heritage, my environment, and my free choices. Rather, God's action is transcendent — and at the same time is immanent. This means that it operates in and through all the other elements that shape me — but not in a way that I can specify precisely.

Furthermore, I believe that God not only shapes me but also moves me. Once again, God's action is at once transcendent and immanent. A person who is moved by God to do some action may find it difficult to specify where exactly the call of God is experienced. God does not normally operate in a way that goes against what is most human in me. Rather, God's call, his 'movement' in me and of me, works through the most authentic movement of my own spirit. St Paul, in Chapter Eight of the Epistle to the Romans, indicates how the Spirit of God touches and cooperates with the human spirit — helping us in our weakness and enabling us to live in the assurance of being God's children.

If what I have been saying above is correct, then the 'place' in which I can come nearest to experiencing the presence and call of God is my 'heart' or my 'gut'. For it is especially there that the challenge to be fully human comes to consciousness. The place where I can 'meet' God most primordially is on the boundaries of my spirit — where I am so stretched that I can

21

no longer be sure what is 'me' and what is beyond me, transcendent. In the experience of some great tragedy of a whole people or some deeply human struggle of a people for freedom I am called out of myself. Similarly, there are certain profound experiences of a personal or interpersonal kind in which I am lifted beyond myself — in compassion, or tenderness, or the sense of being at peace with the world. All of these can be felt 'in the gut'. All of them are experiences so deeply human that they offer a privileged opportunity for being aware of God's presence in our lives.

Of course God remains transcendent, so there is no way in which I can pin him down. I cannot say God is here rather than there. To be more precise: if God is present to me in one situation rather than another, that is simply because of something in my attitude rather than in the objective situation. God can be 'reached' in any human situation — precisely because God is always reaching out to us. Nevertheless, this availability of God does not happen in some automatic or mechanical sense. It is a presence to me as human. And the more deeply human I am, the more easily I can be touched by God. I have been suggesting that a person is most profoundly human in those experiences which move one 'in the gut'. In that qualified sense I would venture to say: 'God is located in the gut!' The sense of the presence of God is by no means confined to such depth experiences. But they are special occasions which can provide nourishment for the more humdrum parts of life. If I welcome such experiences of grace, then my awareness of God's presence can overflow and expand into everyday living.

It is important not to assume that being touched by God is something that happens mainly in connection with purely individual and private experiences. For too long we have been inclined to 'privatise' spirituality in this way. In fact, however, the depth experiences in which we can most easily allow God to touch us may be associated with any of the three major aspects of life outlined in the previous chapter — the personal aspect, the interpersonal aspect, or the public sphere. I have tried to bring out this point in the examples used above.

## Grace and Morality

I have been saying that my spirit is shaped by my history. One effect of that shaping is that some parts of my personality are carefully fenced off; nobody is allowed to trespass on that area. Indeed some of these fences are so thick and high that even I myself do not really know what lies behind them. I sense obscurely that these are untouchable areas and I tend to shy away from anything that might open up these zones even to my own scrutiny, not to mention that of others.

It is not very helpful to assume at once that all such fences are bad, that they are to be found where sin has taken control of my life. Nor is it wise to presume that moral progress and the work of grace consists in pulling down all the barriers. That may eventually turn out to be true. But a more immediate moral call is simply for me to recognise that there are such fenced-off areas in my personality. I have to be gentle with myself, to accept that I may not yet be ready to burst into the unknown territory. The fences are *de-fences*. They are there because I needed them at some time; and I may still need them to protect me from some of the more unacceptable or frightening aspects of myself. Morality is not normally a matter of doing violence to myself; and the action of God's grace respects my present limitations.

Once I acknowledge the existence of such fenced-off areas in myself I can begin to take personal responsibility for what I do about them. Some delicate scouting around the perimeter may indicate that it is safe to dismantle the barriers around some areas, while others are still too threatening force me to enter. To take down some of the barriers is to change the shape of my spirit. This reshaping is the result of something that moves me deeply and calls me out of myself. One could call this a movement of grace, opening me up more fully to myself and others, increasing the area of freedom in me. When I feel the barriers crumbling it can come in unexpected ways. There is in it a certain sense of gift – an experience of God's power working in me. Quite frequently it comes also as the gift of another person or a community who make it safe for me to lower the barriers, or (changing the metaphor) to come out of my shell.

Not every call to change the shape of my spirit is to be

23

followed. Some calls may mis-shape me further, lessening rather than increasing the area of my freedom of spirit. How is one to know which calls to follow, which are the authentic movements of grace?

All of us have some code of morality which lays down general guidelines about the direction in which we ought to grow. But such a general code is really just the distillation of the experience and wisdom of the past. It cannot always provide the very specific guidance we need in regard to some deep challenge experienced here and now. For instance, I may be wondering whether this is the right moment for me to drop everything and go off for a long retreat; or whether I should take the risk of sharing some intimate secret with another person; or whether I ought to spend some years working with the poor in the Third World. (Note that these three examples are taken from the three areas of life mentioned earlier – the personal, the interpersonal, and the public spheres.) General moral norms may not provide an answer to such existential questions. What is required is a process of discernment to distinguish which of the calls I experience are the most authentic.

There is a very interesting text in St Paul's letter to the Romans which can be helpful here. Paul says:

> Offer yourselves as a living sacrifice to God ... let God transform you inwardly by a complete change of your nature. Then you will be able to discern the will of God and to know what is good and is pleasing to him ...
>
> (Rom 12:1-2)

This text suggests that discernment is not a purely intellectual process, a teasing out of the arguments on one side and the other. It is more a matter of sensing a conformity with the will of God – of 'sussing it out'. It is an intuitive rather than a rational activity. More important than the process itself is the presupposition – namely, that one should be totally dedicated to God, fully converted. Paul suggests that once that has taken place, it will be a relatively simple matter to discern the right course of action: '*Then* you will be able to discern ...'

The crucial thing, therefore, is the dedication of oneself. What is in question is not an act of fanaticism but a process of allowing oneself to be committed deeply to certain fundamental values. These ideals have the ability to attract one to such an extent that the whole personality is gathered around them. When the Gospels report Christ as saying, 'Blessed are the pure in heart', I take it that this refers to the dedicated ones, those who are single-minded — or, more accurately, single-hearted. These are the ones who are able to discern what they ought to do and in what direction they are called to grow. One can say that they have an experience of a personal call from God. It comes, not in the form of a disembodied voice, but rather as a movement of the whole person, centred in the heart or in 'the gut'.

## The role of Theology

If one gives priority to spirituality, does this eliminate the need for theology? Not at all. Theology is a reflective activity — and the primary material for this reflection is the person's own spirituality. We all experience in some degree the urge to articulate our fundamental values and beliefs. This is the urge to do theology. It follows that everybody is called to be a theologian, at least in some rudimentary sense. Most people keep this urge to theologise under a tight rein; it may find expression only in the rather inappropriate setting of a bar or a cocktail party. Perhaps the fact that it breaks through in such situations shows just how strong the urge really is. It would be wrong to sneer at such amateur theologising; for the work of professional theologians must be rooted in the fundamental need, which we all share, to reflect on our beliefs.

Theology does more than simply give expression to our value system and beliefs; it also involves some attempt to introduce order and consistency into them. Some people experience a very strong urge to be coherent and systematic. Until quite recently I believed that such consistency was one of the very highest values in theology — so much so that I had great difficulty in coping with any religious ideas which I could not fit into a system. But now I think that to be a good theologian one must be able to juggle with different systems. The juggler can handle many different objects more or less at the same time, by taking each one in turn while keeping the others in the air. In somewhat the same way I

25

now try to switch from one thought pattern to another, recognising that some of the most important truths about life and God may not be adequately expressed if I stay in a single system. By way of example I may refer to what I said in the previous chapter about the need to relate to God in two very different ways — in a childlike mode where one can ask for anything, and in a mode which borders on the agnostic. Neither of these approaches is sufficient to express our fundamental religious attitude; but each can supplement the other.

From what I have been saying it should be clear that there is a sense in which theology, like religion, is first of all a personal matter. Once this is recognised one can then go on to try to make sense of a theology which is shared by a whole community of people. Quite a lot of people who use theological words and propound theological ideas are not really doing theology at all; they are merely mouthing phrases that do not truly represent their deepest beliefs and values. But a person may be so much part of a community that both the religion and the theology of the community represent the basic outlook of that person. Such a community value-system may be carried on from one generation to the next; in this way an authentic tradition may come into being. Christianity is one such; and the reflective part of that tradition of belief is its theology.

### Do Christians need Theology?

Does it undervalue the Christian faith to speak about it as one of a number of different religious traditons? I do not think so. It is true that to believe in Jesus Christ is rather different from accepting a traditional community religion: the Christian faith may be shared by a whole community of people but it remains, nevertheless, deeply personal. So much so, that for any individual to claim to be a believer is to affirm that he or she has had a conversion of heart. But, on the other hand, this deeply personal faith, even though it is the pure gift of God, does not simply drop down from Heaven. It is normally mediated to the individual through the Christian community. And this community carries the Christian faith from one generation to the next. We cannot really 'pass on' the faith to our children; we cannot even

26

'offer' it to them, since we do not own it. But we can try to live by it and embody it in our way of life, hoping that this witness will be used by God to dispose new people to accept the gift of faith. There is a sense in which much the same could be said of any really profound religious faith — though Christianity does seem to put a special stress on faith as the gift of God.

Christian faith combines an insistence on the centrality of the *historical* figure of Christ with a strong emphasis on the *personal* relationship of each individual believer with God. This caused no difficulty for the very first Christians because they had been disciples of Jesus during his life on earth (cf. Acts 1:21-22). But we are separated from the historical Christ by a gulf of almost twenty centuries; and most Christians today live in a very different cultural setting to that of Palestine in the first century. Surely this must cause some difficulties in reconciling the personal and the historical dimensions of Christianity? Can we really understand the message and mission of Christ across such a gap of time and culture? Can we share his value-system in our own very different world?

Generations of Christians have believed that they can answer 'yes' to these questions. People in very diverse ages and cultures have felt that Christ has spoken to their hearts. Such a claim is not too surprising. But what is astonishing is the extent to which Christian belief has remained constant through the ages. As one might expect, there have been differences of emphasis at different times, and not infrequently there have been some distortions in the understanding of the Christian faith. But the tradition has incorporated a critical strand which has helped Christians to correct distortions and deepen their understanding of the faith.

I have just mentioned two key elements that help to explain how Christianity succeeds so well in combining the personal with the historical. The first is that Christ appeals to the heart, not just to the mind. Christian faith is not primarily a message which can be expressed in a purely rational form. Rather it is a response to the person of Christ as he comes across to us even today in the pages of the Gospels and in the witness of believers. Something similar applies in the case of the Old Testament: it is a story before being a message. The

27

parts that touch us most deeply — for instance the prophets and the psalms — speak to the heart. The gap of space and time can be bridged to a remarkable extent by the appeal to the heart. There is something universal in the Bible; it finds echoes in human experience in every age.

The second element I mentioned was the critical strand in the Christian tradition. This is where theology comes in. For theology is a reflection on the faith and it can help to ensure that distortions are detected and overcome. Theology can help us to avoid the mistake of the fundamentalists, who fail to take account of the different cultural settings in which the books of the Bible were written. They want to take the Word of God 'literally' — and they presume that this means understanding it as though it were a factual newspaper story written today. What theology can do is help us to understand the original significance of the words of the Bible. It can reveal the different literary forms which one finds, say, in the Gospels (not to mention the Old Testament); and it throws light on the different stages of the composition of the various parts of the Scriptures. All this helps one to cross the culture barrier and discover the original sense of the text — and so what God is really saying to us in the Bible. This same process of critical interpretation has to be applied to various statements of Church authority and the great religious writers.

A famous historian is said to have remarked that one major purpose of writing history is to correct the bad history written by others! Much the same could be said about theology: one of my most important tasks as a theologian is to help people to discover and avoid various misunderstandings of the Christian faith. Good theology does more than help correct misunderstandings of the Christian faith. Its more positive side is that it can mediate between the religious experience of people of different ages and cultures. This is particularly important for us Christians, since we believe that Christ's relationship with God provides us with a model and a norm. It is true that on many occasions the Gospels speak directly to my heart, without any conscious use by me of theology. Nevertheless, parts of the Scriptures, even of the Gospels, remain opaque to me or are open to serious misunderstanding unless I have some theological understanding of what the text originally implied. For instance, I need

28

to know what St John really meant by such phrases as 'the world', 'the Jews', 'the Advocate'. Otherwise I will miss out on the full riches of his Gospel.

Theology, then, can play an important role in combining the historical dimension of the Christian faith (Christ and the whole tradition before and after him) with the uniquely personal dimension (the fact that it is my individual spirituality that is ultimately in question). Recall the three major spheres of spirituality outlined in the previous chapter — the personal, the interpersonal, and the public spheres. When I proclaim that I am a Christian, I am saying that in each of these spheres I find that the experience of Christ is in some way normative for me. For instance, his way of addressing God as 'Abba' teaches me to do the same. His washing of the feet of his friends shows me how to relate to others. His silence before Herod and his words before Pilate suggest ways in which I might take a stance in public affairs. Some aspects of the life and words of Jesus speak directly to my heart, despite the gap of space and time. Others are mediated to me through a more scientific theological understanding. In this sense theology should be seen as being in the service of spirituality: at its best it mediates between Christ's religious experience and my own.

## Distortions

Theology is the articulation in an ordered way of the faith of a person, or a community, or a whole people. But it is not simply a matter of using the faith as the object or raw material of theology. Rather, the reflection is itself a faith activity, a dimension of the faith itself. This means that doing theology is not a neutral activity, quite independent of the content of one's faith. The very way in which theology is done is deeply affected by the person's beliefs and values. This has very important practical consequences, which can be shown by taking examples from each of the three spheres of human living which I noted above — the personal, the interpersonal, and the public spheres.

Suppose that I am not religiously converted in the sense described in the previous chapter — or at least not adequately converted. Let us say that I have not opened myself to the presence of God in my life, or to the Lordship of Jesus Christ;

my life is governed by other forces such as anxiety or ambition. Does this affect my theology? Yes indeed — and in a very subtle way. While continuing to use the traditional theological language of Christianity, I will find it more and more unreal. I will be half aware that the more deeply personal and experiential aspects of the Christian tradition are simply not relevant to my own religious experience. But I may still be trying to articulate my ultimate beliefs in the language of Christian theology. In that case it is likely that I shall lessen my sense of inadequacy and embarrassment by playing down the more openly experiential aspects of the tradition — for instance, any reference to the experience of grace or of God, or any very explicit theory of providence. Instead, I shall fasten on those parts of the theological tradition that seem to support my own experience.

It is unfortunately true that Western theology in recent centuries contains a good deal of material that will give some appearance of legitimacy to such inadequate theology. Western dogmatic and systematic theologians were very hesitant to speak about the experience of God — they left that to those who were specialising in the area of mysticism. There developed a theology of grace which opposed it to nature — and insisted that the whole order of grace remains beyond the realm of human experience. This kind of theology is ideal for people who want to see themselves as Christian theologians but who in fact have little or no experience of grace and little living contact with God. It eliminates the embarrassment that should be felt by anybody who talks about God in a way that is not rooted in personal experience!

This example shows how a person's deepest beliefs and values can affect his or her theology. A kind of *editing* process takes place — a selection of the parts of the tradition that are more compatible with that person's values, and an overlooking of those that would prove awkward to handle. The most unfortunate effect of this editing is that the resultant theology functions as a support and justification for the inadequate religion of the person concerned. If I have little sense of the presence of God in my daily life, and if my theology tells me that that is exactly what I ought to expect, then what incentive do I have to become more open to the awareness of God? In that case, my theology justifies my lack of religious conversion. It functions as an ideology — a set of theory which is a defence of my present outlook. It disguises the weakness of my position — from myself and from others.

The same kind of distortion of theology can take place in relation to the interpersonal sphere of life. If I am partly or totally unconverted morally (in the sense outlined in the previous chapter), if I am closed to others and distrustful of them, this will probably result in the kind of theological editing which I have just been describing. By way of example I may mention one instance which struck me very forcefully. I knew some theologians who were living in an institution where there was very little experience of community. Even the word 'community' was seldom spoken, and when it was, it sometimes evoked a sneer. But some of these theologians were well aware that the concept of community lies at the very heart of the Christian experience. So they could not easily ignore it entirely; a more radical solution had to be found. One Sunday morning I was astonished to hear one of these men preach about community. But I was even more astonished to hear his account of it. Basically he was claiming that the group constituted a community because they all followed a common timetable! The preacher had redefined the meaning of the word 'community' to make it fit in with his current way of life. I do not believe he was being deliberately hypocritical; it was simply that his theology was shaped — and in this case distorted — by his practical living.

This example shows that theology can be a dangerous weapon. At its best it enriches a person's faith by articulating it in an ordered way. But at its worst it can be used as a defence against anything that might challenge the theologian's beliefs and way of life. This defensive element is most common in the theology that is concerned with how we relate to society at large, in the public sphere. In the previous chapter I suggested that the Christian is called to be 'politically converted', that is, to be fully committed to bringing justice into society. But suppose my conversion in this sphere of activity is lacking or inadequate. What will be the effect on my theology? Once again there will be a tendency for me to play down those aspects of the Christian faith and tradition that are a challenge to my present stance. And I shall be favourably disposed towards any kind of theology that seems to justify my position. ✳

31

Distortions of this kind have occurred at various times in Christian history. Quite a lot of the Western theology of recent centuries is marred by a tendency to make religion a rather private relationship with God — or to extend it at most to cover interpersonal relationships but not public life. A particular kind of dualism has also affected much of Western religion and theology — a tendency to make too sharp a distinction between the spiritual and the temporal. This kind of poor theology has led people to assume that Christianity is not primarily concerned with political or economic affairs. A person who accepts such a dualistic and privatised theology can use it to stifle the voice of conscience. Touched by the injustice of the world, such a person may be falsely reassured by this poor theology. Not that it would go so far as to suggest that social injustice is acceptable, but it could convince the person that more 'spiritual' issues should be given a higher priority.

An example from Christology may help to illustrate the kind of imbalance that can easily take place. Christ is often presented as the supreme model of obedience and non-violence. Passages from the New Testament are quoted in support of this position. But there are other passages which do not fit so easily into this presentation of the attitude of Jesus. For instance, the Scriptures present him as challenging all the religious and civil authorities of his time — the Jewish leaders, Herod, and Pilate. Theologians who themselves are part of a comfortable establishment are quite likely to ignore or explain away this aspect of the life of Christ. Anybody who is looking for a clear example of the political implications of different theological outlooks will find it in the description by Peadar Kirby of the situation in Nicaragua — 'a country where the political power struggle between two social classes is at a very advanced stage'. ('Church and State in Nicaragua' in *Doctrine and Life* 33, Dec. '83, 610-17).

To recapitulate: spirituality underpins theology; and theology can be seen as an articulation and ordering of a basic religious outlook or spirituality. But precisely because our theology is rooted in our fundamental values and beliefs we tend to select those parts of the theological tradition which fit in comfortably with our present stance. Then the theology which we espouse not merely expresses our basic outlook but also functions as a support and defence for it.

Theologians are in a privileged but dangerous position, because of their specialised training and their familiarity with the various traditions. On the one hand, they may allow themselves to be challenged by what they are studying, and led to a deeper conversion at every level — religious, moral, and political. But on the other hand they may use their expertise to construct an elaborate theological justification for their own lack of effective conversion in any or all of these aspects of life. In that case they are deluding themselves and others in a very sacred matter. There is something that comes close to idolatry in what they are doing — making use of the Word of God to bolster up their own prejudiced positions.

I have suggested that in cases like this, genuine theology is being replaced by an ideology. Why use the notoriously ambiguous word 'ideology' to describe a theology that has become distorted by the theologian's lack of adequate conversion? One reason for doing so is that the word is widely used by others, so it may be worthwhile trying to disentangle the different strands of meaning in it. Another reason for using the word 'ideology' is that, for all its ambiguity, it has a connotation that is peculiarly appropriate here and that is not conveyed by any other word.

There are two main strands of meaning in the word. Firstly, it suggests ideas that are not merely incorrect but also illusory in the sense that there is an element of self-deception in them; the person who holds these ideas is not in touch with the full reality of the situation. Secondly, 'ideology' is used to refer to a set of ideas that reflect the *class interests* of a particular group. Marxists tend to use the word mainly in this latter sense, while retaining most of the former meaning as well. When I apply the word 'ideology' to distorted theology I do so in both senses. I have been describing a process by which a theologian writing about grace may 'edit' the Bible or the Christian tradition, omitting those elements that challenge the writer's own failure to experience God or grace. This editing arises from self-deception and is the cause of further self-deception. It tends to cut off this theologian from the authentic Christian revelation. Its effect is the building up of a set of ideas and theories that are quite inadequate as an expression of the Christian faith. These ideas are, at least partly, *illusions* rather than truth.

33

Furthermore, as I noted earlier, these ideas serve the purpose of being a defence of the present stance of those who hold them. This is brought out by the example I gave above of the sermon on the meaning of the word 'community'. Abundant instances of this kind of defensive use of theology can be found as soon as theologians begin to treat of political and economic issues. In this sphere, theology is especially likely to reflect the self-interest of the theologians who write or teach it. I see no reason to deny that that interest may often be a *class* interest. For the fact is that most Western theologians belong to a particular class in society — and many are content to fit rather comfortably into the privileged niche which society gives them.

I gave an example earlier of the way in which the theology of authority can become impoverished when theologians play down the more confrontational incidents in the life of Christ. In general, the whole theology of social justice and of poverty, together with the theology of peace and of violence, is open to serious distortions; such distortion comes when theologians, however unconsciously, are propounding ideas which serve their own interests and those of the class to which they belong.

This topic is so important that I propose to deal with it at greater length in the next chapter. There I shall indicate how, in recent years, theologians from the Third World have challenged the dominant theology of the West on the grounds that it has condoned and even supported injustice. They accuse most Western theologians of having failed to make an authentic option for the poor. They believe that this failure in what I have called 'political conversion' has infected Western theology as a whole — turning it into an ideological defence of the unjust structures which divide our world into the rich and the poor, the oppressors and the oppressed.

# 3

# Challenge from the Third World

Just before I returned to Africa early last year I visited a cleric who holds a very senior position in the Church. His sitting-room was lavishly equipped with elegant, expensive furniture. Proudly he told me that he had not bought any of these items; they were all gifts from benefactors and friends — wealthy people, some of whom are prominent in the political world. Perhaps he sensed in me a certain questioning, for he went on to offer me this word of advice out of his experience and success: 'We have to learn how to receive . . .' Later on, the conversation turned to Central America. It was evident that he disapproved strongly of the Sandinista government in Nicaragua. I ventured to ask, did he not think that at least it was preferable to the Somoza dictatorship which preceded it. He replied that there was little to choose between them . . .

Living now in an area where children are dying of malnutrition and where most people have to struggle to get enough to eat, I often reflect on that visit and that conversation. I ask myself: what did this clergyman give in return for those beautiful gifts? His soul? His integrity? Not really; for he remains a good, sincere, kind person. But I feel sure that, without realising it, he paid a high price — not so much for the gifts as for the friendships which they sealed. He came to share more and more of the values of his benefactors and friends. This lessened his chances of developing close friendships with poor people, or at least with hurt and angry people, alienated from respectable society. He lost sympathy for the struggles of people against oppression — except, of course, Communist oppression. His benefactors may not have bought his soul; but on the whole they got good value for their gifts.

The incident makes me more willing to listen to the accusations made by some Third World theologians against Western theology, even if at first sight their claims seem rather extravagant. They say that our theology functions as an ideology, a defence of political and economic injustice. Of course I'm tempted to reply that the political outlook and prejudice of Church leaders is not determined by theology. But that brings me to the crux of the matter: we have turned theology into something so limited in scope and so abstract that it scarcely affects everyday life. The result, paradoxically, is that our attitudes are determined less by our official theology than by an implicit theology which we think of as commonsense. This applies not merely in the political sphere, where it is most obvious, but also in the personal and inter-personal spheres. (That should be evident from the examples of 'editing' which I gave in the last chapter.) The challenge from the Third World is to discover, or rediscover, a different way of theologising, resulting in a different kind of theology, one that is much closer to life, affecting all our commitments, our attitudes, and even our feelings. I shall deal with this topic in two chapters of this book. In the present chapter I propose to give a general account of Third World theology in so far as it is centred on the theme of liberation, and to note the ways in which it challenges the dominant Western theology. Much later in the book — in Chapter 11 — I shall give a more detailed account of the various currents which have been converging to form Third World theology; and following that I shall consider in more detail the issue of the relevance of this theology to Christians of the First World.

## A Biblical Example

I do not want to give an abstract theoretical account of Third World theology, for that could lead one to miss what is central to it — its dynamic, inspirational quality. So I propose instead to begin with a practical example of it, a passage taken from the Bible itself. It is the song of praise attributed to Mary in the first chapter of the Gospel according to Luke:

My whole being proclaims the greatness of God
And my spirit rejoices in God my saviour.
For he has remembered me, his lowly servant,

36

And from this time onward people of all times will call me
   blessed,
Because of the marvels the Almighty has done for me.
His name is holy;
He shows mercy from age to age to all who fear him.
He stretched out his mighty arm
To shatter the plans of the arrogant.
He has brought down mighty rulers from their seats of
   power
And lifted up the little people.
He has filled the hungry with the best of food,
While the rich were sent away empty.
He has come to the help of Israel his servant,
Fulfilling the promise he made to our ancestors,
A promise of mercy to Abraham and his children's children,
   for ever.

(Lk 1:46-55)

The most obvious thing about this passage is that it is a
beautiful prayer. But that does not prevent it being at the
same time a profound theological reflection. In that sense it
is what Third World theology would like to be at its best. It
is not an academic statement propounded in carefully detached
and objective language. Rather it is a proclamation of personal
faith and hope, rooted in Mary's own experience — while
being at the same time a theological interpretation of that
experience.

The deeply *personal* element can be seen in the way Mary
speaks of 'my soul', 'my spirit', and of God's marvels done
'for me'. However, the experience on which Mary's reflection
is based, though personal, is not a purely private one. It is
rather the experience of a whole *community* — 'my people'.
It is not even confined to what is happening to this people
at the present time; for it extends to the whole *history* of
her people. She speaks of God's mercy and power being at
work 'from age to age'. Her prayer is a biblical reflection
which takes the form of a mosaic of texts from the Old
Testament, the religious history of the Jews. They bring hope
because they recall the saving presence of God throughout
that history — and therefore give the assurance that he is
still at work today. Mary is led to believe that God is doing

great things in a situation which, from the point of view of the powerful of this world, seems to have little significance.

## The lowly ones

Mary's reflection centres on the on-going history of her people. But who are these people? They are not just a particular racial group. Rather they are, in Mary's own words, the lowly ones, the hungry. For Third World theologians this point is crucial. They believe that if Christian theology is to be authentic it must be done from the perspective of the poor, the oppressed. As they say themselves, it is a theology done 'from the underside of history'. This theology is a radical challenge to the implicit assumption of our world that 'the little people' of society are unimportant. Its fundamental claim is that the apparently insignificant ones — people like Mary, and David, and Ruth (and, above all, Jesus himself) — are the people called by God to play the central role in the making of human history. This belief of Third World theologians is of particular importance in today's world. For this is a time when many of the forgotten people and peoples are waking up to their situation and shaking off the silence of oppression. To use the language of the Ecumenical Association of Third World Theologians, there is an 'irruption of the poor' on to the stage of history.

This people of which Mary speaks is also the community of those who 'fear God'. I take that to mean that they recognise and worship the true God rather than an idol. Idols, false gods, are as common today as they were in Mary's time — and perhaps more powerful than ever. The National Security State may not be called 'God' by those who serve it; but its claim to the total allegiance of the citizen makes it a false god, an idol. Other ideologies make similar absolute claims. The people who 'fear God' are those who know what God really stands for. They try to live out the values of the Kingdom — values that conflict sharply with those that are dominant in our world. (In later chapters I shall give a detailed account of some of these Kingdom values.)

The poor and the hungry are the 'lowly ones' not simply because they are at the bottom of the heap from an economic and political point of view. As a result of their deprivation it is very likely that they are also wounded in spirit. The experience of being harassed and down-trodden causes psychological damage: it leaves people with a very poor self-image. They will be lacking in confidence — and even to some extent in the basic knowledge and skills needed to live a dignified human life.

There are two ways in which people respond to such deprivation. The reaction of some is one of resentment: hurt and bitterness exacerbate their psychological wounds. On the other hand there are some who are able to draw good out of their loss and their inadequacies. These are the 'lowly' ones — people who accept their weakness. This does not mean that they lie down under it but that they recognise their hurts and deprivation while struggling to overcome them. The truly 'poor and lowly' person believes that weakness and hurt can, paradoxically, become a source of strength. That faith is summed up in St Paul's statement: 'For those who love God, all things work together for good.' (Rom 8:28). This is not purely a matter of blind faith. There are times, at least, when it is confirmed by personal experience and by the facts of history — especially the history of salvation recounted in the Bible. It is this faith and this experience that animate the lowly ones in working for liberation — not only for themselves but also for the whole world. They know that they have been given a privileged role by God in bringing about the Kingdom.

These 'lowly ones' are the people who experience what Mary calls 'the marvels the Almighty has done'. The marvellous events to which she refers are not just any kind of amazing happenings. Rather they are the liberating acts through which the Lord shows that he is with his people. The power of God is proved precisely in the way he brings freedom to the poor, the starving, the oppressed. Mary does not fudge the basic issue at this point. She makes it clear that to rescue the poor is to break the hold of the powerful ones who have been crushing them. To lift up 'the little people' is to bring down 'the mighty rulers from their seats of power', and to 'shatter the plans of the arrogant'. While the hungry are fed, the rich are sent empty away. Mary's theological reflection makes no concession at all to those who would like to imagine that the oppressed can be set free without disturbing those who hold power and without dismantling the structures of oppression.

The liberation of the poor is experienced by Mary as the fulfilment of God's promise, made long ago and continually renewed. In relation to this promise her prayerful reflection has two aspects. Firstly, it is a celebration of the way she sees the promise being fulfilled already. Secondly, it is a proclamation of hope in a future in which the fulfilment will be complete. Mary recalls Abraham, the model of all who put their faith in God's promise. The source of hope for those whose situation appears hopeless is their trust that God will continue to 'remember his promise'. That hope is the source of energy of those who choose to work for human liberation and the building of the Kingdom.

## Commitment

I have been using Mary's biblical reflection and prayer as an illustration of Third World theology. In the light of this example I would like now to go on to specify more clearly the main way in which Third World theology differs from the usual kind of Western theology. I can begin by taking an analogy from the realm of literature.

Recently I have been reading similar books by two well-known African writers — Wole Ṣoyinka of Nigeria and Ngugi wa Thiongo of Kenya. Both men were interned without trial; and the books I was reading were the accounts given by each of them of their time in prison. What comes across very clearly in these books is that the authors' commitment as writers is an integral part of their wider commitment. Both of these men are deeply concerned about justice and human freedom; and their writing is one element of the broader struggle in which they are engaged. This does not mean that they have subordinated their art to politics, in a way that turns them into mere propagandists. Instead, their moral and political commitment provides the context within which their art is exercised.

Much the same applies to the kind of Third World theology of which I am writing here. It makes sense only as part of a wider commitment to human liberation. This theology is an articulation of an engagement in the task of working for justice, for human rights, and against oppression. It is genuine theology, not mere propaganda. But it does not stand in isolation; it does not have the kind of autonomy that would

40

leave it unrelated to the rest of life in those who practise it. Third World theologians express this idea by insisting that their theology is 'a second act'; it follows on 'the first act' which is involvement in the struggle of the Christian for human liberation and the promotion of the Kingdom.

This way of thinking about the nature of theology is not entirely new. For a long time theologians have been insisting that theology is a reflection on the Christian faith; so faith precedes theology. But what the Third World theologians are particularly insistent on is that the kind of theology done by a person is determined to a very considerable degree by the way that person interprets the faith in practice and lives it out.

For Third World theologians of the kind I have in mind the most notable feature of our world today is the structural injustice which splits each nation, and the world as a whole, into the rich and the poor, the powerful and the powerless. These theologians hold that anybody who fails to challenge this massive evil is not really living out the Christian faith in practice. For the injustice is so much part of life that nobody can really ignore it. To play it down and suggest that for the Christian it may not be a very urgent issue is to condone it. The crucial point is that before ever the theologian engages in 'the second act' of theological reflection, he or she will have taken some option in practice — either to challenge or condone the evil. There is no room for neutrality. Third World theologians hold that the only theology that is authentically Christian is one that is preceded by, and springs from, the 'first act' of an option for the poor and a commitment to liberation.

Most theologians in the Western world are by now well aware of the injustice of the world economic order — the wide and growing gap between the rich and the poor. But they do not appear to feel any particular responsibility for this injustice. Nor do they indicate that they see themselves as called to do much to overcome it. Individuals among them have, of course, taken on various pastoral commitments; and some of these are related to the problems of poverty. But there is no evident *intrinsic* connection between the practical commitments of these people and their theology.

Western theologians see themselves as called to reflect on

41

the deepest meaning of the Christian faith. They take it that this task requires a certain detachment from the immediacy of involvement in a struggle to change the world. It is accepted, of course, that theologians do at times engage in a highly specialised type of struggle — a controversy about ideas. It is not uncommon for theologians to engage in intellectual jousting about the meaning of words. Obviously, such controversies have practical implications. But these are seen as a matter of applying the theory to life; the truth itself is to be discovered not by living it but by study. For the most part it is assumed that the theologian is to seek the truth by examining the documents of the past with as much scholarship and detachment as possible. Involvement in, say, work with the poor would be a distraction from this theological task. No wonder, then, that most Western theology is carried on in the security and relative comfort of universities or seminaries.

Few Western theologians would wish to be 'activists', people working to change society and the world. For the activist would not have the detachment to achieve the objectivity which, for them, is the essential virtue of a good theologian. Third World theologians challenge this point of view. They maintain that Western theology, which purports to be the fruit of detachment and objectivity, has a role that is not at all 'neutral'. They hold that the theology of the West plays an important role in society: it may not explicitly support the present unjust world order, but it lends it a certain respectability.

The point is that most university and seminary theologians are part of the intellectual establishment. In fact they are a particularly important part of it, because their area of specialisation is God and the deepest meaning of human life. If these theologians are content to live comfortably within the present system, this suggests that they see nothing in their studies that would call them to reject the system. It could even be taken to indicate that, in the view of those who are the 'experts' on God and on divine revelation, God is not particularly concerned about the injustice and oppression that seem to be intrinsic to the present world order. In that case, the would-be detachment and objectivity of the dominant theology of the West would in practice amount to collusion in the social evils that mar our world.

*Objectivity?*

First World theologians may argue that theology, as a search for understanding, requires that they dedicate themselves single-mindedly to a world of scholarship and of theory, without the distraction of worrying about practical applications. I would agree about the importance of scholarship and scientific theory; and I accept that some aspects of theology require a certain distancing of oneself for a time from the immediacy of practical issues. But I have recently been asking myself whether theology has not lost as much or more than it has gained by the rather secluded and privileged life which most of us Western theologians have led.

No doubt we had the leisure and the research facilities to pursue our studies into the meaning of the Judaeo-Christian tradition. But I suspect that an element of selectivity — perhaps even of bias — crept into theological research as a result of the fact that the study was done mostly in an atmosphere that was clerical, male, middle-class, and privileged. Some examples may bring out this point:

— The fact that there have been very few women theologians may have contributed to the playing down of the 'feminine' aspects of God as revealed in the Judaeo-Christian tradition (e.g. the Greek word for wisdom is feminine; and the Hebrew word for divine compassion in the Bible is the word 'womb').

— The over-spiritualising of the meaning given to the word 'poor' may be due partly to the fact that not many theologians have lived in poverty.

— The theology of authority has come close at times to being an ideological defence of the power of those who exercise authority in the Church.

— The fact that most Catholic theologians have been clerics seems to have left its mark on our theology of priesthood — and the way the role of 'the lay person' was understood.

This question of objectivity needs further probing. The theology which has been dominant in Europe and North America is not a single monolithic system; there are different varieties in it. But one thing they have in commmon is an explicit or implicit claim to be so scientific and objective that what they propose as the truth is universally valid. Western theologians are concerned above all with the interpretation of the Bible, which consists of writings from a variety of non-

43

Western cultures. It is ironic, then, that they have seldom adverted to the possibility that their own statements are as culturally conditioned as those of the Bible. The theologians who see themselves as interpreting the Bible in universal terms are not nearly so objective as they would like to believe. They make use of Western conceptions of morality and law, and also of society, nature, and human fulfilment. Consequently, when they speak of such things as 'the nature of development' or of what it means to act in a human way, they are putting forward Western concepts as though they were 'the truth'. This kind of cultural arrogance touches all the basic themes of theology — even the very notion of God.

Third World theologians point out that the cultural and religious imperialism of the West has had some disastrous consequences. In the past it led Church leaders and theologians to give religious legitimation and support to Western colonialism — and even at times to racism. More commonly the Churches and theologians of the West have tended to undervalue the way of life and the traditions of the peoples of the Third World (— and also, I must add, of what I would call 'the little peoples' of Europe). As a result, Western theology has given legitimacy to the destruction of the cultures of the peoples dominated by Western colonialism or neo-colonialism — or has at least failed to challenge this effectively.

For the most part this has been due to unconscious bias on the part of Western intellectuals. Very recently, however, a small group of theologians in North America have set out more consciously to defend the present world order and to justify aggressive action by the West against those who dare to challenge it. For them, the great enemy is liberation theology, which they see as an ideological defence of violent revolution. They respond by providing a theological justification for 'Western democracy' — and for the international order imposed by Western economic and political power. So there is a very sharp polarisation among the theologians — and the controversy has major implications for the life of the Church and of every Christian.

The theological world is now the arena for what has aptly been called 'a battle of the gods' ('Doing Theology in a Divided World': Final Statement of the Sixth Conference of The Ecumenical Association of Third World Theologians

[EATWOT], Geneva, 1983, section 33). On one side is the true God — the God who takes the poor and oppressed as his people. Ranged against him are the false gods — the idols that give religious legitimacy to injustice. For instance the racist authorities in South Africa claim the backing of God for their system; so the god they worship is a total distortion of the God who reveals himself in the Bible. More commonly, many unjust regimes have adopted the ideology of the National Security State. This means they have set up the State as the ultimate value. It has become an idol. The effect is that anything can be justified in the name of the security of the State — which in practice, of course, means the interests of those who hold power. In many National Security States a deliberate effort is made to 'harness' religion in support of the regime. This is usually done by stressing the need to defend tradition and the national culture against external enemies and subversion from within.

The so-called 'battle of the gods' is really, of course, a struggle between people with different conceptions of God. Those theologians who have taken liberation as their basic theme see the issue as one of choosing between, on the one hand, an authentic religion and theology and, on the other hand, a religion and theology that support injustice. For them, however, the enemies are not just the obvious forms of 'idol worship' as exemplified in racist or National Security regimes. They believe that there is also a more subtle version of idolatry. This is the consumerism and competitiveness that is common in Western countries. The values underlying this style of life are in direct conflict with those to which the true God calls us. Though less explicit it is perhaps just as damaging as more overt forms of idolatry. Any theologian who fails to challenge the Western way of life and the unjust world order to which it gives rise, is acquiescing in a form of idol worship.

From what has been said it should be clear that the difference between Third World and First World theology is not simply one of content. There are, of course, obvious differences in the content — the way different topics are covered and the priority given to certain truths. Some of these differences are indicated in the previous chapter and in the remainder of this book. So at this point I need only briefly note that Third World theologians have a very distinct emphasis in the way

45

they understand God, revelation, the mission of Christ, and the role of the Church. But behind this distinctive content of Third World theology lies the more fundamental difference — one of context: Third World theologians see their work as rooted in a commitment to challenge oppression and struggle for integral human liberation. Indeed they see their theologising not just as following on action for liberation but as an intrinsic — and important — part of the process. Their theology provides religious justification for the struggle against injustice; and when the odds seem to be impossible it offers *hope*, by assuring the poor that God has heard their cry and intends to rescue them (cf. Ex 3:7-8).

## Who does theology — and how?

This difference in context gives rise to other major differences between the two kinds of theology. Third World theology differs notably from more conventional theology in its sources, its methods, and even in its answer to the question: 'Who does theology?' Whereas Western theology has concentrated mainly on documents from the past as its *sources*, Third World theology puts much more stress on the present experience of people — above all of the poor — as a source of theology. They hold that God is present to our world especially in the struggle against oppression; so theologians must look for God there. The Bible is used perhaps more widely than ever before. But there is a major difference in the way in which it is used. Instead of starting by trying to interpret this sacred book from the past, the aim is to begin with the present reality, and to use the Bible to throw light on it. This, as we have seen, is precisely what Mary is presented as doing in her song of praise in Luke's Gospel.

The *methods* that are considered appropriate for theology depend very much on the sources that are being used. So long as the main sources were documents from the past, traditional methods of scholarship were called for. But, with the new emphasis on the present experience of oppression and liberation as a source for theology, there is need for new methods. The theologian can no longer afford to be cut off from the experience of the poor, and from the struggle to overcome injustice. Rather, he or she must seek ways in which that experience can be articulated. One fascinating example is

46

Ernesto Cardenal's series of books, *The Gospel in Solentiname* (Orbis, 1976—). The author set out to make it easier for the members of this poor community to express their understanding of the Word of God in relation to their own lives:

> Young Oscar: 'That Herod was a coward. It was because he was a coward that he committed all those murders . . .'
> Young Alejandro: 'It's the same nowadays: As soon as they see the first signs of anything new, they get scared . . . and it's cowardice that makes them kill defenceless people.'
>
> (*The Gospel in Solentiname*, Vol 1, p. 74)

Third World theologians are well aware that the need for scholarship is not gone. In fact the new approach requires even more technical skills than the old one. For, while the need for biblical and historical scholarship remains, there is now a stress on the importance of being able to do a 'social analysis' of the present situation. But no scientific technique can substitute for sharing with the poor as they experience God in their struggle for justice and dignity. The Ecumenical Association of Third World Theologians is very explicit on this point: '. . . it is not possible to do Christian theology without making a political commitment in solidarity with the poor.' ('Doing Theology in a Divided World', Geneva, 1983, section 39).

Closely linked to the question of the method of theology is that of the 'subjects' of theology — that is, the people who are called and qualified to engage in theological reflection. At this point there is a very clear contrast between the two approaches. In the First World, theology has become a preserve of 'experts'. In fact it has become so specialised that the scholars in the different branches of theology find it difficult to share even with each other the fruits of their researches. The communication of the 'experts' with the mass of Christians is not normally done directly. What happens is that the specialists try to teach theology to those who are training for the ministry — and also, more recently, to lay people who will dedicate themselves to religious education. So theology is passed on at second hand to 'ordinary Christians'; and the dominant mode in which this takes place is one of instruction.

In the emerging Third World theology this whole approach

is questioned. It is assumed that all Christians have the right and the duty to reflect on the meaning of their faith. And it is presupposed that such reflection is the initial and fundamental form of theology — a form that cannot be ignored or played down by any experts. More specialised theologians still have a role to play in the Christian community. It is a service role: helping Christians to articulate their reflections and to relate their Christian experience to that of people in other places and times — and above all to the salvation history recounted in the Bible. The specialist theologian is not just one who 'teaches' in the sense of handing down ready-made truths. There has to be a two-way communication. The specialist must try to respond to the need and questions of the community — though as a member of that community he or she is also, of course, entitled to challenge the others.

I have been giving a rather abstract account of the role of the professional theologian and how it relates to the theological activity of individual Christians and the community as a whole. I feel this fails to bring out both the challenge and the excitement of what is involved. So I venture to recall two experiences which helped me to understand the relationship. I was a member of a very diverse group of Christians who had been meeting occasionally to share our faith and our reflections. In preparation for dialogue with theologians from the Third World, a minibus-full of us travelled to a meeting with Christians from other European countries. During the meeting we found that we had much in common with people in other countries who were trying to work towards an alternative way of doing theology; and we found ourselves at times in sharp conflict with some of the more academic theologians. For us the most exciting part of the conference was when we met together in the evenings to pray and reflect and celebrate. There we shared faith in a way that broke down all kinds of barriers. Two married women from Dublin — one from the inner city and one from a working-class suburb — began to speak of how they found God both in their struggles to survive and in their experiences of joy and love. They were quite distressed that their views did not conform at all points to what they were hearing every Sunday from the pulpit. Suddenly one of them turned to me and asked in all seriousness: 'Do.you think I am a Christian at all?'

In that moment I realised more vividly than ever before the kind of power that I had been given — a power that had been withheld from most of the 'lay' members of our group, especially the poorer ones and those with less formal education. It is a power over words, over the words we use to speak about God, and Christ, and the meaning of our faith. When I hear a sermon that does not fit in with my understanding of how to follow Christ, I try to allow myself to be challenged. But I am not at the mercy of the preacher; I know he may be wrong even if he is quoting the Bible or the highest authorities. I have been taught to interpret the words of Scripture and of other authoritative documents. This gives me the power to work out my own understanding of the formulas of our belief, without doubting the authenticity of my faith.

So my training and status as a theologian give me real power. It is a dangerous power, for I may abuse this ability to interpret the words in which our faith is expressed. But the Christian community has to trust some of its members with this power. Otherwise the Church would find itself bound hand and foot to a rigid, literal acceptance of its sacred documents, with no possibility of making allowances for the blind spots of ancient cultures, and no hope of a deepening understanding of revelation. (This has happened to a considerable extent in Islam and in some fundamentalist Christian groups.) Theologians are entrusted with this task of interpreting the formulas of our faith. I must add at once that, in the past few years, Church authorities have become more reluctant to make this act of trust; they feel that the theologians have been abusing the freedom they have been given.

The Church in the West is now in a rather odd situation. There is a kind of competition between two sets of authorities: the theologians who have the authority of scholarship and expertise; and the Church hierarchies and officials who have the authority of office. The latter group are anxious to protect the 'simple faith' of the Christian community against 'far out' theological opinions. At the same time they sometimes justify their disagreement with the views of theologians by invoking the faith of the community. Meanwhile the professional theologians are also claiming to be articulating the authentic faith of the Christian community. But neither of these two authority groups show much inclination to really listen to the 'ordinary' Christians; very little effort is made to enable the members of the community to articulate their own Christian experience.

I find it hard to take sides in this disagreement between the two sets of authorities; I do not think it would be good for either side to win. The way forward seems to me to be an act of relinquishment by both groups — not a yielding to the others but rather a determined effort to share power with the wider Christian community. As a theologian I would not be giving up my right and my call to reflect on and interpret the faith. But I would be letting go any claim that theologians have a special or exclusive right to do so. It is easy to do this in words; but to carry it through in practice would involve a determined effort to share theological skills, knowledge, and confidence with non-professionals.

It is time for both theologians and Church authorities to make an act of trust — for us to share as much of our power as possible with our fellow-Christians. For they have as much right as I have to reflect for themselves on what Christ means to their lives. If most Christians seem apathetic about engaging in theological reflection that may be because they have been given little encouragement to do so. And this brings me to the second incident which I wish to recall. A couple of years ago when I had just returned to Ireland from Africa I was invited to join a group for a Eucharistic celebration followed by a Christmas party. The Eucharist was deeply moving — prayerful, 'easy', and very participative. One member of the group was a man from the West of Ireland who had left primary school to work as a migrant labourer in Britain and had later returned to his home in Connemara. He said: 'I am happy to be able to take part in this Mass and I am delighted that there are some priests who are willing to allow us to celebrate in this way. For too long the priests kept God locked up in a box in the Church . . .'

To 'keep God locked up in a box'. What an apt and challenging phrase! Control over the tabernacle is a perfect image for control over the religious beliefs of the Christian community. The remark brought home to me very vividly that what is at stake is a matter of justice. I have no right to imagine that I 'own' God, that I can control what people believe about God. Neither can I disclaim responsibility for

50

the way in which, in our world, power has becom
trated in the hands of a relatively small number of pe.
For I myself am one of those who have power. Not economic
or political power — but a power that can affect people at a
deeper level. Furthermore, such religious power has often
been traded off for monetary or political benefits.

At the heart of the evil of injustice in society lies the fact
that power of different kinds has come to be held by privileged
minorities. It is clear that, if I am not part of the solution to
this problem, then I am part of the problem. The writing of
this book is one small way in which I hope to contribute to a
solution. I propose to go on in the next chapter to explain
the causes and effects of such concentration of power — and
how it results in what is called 'structural injustice'. In subsequent chapters I shall try to spell out how the Christian can
try to overcome such injustice in various spheres — including
the sphere of Church structures.

# 4

# Structural Injustice

Why is there such a thing as 'The Third World'? Why are the majority of its people trapped in poverty? Why is it that, even in the First World, the gap between the rich and the poor grows wider? To answer these questions adequately one would have to give a long historical account of the way our world has developed in recent centuries. But in any account of the relationships between the rich and the poor there is one crucial point that must be understood; it is the difference between personal injustice and structural injustice. Unless one makes that distinction one cannot really understand the problem of social injustice. Furthermore, if one fails to distinguish between these two types of injustice there is little hope that one can understand what is meant by 'an option for the poor'.

The sad fact is that many sincere people who are actively involved in trying to help oppressed people are at the same time helping to maintain unjust structures in society. For instance, I may become involved in a movement against apartheid in South Africa, while continuing to exercise authority arbitrarily as a priest in a highly clericalised Church. Somebody else may play an active role in a Prisoners' Rights organisation, while taking a large salary from a multinational company that is failing to pay Third World workers a living wage.

It is very important, then, that those who wish to work for social justice should take part in some kind of 'social analysis' that will help them to locate the structures that maintain injustice. A study of this kind has to be specific. It should begin from the local situation. So there is no possibility that it could be done in a general book like this one.

What I can do, however, is to offer a very broad historical outline of the development in our world of structures that embody and promote injustice. I shall then go on to suggest a framework which may help people to identify the main types of structural injustice, and to see how they support each other.

*Trapped in poverty*

A few hundred years ago the different regions of the world were largely self-contained, self-sufficient, and linked to each other only through a relatively small amount of trade in luxury goods. Then came the imperialist expansion of four or five European countries. They set up colonies in most of what we now call the Third World; and the economy of the colonised areas was reorganised to serve the interests of the imperial powers. Colonialism is almost gone, but it has been replaced by a neo-colonial system. This means that control over poorer countries is not usually exercised now by overt military and political power but mainly in economic ways. This economic control can create even greater hardship than the old-style colonial rule because it affects every sphere of life.

The typical poor country is dependent for foreign earnings on the export of one or two agricultural products such as tea, coffee, bananas, sugar-cane, or beef. Trade in these products is grossly imbalanced in favour of the rich countries of 'the North' and at the expense of the poor countries in 'the South'; prices are low and unstable; and the market is controlled by foreign companies. A country in this situation sinks ever deeper into debt; and so it is no longer in a position to make important decisions about its economy — these are made by the foreign countries and banks to whom it owes money. Locally owned crafts and industry (e.g. the manufacture of clothes, footwear, soap, and food products) are largely replaced by multinational companies which have no interest in the long-term welfare of the country; their only concern is to make as much profit as possible as quickly as possible. The country does not have the money to extract and process its own mineral and energy resources. So mining corporations and oil companies are invited in to exploit these resources; and *exploit* them they do. In most cases even the agriculture of the poor country comes to be controlled by foreign interests: land that could produce food for the poor is given over to growing crops for export at very low prices.

The result of all this is that poor countries are trapped in their poverty. No matter how richly endowed they are with natural resources or how hard their people work, it is highly unlikely that they can ever catch up with the rich countries — so long as the present system continues. The poverty of the Third World is not due to a lack of resources. Neither is it to be explained by saying that the people are lazy, or not interested in work, or not good at looking after machinery. These accusations may be true in some cases — but they are not the crucial issue. Poverty on this global scale cannot be accounted for in terms of the character and behaviour of those who are poor. It is not a *moral* matter but a *structural* one; the structures of the international economic order are biased against the poor.

So much for poverty at the global level. But what about the poverty of a large minority of people who live in the wealthy countries? This poverty also has to be explained mainly in terms of structures rather than in terms of moral behaviour. If the poor are apathetic, that is the result of their poverty rather than its basic cause. In Chapter 1 of this book I noted a variety of ways in which our society is biased against the less well-off. The wealthy and privileged groups 'have everything going for them'. It is not mainly their industry or wisdom that leads to the widening of the gap between rich and poor; rather it is the economic, social, and political structures of our society.

This has important practical consequences. It means that if I want to 'act justly', as the Lord asks through the prophet Micah, then it is not enough for me to ensure that I work within the existing economic structures, either at the international or the national level. Justice requires that I make a serious effort to replace this unjust order with one that is more equitable, one that gives much greater opportunity to the poor. If I am committed to justice, one of the first steps will be to locate the different spheres where structural injustice exists.

*Four pyramids of power*

I have already pointed out how, at a global level, economic power has come to be concentrated in the hands of the relatively small number of rich countries of the industrialised 'North'. But this concentration of power is not confined to some *nations* or *regions* as against others; it is also a matter of some *classes* or groups of people being vastly more wealthy and powerful than others. Even in the poor countries – in fact especially in the poor countries – a small minority control almost all of the wealth. In poor countries these people usually act as the agents of foreign companies; and their interests coincide with those of the foreigners rather than with the mass of their own people.

It is not only in the economic sphere that power has become concentrated in the hands of a few. This also happens in the political sphere. There is a close link between economic and political power. In some cases this is overt: wealthy people go into politics, or politicians become very wealthy by making use of their political power. At times the links between the two are more subtle. For instance it often happens in Third World countries that local politicians have a trade-off arrangement with foreign companies or with wealthy ethnic minorities within the country (such as the Asians in some East African countries): in exchange for money, the politicians offer the privileges which they control. This kind of trade-off does not have to be illegal. For instance, a multinational company may agree to invest in a country only under certain conditions – such as the curtailment of trade union activity or the adoption of certain economic policies by the government.

In addition to the concentration of power in the economic and political spheres, something similar takes place in the less tangible sphere of communications, information, and ideas. A relatively small number of people own or control much of the world's mass media; a few fashion designers decide what people will wear; and the form and content of education is under the control of a small elite.

Even in the religious sphere a similar concentration of power has occurred. One can see this taking place very clearly in African countries as Christianity replaces traditional beliefs. In the past, each local community had a number of people who specialised in divining, healing, and the provision

55

of protection against evil. They had religious power which could be used as a source of money and influence. But normally they were part of the local community, not subject to any outside power. Nowadays the clergy are taking over the position of these people; but the local clergy are themselves functionaries of a much larger organisation where the real power is held by the bishops and higher Church authorities.

The typical pattern in modern society may be represented visually by four narrow pyramids. Sitting on top of the first pyramid are those who have 'money power' — the small number of individuals, companies and countries who are dominant in the economic sphere. At the top of the second pyramid are the few who have political power. On the third pyramid are the people and organisations with a near monopoly in what I would call 'idea power' — the power to influence how people think and feel. At the top of the fourth pyramid are those who hold what might be crudely called 'God power' — i.e. power in the ecclesiastical or religious sphere. All four pyramids have the same base; this common base represents the mass of ordinary people who have little power in any of the four spheres. The people at the top of the four pyramids negotiate with each other about the distribution and exchange of power between them. They may call this a 'dialogue' — but it is one that excludes the mass of people at the base of society. Those at the bottom are likely to lose whatever little power they had, and to become more and more marginalised and alienated. For they are not involved in the decision-making that goes on over their heads; and their voices are scarcely heard and seldom heeded.

### The 'Service People'

How do just a few people manage to exercise so much power? By setting up a large administrative 'machinery' in each of the different spheres — economic, political, cultural, and ecclesiastical. There are the economic organisations such as banks, insurance companies, and large business concerns; and one might also include in this economic sphere almost all the agencies dealing with sickness. Then there is the political bureaucracy — the civil service and the law enforcement agencies. There are organisations in the cultural sphere, such as news agencies, publishing companies, and the whole educational system. The Churches too have a highly centralised administrative system. By means of these different organisations the decisions of those at the top are implemented at the various levels until they reach the ordinary people at the bottom of society. These decisions determine how the common people live their lives; but quite often those who make the decisions are not accountable to the community.

The administrative 'machinery' requires a lot of people to staff it. These are the 'service people' whose work is to operate the economic, political, cultural, and ecclesiastical institutions of society. In feudal times a relatively small number of people was sufficient — clerks, clergy, artists, law enforcement people, and soldiers. In modern society there is a very large organisational superstructure, giving employment to perhaps 40% of the working population in some countries. The organisations have a hierarchical structure. The clerks and functionaries at the lower levels implement the decisions of those above them. The higher executives are allowed a greater degree of discretion in applying the existing policy. But real power remains in the hands of those at the top.

The result of all this is that modern society has a large middle group of people, employed by those who hold power of different kinds, and accountable to them rather than to those over whom they exercise their authority. These people are not very wealthy or powerful themselves; but the work they do maintains the power of those at the top of the pyramids. The organisations which they staff have a double purpose. On the one hand they are (normally) there to meet a real need of the community — e.g. the need for health services, security, information, food, religious services etc. But they also have a second purpose, which is less obvious: to promote the interests of those who control the 'machine' and ensure that they do not lose their power.

The 'service people' occupy a middle place in the four pyramids of power. In running the various systems they act as the agents of those who have power, imposing that power on the common people. But of course the very people who are running one system are themselves part of 'the common people' in relation to other systems. For instance, prison officers help to run the system which enforces the laws on ordinary people, but are themselves part of the common people whose economic lives are regulated by banks, insurance companies, and the government's department of finance.

There is, however, a *social* stratification in society which causes most of the different service people to have broadly similar aspirations and life-style — distinctly different from those of 'working class' people. This social division of society may originally have had an economic basis; for there was a time when manual workers as a whole were paid much less than 'white collar workers'. That has changed in Western countries; but the social stratification remains and plays a major role in determining how people feel and act.

By the very nature of their work the 'service people' are tied into the existing system. Their jobs depend on it, and their status in society, and frequently even their sense of their own identity. So it is not very common for such employees to challenge the system. In the first place, it does not normally occur to them to evaluate the organisation that employs them; most people think of it simply as the agency that gives them a job. Secondly, if they do begin to question the purpose or structure of the organisation, to wonder whether it is unjust, they will find it very hard to raise the issue; for they are likely to be seen as trouble-makers.

Most of what I have just said applies not merely to the 'service people' but to all employees. But industrial workers generally feel less identified with the system. For social and historical reasons they tend to feel more solidarity with fellow-workers than with the agency that employs them. (Perhaps Japan is an exception in this regard.) But for any of the service people to challenge the system would involve a deliberate choice to go against the stream. This is partly due to their place on the social scale. Being halfway up, they generally aspire to climb higher. Furthermore, their work is of a different kind to that of manual workers. They are not concerned with making objects but mainly with telling others what they must do. This exercise of authority leads them to identify more closely with the system.

*Structural, not personal, injustice*
One could talk in a general and abstract way about the difference between personal and structural injustice. But I decided instead to give the foregoing outline of the actual

58

situation in our world so that what I say about structural injustice may be more specific. I want to insist that any treatment of injustice is seriously deficient if it deals only with the unjust actions and attitudes of individuals. Over and above such personal injustice there is the injustice that is built into organisations or the structures of society.

There are two ways in which organisations may be unjust. Firstly, they may be unjust in what they do — e.g. exploiting the Third World, or depriving poor people of their rights, or charging excessive interest on loans. Secondly, they may be unjust in the very way in which they are designed. *Both* types of structural injustice are common in our world today. Firstly, the activities of many organisations and agencies are unjust. This should be evident from the account I gave earlier in this chapter of how the poor of the world are trapped in poverty. The world economic order has serious injustice built into it; there is a lack of equality in the bargaining between rich and poor. Secondly, there is an injustice built into the very way most of the large organisations in today's world are designed. They concentrate almost all power at the top; and that is itself an injustice, built into their structure; it deprives the ordinary workers of any effective control over the policies of the organisation in which they work.

If an organisation is unjust in either of these ways, then those who staff it are contributing to that injustice. No matter what their private attitudes and values may be, by their work they are promoting the injustice of the agency, or at least allowing it to continue. This is the really crucial point about structural injustice: it does not depend directly on the personal moral behaviour of those who are operating the system, but is rather a quality of the system itself.

How does structural injustice relate to personal injustice? In the first place unjust structures are the creation of people. Sometimes we establish structures that are unjust without really intending to do so; but normally it is done deliberately. Once structures come into existence it may be very difficult to change them. The crucial question then is to what extent anybody can be held responsible for the continued existence of unjust structures. Individual accountability varies. But, in general, the degree of responsibility corresponds to the position one occupies on the social pyramid.

The people at the bottom of the social pyramid are mainly the victims of structural injustice — although even they are to some extent involved in the working of the system. They have most to gain from a change; but normally they have little opportunity to change the structures from within. It should be noted, however, that the working-class in the First World often benefit from the structures which allow the Third World to be exploited. So it cannot be assumed that workers all over the world have identical interests.

The people at the top of the pyramids of power are the ones who must be held mainly accountable for structural injustice; for they are the ones who could most easily change the system. But they are the people least likely to replace the unjust structures, since they have most to lose. At times they use the structures as a way of shirking personal responsibility for injustice: they blame the system. There is some truth in this; for even they are to some extent trapped in a system. For instance if one big company 'goes soft' by paying more for raw materials from the Third World, it will soon be put out of business. Similarly, any managing director who makes changes resulting in reduced profits is quite likely to be dismissed by the share-holders. As for individual share-holders: they find it very difficult to push through changes that would make a company more just either in its own structures or in its activities. Even those at the top of the different pyramids could change unjust structures only by concerted action.

The problem of structural injustice affects the 'service people' most acutely. For they are the ones who staff the organisations through which it exists. They are in a better position than the working class to understand what is going on, and how the system discriminates against ordinary people. Those who have a sensitive conscience may feel somewhat guilty about the effects of the system they are operating. Yet they find themselves prisoners of the system, unable to know how to change it. Quite commonly such people get involved in some 'good cause' in their free time. That may be a way of salving their consciences; they are compensating for the complicity they feel in being part of an unjust system. This has the unfortunate effect of splitting the person's life into two very different sectors, each of which has its own

60

morality. It may lead people to abdicate responsibility for the injustice of the organisation in which they work.

I have spent a good deal of time trying to clarify the distinction between personal and structural injustice. That is because even those who understand the distinction seem to forget it in practice. Just one example: I know several Catholic dioceses where the relations between the bishop and the priests are strained. In discussion on the matter I often hear such remarks as: 'the bishop won't listen to the priests', or, 'the priests are not concerned about the welfare of the diocese as a whole'. This shows that attention is being focused on the moral behaviour and attitudes of the particular bishop and priests. There is very little awareness of the structural causes of the problem, as distinct from the moral causes.

The role of the bishop is defined in such a way as to give him a monopoly of power in the diocese. He does not require the approval of priests or lay people for most of his important decisions. This is a structural weakness, rather than a moral one. The proper remedy is a change in the structures rather than just a moral conversion. However, a moral conversion may also be required, because the structures tend to promote certain types of attitude and behaviour. The Church structures tend to make the bishop isolated from his fellow-priests and arbitrary in the way he exercises power; and the priests will find it hard to be concerned for 'his' diocese. The attitudes are more immediately obvious than the structures; so people fail to advert to the underlying structural causes of the problem. I shall return to this issue when considering the Church towards the end of Chapter 10 of this book; there I shall have more to say about the need for changes both in attitudes and in structures.

### Structural injustice and development

There has always been structural injustice in the world; and I do not see how one could measure whether it is more widespread and serious today than in the past. But, in the modern world, structural injustice is particularly odious for a number of reasons:

— First of all, it is global in a sense that was not true in the past. For there is now a single economic network linking almost the whole world; and this international order is grossly biased in favour of the industrialised nations of 'the North'.

61

— Secondly, there is less excuse than ever for injustice. Modern science and technology have made it possible for all peoples and classes to live in reasonable comfort. It is only the excessive demands of some — and lack of proper organisation — that leave others short.

— Thirdly, the mass media have made structural injustice much more evident than in the past. Television shows an undernourished Third World child and links it to the confiscation of peasants' land to grow cheap tomatoes or coffee for the First World.

— Fourthly, there is a peculiar hypocrisy associated with the new forms of structural injustice that have come into the world in recent times. For these new injustices have frequently been perpetrated in the name of 'development'; and this 'development' is presented as the way in which poverty and social inequality are at last to be overcome. This is a point that is missed by most people. It is so important that I propose to devote the remainder of this chapter to clarifying it.

In the name of 'development' peasant farmers in Kenya today are forbidden to cut down their coffee bushes to plant maize — even though the price they get for the coffee (if they eventually get it) would not buy the amount of maize they could have grown. In the name of 'development' inner city residents in the cities of Europe and America are being forced out of their homes and communities. To promote 'development' in Brazil, huge tracts of land which are badly needed to grow food, are now producing sugar-cane which is turned into *gasohol* to drive the cars of the wealthy elite. 'Development' has left many First World farmers hopelessly mortgaged to the banks that encouraged them to take out heavy loans to 'develop' their farms. In the search for 'development', small countries all over the world have lost whatever degree of economic independence they once had; they have become dangerously dependent on international companies, and on an international market that is both unstable and unresponsive to the human problems it generates.

The foregoing examples suggest that I am not very enthusiastic about many of the things that take place in the name of 'development'. In the following pages I shall have further harsh things to say about the process called 'development'.

So it is necessary to insist beforehand that I am not condemning any and every kind of economic and social development. What I shall be criticising is the particular model of development that has been adopted so enthusiastically in many countries over the past generation. This particular approach has been so universally and uncritically accepted that most people do not realise that it is only one of the ways in which people can seek to overcome poverty. It would be unfortunate if it were thought that in criticising it I am advocating a policy of stagnation. In later chapters it will, I hope, become clear that I am advocating an alternative approach to development rather than no development.

There is a serious language problem in regard to the word 'development'. The word has a value-judgment built into it; few people would claim to be against development. But at present the word is associated almost exclusively with a particular approach; and there are good reasons for being critical of the process that is generally called 'development'. I am reluctant to allow such a good word as 'development' to be 'high-jacked'; yet I have to take account of current usage. So I shall generally put the word in inverted commas when I am referring to the present dominant model of development.

## The myth of development

Over the past generation the process of 'development' has spread from the industrial centres of Europe, North America, and Japan to the Third World, as well as to the 'underdeveloped' periphery of the First World. Its spread has been fostered by a set of myths that have made it seem inevitable and respectable − the only way of achieving progress and of overcoming poverty. These myths have led governments − and many of the people − to justify the enormous human and environmental costs that have been paid as the price of rapid growth of the economy.

In some cases the process has 'worked' in the sense that economic activity in the country or region expanded rapidly and more wealth became available. On the other hand I know some African countries where the whole process of 'development' has been a ghastly failure, even from a purely economic point of view. It has undermined the traditional subsistence economy and replaced it with an economic system designed

63

to exploit the resources of the country in return for 'pay-offs' to a few people in power. There are places where the newly imposed system is so alien that even the exploitation carried out under the guise of 'development' has not worked effectively! So much so that one could hardly say which would be better for the country and the people: for the development plans of the government to work or for them to fail.

In most Third World countries the economic results of 'development' lie somewhere in between the extremes. New wealth has been generated; but there are doubts about whether the process can be sustained when the easily available resources (oil, minerals, etc) run short. Or agricultural production of export crops has been greatly expanded, but the market prices have dropped or become dangerously unstable.

Even in situations where the process has worked reasonably well from an economic point of view, serious questions arise about the overall human effects of this 'development' of the poorer countries. In most of those parts of the Third World where new wealth was generated, poverty has not been overcome — because the wealth was not fairly distributed. It is true that in some countries of East Asia industrialisation has led to a general rise in the standard of living; but this has been linked to serious deprivation of basic human rights — the right to join trade unions, to proper standards of industrial safety, to engage in political activity, etc. Another problem about 'successful' economic development is that it is very costly from an ecological point of view: it leads to serious depletion of precious resources and it often overloads the land, water, and air with poisonous wastes. In the Third World there is generally less control over such ecological damage than in the First World.

If 'development' gives rise to so many problems why is it that newly independent countries embrace it so uncritically? There are two basic reasons. Firstly, those who act on behalf of these countries are generally a small and privileged minority. They have much to gain, at least in the short term, from the 'development' process, even if it causes troubles for the country as a whole. Secondly, the dominant elite have swallowed the myth of development — and they often succeed in 'selling' it to the masses as well. These people are shrewd; they will not be convinced by some abstract theory about development; but they have before their eyes the success of the Western countries in becoming rich and powerful. The myth of development consists above all in *the belief that the First World has led the way*; the Third World can follow the same path and become rich and powerful in its turn.

This belief is an illusion. It is simply not true that the rest of the world can develop in the same way as the Western countries. For a crucial factor in the history of Western development has been the fact that the 'undeveloped' countries were there 'beneath' them. In fact the whole purpose of the colonial system and the neo-colonialism which has replaced it, was to make use of the countries of 'the South' to enrich 'the North'. This took place in different ways at different stages of history. At first the poor countries provided cheap *labour* in the form of slaves. Later, as colonies, they were the source of cheap *raw materials* (e.g. cotton), for Europe's industrial revolution. At the same time they provided a ready *market* for its products. When the industrial 'North' began to run short of energy sources the 'underdeveloped countries' became a source of cheap *energy* (oil, uranium). More recently 'the developed countries' have benefited again from the cheap *labour* of people from the Third World. This time it came in two forms: multinational companies came to Asia, Brazil, South Africa, to exploit their cheap and strictly controlled labour; meanwhile migrant workers came 'North' to harvest crops at slave wages or to take menial jobs in industry or the service sector. In very recent times the Third World has become the place where 'dirty' industries can be sited without too much concern for the *environment*.

It would be very convenient if the Third World could find another 'undeveloped' region 'below' it – a vast region that could be exploited in the way 'the South' was used by 'the North'. Science fiction suggests that other planets might be treated in this way. But the present reality is that we live on 'Space-ship Earth', with no further 'undiscovered' continents available to Third World countries for exploitation. So they cannot repeat the pattern that worked so well for the First World.

There is no easy solution to the poverty of the Third World. What we have to look for is a better distribution of the present resources of the earth and careful conservation

65

...e. In Chapter 9 of this book I shall discuss the ...'an alternative economics', which would work ...ese goals. At present my main concern is to ...now illusory it is to suggest that poor countries ...ow the same pattern as the rich ones in becoming ...ped'. Of course, a small number of poor countries may manage to squeeze into the First World. But the present favoured model of development cannot be repeated all over the world. There is room for only a relatively small number of people or countries at the top of the pyramid; they are there because others are at the bottom.

For the individual the advantages or disadvantages of 'development' vary according to one's place on the social pyramid. For the top 5% in both First World and Third World countries it has meant a massive increase in wealth and power. For those in the middle it has generally meant a significant increase in their standard of living. This middle group covers perhaps 15% of the population in Third World countries. But in the First World it can be as much as 65% or 70%. For those at the bottom it has meant being left more and more on the margins of society — not only trapped in poverty but also voiceless. This group may include as many as 80% of the population of some Third World countries. In the First World it includes 'only' about 20% to 25% of the population.

To finish this section I shall try to spell out clearly the close connection between 'development' and structural injustice. It is this: the process called development consists mainly of the replacement of traditional economic structures with what are called 'modern' ones. The effect of the change is to render inoperative or ineffective many of the traditional checks and balances which ensured a modicum of social justice. There are many new opportunities for the strong to take advantage of the weak.

This kind of thing is liable to happen whenever there is rapid social change. But it is made much worse when countries deliberately adopt the current model of 'development'. For it is one that puts stress on rapid growth of the economy. This is to be achieved by allowing entrepreneurs to be 'rewarded' by high profits. Better distribution of wealth is postponed until after growth has been achieved. So, not only does the new system give advantages to those who already have power,

66

but even the *theory* of 'development' justifies a widening of the gap between rich and poor.

But what about 'the Welfare State'? Does it not offer a country the best of both worlds — development combined with social welfare? It is true that about twenty years ago some First World countries succeeded in combining economic development with the maintenance of a Welfare State. But in those cases there were special circumstances which are unlikely to be repeated: notably, the availability of very cheap oil and raw materials from the Third World. In fact the problem of the poverty of the working class in the First World was being alleviated by the use of resources taken partly from the Third World and partly from reserves that should have been saved for future generations. One might say that poverty was being internationalised and exported — and also passed on to the next generation. In recent years these Welfare State systems have come under increasing pressure. In many places they are no longer keeping pace with the social problems. Of course it would be possible for the relevant countries to give a much higher priority to the elimination of poverty. But that would involve abandoning the present conception of 'development'; and in fact the tendency is in the opposite direction. (In my book *Option for the Poor: A Hundred Years of Vatican Social Teaching*, pp. 93-9, I have discussed at more length the question of the possibility of overcoming poverty through rapid economic growth, combined with a Welfare State approach to social services.)

## A time to shout 'Stop'

More and more committed Christians are coming to realise that to commit oneself to social justice at the global and local levels means in practice a radical questioning of the present dominant model of development. We are beginning to see just how inimical to human life it really is, and how deceptive its promises have proved to be. I have already pointed out many of the problems to which it gives rise. But at this point it may be useful to list various serious objections that have been raised against it — not by wild radicals but by respected scientists and cautious Church leaders such as Pope John Paul II:

— Far from solving the problem of poverty, 'development' has actually widened the gap between the rich and the poor.

— Its undermining of the traditional economic and social structures has left many people powerless, deprived of the opportunity to share in the making of decisions that affect their lives and their livelihood.

— 'Development' also threatens the traditional cultures of many non-Western peoples.

— It requires excessive specialisation in work; this means that many people have no sense of fulfilment in their work, so they become alienated.

— It poses a serious threat to the environment by poisoning the land, the water and the air.

— It causes the resources of the earth to be used up at a rate that cannot be sustained.

— It leads to sharp competition between nations for access to scarce resources; this competition is a major factor in the arms race — which itself involves the squandering of resources, and which threatens to wipe out the human race.

Later in this book, particularly in Chapters 7 to 10, I shall take up many of these points in more detail. But at present I want to raise a more general question: what is it about the process called 'development' that causes it to be so damaging to human life? If we could find an answer to this question it could help us to design an alternative model of development, one that would make use of modern science and technology in a way that is 'friendly' to human life in all its aspects. It seems to me that in the process of 'development' there are two crucial weaknesses which are the source of most of the problems listed above.

The first major weakness in this model of development is that it is a system which contains an unregulated 'growth imperative'. Putting it in popular terms one might say that it has a very powerful acceleration system but no brakes. Once the growth rate of a country slows down, the whole development process runs into trouble, and there is danger of complete collapse. This applies with even more force to the world economy as a whole. It is even true at the level of the individual company; almost as soon as it stops expanding, it is at risk. I do not want to go into the technical reasons why continual economic growth is so crucial; I shall merely say that it has to do with the motivating forces which are the 'fuel' of this model of development. This brings me to the second basic flaw in the system.

The second weakness is closely related to the first, since it too removes the brakes from the system. It is that this model of development fosters a very high degree of competitiveness. The only virtue recognised and rewarded by the system is strength. Any concession to humanity becomes a weakness; so too does any concern for the long-term welfare of the community; or any special care for the environment. Concern in any of these areas may of course be worth while as an exercise in public relations; but the inner dynamic of the system requires that these be kept to a minimum and that they be 'milked' for publicity rather than undertaken for their own sake. In general, long-term welfare is subordinated to immediate or fairly short-term gain.

The result of this in-built competitiveness is that there is no effective mechanism to regulate the speed and manner in which new technology is introduced. On the rare occasions when a new invention is not made use of, this is because it threatens the interests of some powerful cartel. But the fact that a new invention will put people out of work is hardly ever allowed to delay its introduction. The argument is: 'If we do not introduce this new technology, our competitors will do so.' In other words, the system is able to defend itself but not the people who work for it. On rare occasions strong trade unions may be able to resist the change for a time; but their concern is to help their own members rather than to limit unemployment in general.

Because of the 'growth imperative' and competitiveness that are intrinsic to the system, even governments find themselves trapped into supporting a policy that creates unemployment. They have to accept the logic of the claim that the only way to save jobs is to make industries more efficient — and this means approving of more redundancies. An example will illustrate the point. Suppose the footwear industry in Britain introduces new technology which puts half its workers out of a job. It may then be so efficient that it is a threat to the footwear industry in other countries. So they introduce still higher technology, with the loss of even more jobs. And so the spiral continues. What is horrifying is that this irrational behaviour is described as 'rationalisation'. Those who resist it are branded as irresponsible, if not actually irrational. The 'rationalisation spiral' has the same kind of crazy logic as the arms race: each stage of the process is necessary because people have failed to question the presuppositions of the whole system.

We are told that competition is justified because it enables people to have a choice. But what kind of choice? We can choose between Ford and Toyota, between Heinz and Nestlé. But the system does not give us the opportunity to make the kind of choices that really matter:
— between a really effective system of public transport and the proliferation of costly and wasteful private transport;
— between a lifestyle that conserves resources and respects the environment and one where we rob future generations by squandering resources on arms and useless luxuries;
— between the use of an appropriate technology that permits everybody to have employment, or high technology and cheaper goods at the cost of massive unemployment.

These are the kind of choices that really matter; and I shall have a good deal to say about them in chapters 7-11 of this book. I mention them here simply to bring out the point that I am not advocating *no* development but an alternative model of development. The time has come when we must cry, 'Stop' to the present model. There are sound moral and cultural and ecological and political and even economic reasons for doing so. Let me just mention one, which should be sufficiently convincing even on its own. Robots on assembly lines are putting thousands of workers out of a job for the rest of their lives — and soon it will be millions. Surely, then, it is time to question the logic of the system. After thousands of soldiers had been poisoned by mustard-gas in World War I, the nations agreed to ban it. Is it not time that they agreed to regulate the use of high technology which is depriving so many of the fundamental right to work? To do so would be a big step towards the adoption of another model of development.

What I have been saying brings home the point that the present model of development was not really designed at all. It is a monster that grew in a haphazard way. The futile efforts of Western governments to regulate their economies shows that, even in the First World, 'development' is a beast

70

that is no longer under anybody's control. As for the Third World: there it devours country after country, squeezing the life out of hundreds of traditional cultures and turning them into sick caricatures of the Western world. For the process of 'development' is not merely the introduction of a new economic system. It involves massive cultural imperialism as well — the imposition of Western ideas, values, and priorities on the peoples of the Third World. In Africa today I can see the slow death of languages, traditions, and a heritage of human wisdom of incredible depth and variety. Like Esau, these peoples are losing their birthright for a mess of pottage — and most of them are not even getting the pottage.

The damage caused by 'development' is so serious that one is entitled to describe it in the apocalyptic symbols of the Book of Revelation:

> Then I saw a beast coming up out of the sea.... It was given authority over every tribe, nation, language, and race.... Then I saw another beast ... which forced the earth and all who live on it to worship the first beast. ... This second beast performed great miracles ... through which it deceived all the people of the earth ...
>
> (Rev 13:1-7)

The first beast may be taken to represent the economic and cultural imperialism of 'the North'. The second beast, which leads all the people of the earth to submit to the first beast, may be taken to represent the model of 'development', which has produced 'miracles' that deceive the nations of the world into allowing themselves to be trapped into submitting to and worshipping the powers of 'the North'.

In a public lecture last year I used this symbol of the beast. An economist in the audience said: 'Why not call the beast by its name? The beast that is devouring the earth is capitalism.' To this I would want to give a qualified reply. It is true that the present dominant model of development in the West is almost inextricably tied up with the capitalist approach and philosophy. It is true that the Third World is largely the creation of Western capitalism. In that sense my criticism of 'development' is, concretely, a criticism of capitalism. But to say that the basic problem is the capitalist system seems to imply a preference for the State socialism adopted by the

'Second World' (what we popularly call the Communist countries). That is not the kind of alternative I would look for.

The approach to development adopted in the 'communist' countries is simply a variant of the Western model, rather than a radical alternative to it. The ruling elites in these countries share many of the presuppositions and priorities of Western economists and politicians. They have been just as committed as Western leaders to increased production; and, like their counterparts in the West, they have deceived themselves by giving the name 'production' to such processes as the extraction of oil from the earth. They have presumed that the earth is there to be exploited; and the exploitive mentality has been extended to people.

The communists have attempted to correct the economic problems of capitalism by introducing a rigid system of centralised planning; and the result has been the creation of a bureaucracy even more massive and oppressive than that of Western countries. Their professed aim in economic affairs has been to catch up with the West, and even to pass it out. They have not introduced a really alternative approach to the West in the spheres of technology, ecology, or the participation of people in decision-making. Their societies have pyramids of power analogous to those in the Western world.

The 'communist' system has to be understood as a reaction against Western capitalism. From the beginning, the aim of the communists was to distribute wealth more evenly in society. They set out not merely to replace those who were at the top of the 'money power' pyramid, but to break down the pyramid entirely. Their system succeeded in doing this to a considerable extent — though by no means as well as its founders had hoped. There is a better distribution of wealth in the 'communist' countries. In achieving their goal, however, the communists created a State socialist system in which the ordinary people are still dominated — but by another one of the pyramids of power; instead of 'money power' the primary source of domination has become political power. In Western capitalism those who have 'money power' use it to buy power in other spheres of life. In the countries of Eastern Europe the typical starting-point is power within the communist party — and it can be used to gain privileges in other spheres.

Both systems are riddled with structural injustice. Both deprive many people of fundamental human rights — the West mainly in the economic sphere and the East mainly in the political sphere. Those in power in each of the two kinds of society defend their unjust systems ruthlessly — and claim to be doing so in defence of true freedom. It is significant that in recent years one finds both the East and the West using the language of 'the National Security State'; and at least in this regard they are becoming almost mirror images of each other.

Political oppression is the most obvious effect of structural injustice in the 'communist' countries. Economic exploitation is the most obvious effect in Western capitalist countries. And in the right-wing dictatorships that are common in the Third World both kinds of injustice are equally evident. Capitalists and communists each emphasise the injustices of the other system. In the present political climate it is in the interests of those in power in East and West to present their two systems as radically different from each other. For that may lead us to believe that if we reject one then we have to choose the other. But our options do not have to be limited in this way. We can look for an alternative that is truly different, because it is based on different values, 'Kingdom values'. And as Christians we are called to do so. Later in the book I shall be examining these 'Kingdom values' and the ways in which they can be embodied in our society. But before that I want to give an initial account of what it means to make an option for an alternative system — and to look briefly at the biblical basis for such an option, an option for the poor.

# 5

# Option for the Poor:
# what does it mean?

The best writing on the question of option for the poor comes from the Third World — and it is very much coloured by the situation out of which it comes. This makes it difficult for people in Europe or North America to relate it to their own experience. There are two reasons why the difficulty is greater for this topic than almost any other theological issue. Firstly, those in the First World who face up to the question of global poverty are bound to feel troubled. They know they are benefiting from an unjust system and they have to ask themselves whether they are in some way responsible for it. This imposes a heavy psychological burden on them. The effect on some people is that they 'go on a guilt trip', blaming themselves for all the injustices in the world and allowing their guilt to block them from responding in an easy and honest way to people from the Third World. Others try to escape too easily by disclaiming all responsibility for the injustice of the world and blithely assuming that they have made common cause with the Third World; then they are hurt when they find the genuineness of their 'conversion' being questioned.

In addition to this psychological difficulty there is also a more theological one. It concerns the relationship between 'the poor' and 'the common people' (or 'the masses'). Latin American theologians, writing out of their own situation, are quite entitled to equate the two terms; for the vast majority of people in the Third World are really poor. But the situation is quite different in the wealthy countries. In them, only about a quarter of the population can be considered to be poor in the economic sense. It is true that most people may be 'poor' in the political and cultural sense, having little effective opportunity to shape the structures and values of the society in which they live. Furthermore, women are 'poor' in so far as they live in a male-dominated society. And lay Christians are 'poor' in being deprived of an effective voice in the life of the Church. But if one takes the word 'poverty' in its primary economic sense, one cannot identify the ordinary folk with 'the poor'. .

How is a theologian from the First World to respond authentically to this situation? Some very committed people have simply left their own countries and gone to live permanently in the Third World. A number of the more notable Third World theologians are in fact from the First World. I am thinking of people like Jon Sobrino, José Comblin, and Carlos Mesters, who came from Europe but have now immersed themselves completely in the Latin American situation: 'Your people will be my people, and your God will be my God.' (Ruth 1:16). I do not think such total identification is possible for me in an African situation; and in any case I would not want to relinquish all responsibility for my own country, Ireland, which is in an interesting situation on the margin of the First World. (I shall discuss this in a later chapter.) I want to develop a theology which is rooted both in my home situation and in my Third World experience. I would like to be able to speak to people in both of these 'worlds'.

Any authentic theology, no matter what its local roots may be, must take account of the global reality. Therefore a theologian from the First World who wants to help Christians to become 'the Church of the poor' must face up to the fact that the great majority of the world's poor are living in other continents. This means that it is not at all easy for the Church in the First World to be genuinely committed to social justice and at the same time to be 'a Church of the people'. I can clarify this by taking as examples the Church in Brazil and the Church in the USA.

When Brazilian Church leaders commit the Church to being on the side of the poor they can expect opposition from the rich and powerful. But they have the consolation of knowing that these people, for all their power, are only a small minority of the population; the mass of the people rejoice that the Church has become 'their Church'. In the

USA, however, the majority of the people are privileged and wealthy in global terms. So, in the First World, Church leaders — or individual Christians — who wish to make an effective option for the poor cannot presume that they will have the support of the main body of Christians in their own country.

The split in the First World between 'the poor' and 'the common people' causes a difficulty for Christians who wish to make an option for the poor. It can lead them to take up one or other of two inadequate approaches. On the one hand I know some people who have become quite swamped by enthusiasm for the Latin American Church. They are so intense and committed in their efforts to transpose this model of Church to the First World that they allow an ever wider gap to grow up between their own ideals and the views of the people around them. Before long they are dismissed as 'cranks'; and they are likely to become frustrated and alienated. On the other hand, I can think of a number of people who seek to work up mass support for the cause of the world's poor. The danger for them is that in practice they may reduce their option for the poor to what I would call 'Third World do-goodism'. They use all kinds of promotional techniques to whip up support for justice for and in the Third World; but all this bears very little relation to their own everyday life. The poor and deprived in their own area may remark cynically that this is 'cheap charity'.

In writing this book I would like to avoid both mistakes. In order to do so I have tried to rethink what it would mean to make an option for the poor in a First World context. Anybody who reads this book will find nothing in it about supporting revolutionary movements in the First World. For that is not the kind of agenda that is relevant in Europe or North America at this time. However, I do believe that the demands imposed by an authentic option for the poor are 'revolutionary' in a certain sense: those who respond will find themselves making radical changes in their lifestyle, their approach to work, their political concerns, and their model of Church. In all of these areas the crucial change will be a change in priorities. For what affects us most is not the kind of world we would like to live in but the options we are prepared to make in the immediate future. What counts is not our theoretical ideals but where we are prepared to begin.

76

## A 'Political' act

To make an option for the poor is not to opt for poverty but to opt for people. It is to commit oneself to acting and living in a way that respects people, especially those who are not treated with respect in our society. It is to proclaim by one's actions that people are more important than the systems that deprive them of their basic rights — the right to eat, the right to work, the right to participate in decision-making, the right to worship according to their conscience, and even the right to life itself.

In the past few years, as I worked with various groups of Christians who wanted to promote social justice, I have become more and more convinced that, despite its apparent obviousness, such an option is extremely difficult. It is difficult first of all even to understand what it really means and what it involves in practice. Secondly, it is very difficult to carry through on such an option — to live it out day by day. The difficulty in understanding what the option involves is reinforced by the difficulty in carrying it out: sometimes we fail to understand because we are unwilling to take the necessary action.

What makes the problem particularly awkward is that it is generally the wrong people who have the doubts and difficulties. I have worked with some religious groups who took it for granted that they had *already* made an option for the poor — simply because they had decided to give alms or other help to local poor people. On the other hand I know individuals and groups who have really opted for the poor but are still troubled, because they experience a sharp clash between the society to which they belong and the ideals which they are trying to live by. I hope that what I say in this chapter — and in the rest of the book — may help to disturb the complacency of the former group and perhaps console and fortify the latter group. I want to follow on from the previous chapter by showing the relationship between structural injustice and an option for the poor.

To make an option is to make a personal choice. So an option for the poor is not something that can be done for me by somebody else. I want to stress this personal aspect. But I want at the same time to insist that the kind of option that is in question here is not just an act of personal asceticism, performed to promote my own spiritual growth. Neither is it just an act performed out of interpersonal compassion for a poor person, as when St Martin gave his cloak to the beggar. It is an action that is public in character; it pertains to the 'political' sphere rather than to the personal or interpersonal spheres.

An option for the poor is a response to the structural injustice that mars our world at the local and global level. It is a carefully calculated commitment to working for a more just society, a more human world. In my opinion it ought to include a serious effort to change the present dominant model of development; that should be evident from what I said about 'development' in the last chapter. To opt for the poor is to undertake to work for a style of development that is more likely to promote social justice and to protect the weaker sectors of the community — and the weaker nations of the world.

The phrase 'option for the poor' often evokes strong reactions. Some of the resistance comes from the reluctance of privileged groups — and those who serve them — to give up their unfair privileges. But some of the difficulty comes simply from a misunderstanding of what is involved — due largely to failure to grasp the notion of structural injustice. Those who do not appreciate the difference between personal and structural injustice miss the crucial point about an option for the poor. They think of it in purely interpersonal terms as a rejection of wealthy *people*; they fail to realise that it has to do above all with *structures*; it is primarily an attempt to develop a society that is structurally just.

We speak of making 'a *preferential* option for the poor'. This means working for a society in which the poor are given preference. Does that imply rejection of those who are more privileged? Not at all; and that is made very clear when Church leaders like Pope John Paul II speak of 'a preferential but not exclusive option for the poor'. Nobody is excluded. But the poor are given preference and special care because their need is greater. 'Fair shares for all' leads to justice only if everybody already has a fairly equal share. Where some are already victims of injustice it only reinforces the inequality. Therefore social justice does not require that we give equal shares of our time and resources to everybody. What it requires is that we work for some kind of balance in society. The better off groups already have adequate resources; to opt for the poor is to aim to rectify the balance.

Who is asked to make an option for the poor? Everybody. It is part of the universal call of the Christian faith, which is addressed to all people. But what it involves is rather different for those at the top, the middle, and the bottom of society. For those who sit on *top* of the four 'pyramids of power' it is a straight call to conversion. They are called to let the scales drop from their eyes, to open their ears to the cry of the oppressed. For them, the first stage in opting for the poor is the recognition that the structures of society give them an unfair advantage over others. They have no right to a monopoly of wealth or political power; they are not entitled to control the views of others; neither can they claim to be the only ones who may speak and act in the name of God.

As a Christian I am committed to the belief that nobody is too hardened or corrupt to be converted. The New Testament gives some interesting examples. Zacchaeus had 'money power'; Nicodemus had political power; St Paul had power in the religious sphere. Each of them felt called to relinquish his undue power in order to follow Christ (Lk 19:1-10; Jn 3:1; 7:50-2; Acts 9:2; Gal 1:13-14; I Cor 2:1-4). I must add, however, that the Bible indicates that such conversions are the exception rather than the rule; it is not primarily through the conversion of the rich and powerful that God establishes his Kingdom. That lesson has not (yet?) been taken to heart by the Church in most Western countries.

It is only recently that I have come to realise that the people at the *bottom* of society are also called to make an option. For them, to make an option for the poor is, of course, to opt for themselves. At first sight that seems a selfish act. But what in fact is involved is an act of faith and trust by poor people both in themselves and in others who are in a similar situation. That is very difficult. These are people who are likely to be disillusioned and apathetic, frequently broken in spirit or at least deeply hurt. Their first and greatest challenge is to believe in themselves and in each other. Once they recognise their own talents and the gifts of others they can begin to take responsibility for their lives and the world. The story of the liberation of the Jews from slavery in Egypt is very instructive in this respect. One of the most difficult tasks of Moses was to convince his people that they could be liberated: 'they did not listen to Moses because of their broken spirit and their cruel bondage' (Ex 6:9; cf. 4:1-9; 5:21).

### 'The Service People'

The call to make an option for the poor is directed in a particular way to those who belong to 'the service people', who occupy a *middle* place on the 'pyramids of power'. I am one of these people myself; and I imagine that most of the readers of this book will belong to the same group. So I shall talk in the next few paragraphs of 'us'. Once we begin to be aware of structural injustice we start to realise the crucial role played by people like us in society. We are the ones who operate the unjust structures. For this very reason we are also very well placed to devise and implement alternative structures. Not that we are entitled to do so without involving the poor. For it would be a new injustice to exclude those at the bottom of society from sharing in the task of building a more just world. But the poor need us — just as the Jewish slaves in Egypt needed Moses, the man who had been educated to understand how the empire worked.

For us of 'the service people' an option for the poor means a serious attempt to build a just society — one where the undue concentration of power is eliminated or at least greatly reduced. From a purely logical point of view the first step is to *understand* the present unjust system:

— to know who has power in the different spheres, and how that power is maintained;

— to see who or what is a threat to that power — and how the threat is being contained;

— to discover the forces for change in that society, and to see which of them are likely to cause greater injustice and which could lead towards justice. All this is the kind of knowledge that should emerge from a careful 'social analysis' of the particular society.

The second step should be to begin to *disentangle* ourselves from unjust structures. This is extremely difficult. For we find ourselves living in a huge interlocking system where almost all our actions play a part in maintaining structural

80

injustice. It is pointless to cry: 'Stop the world, I want to get off.' So we are forced to make some compromises. General rules are not much help in telling us where or to what extent compromise is acceptable. But I find it useful to have two practical guidelines. The first is: concentrate as far as possible on the sphere of my present work; in other words, do not allow my challenge to structural injustice to become just a spare-time activity. It is not good enough to continue to operate unjust structures in our work, while using our leisure time to look for alternatives. I must add, however, that in the beginning many of us are forced to do that, until we find an opening to make changes in our way of working — or until we change to a different type of work.

The second guideline is rather more personal: to recognise that the crucial thing is to maintain one's personal integrity; for what is in question is a deeply personal option, even though it is concerned with the public or 'political' sphere. Different people have different 'sticking-points' — and I have no right to ask even my best friend to accept my evaluation of where any one has 'sold out'.

From a logical point of view the third step is to begin to construct *alternative* structures. One can easily be mystified or misled by this talk about 'constructing structures'. What it may mean in practice is the setting up of procedures that promote justice. For instance, students may be given the opportunity to share in designing their education, employees may insist on being consulted about the policy of their company, clergy may relinquish some power to parish councils. In practice, of course, this step of working towards more just alternatives will go hand in hand with the second step, of disentangling oneself from the unjust system. Indeed, it is quite likely that one's social analysis, which from a logical point of view is the first step, will be undertaken formally only after one has already attempted the other steps in some initial way.

Where should one begin? As I have said, I think it is important if possible to begin in the area of one's daily work. This means in practice that the starting-point will vary for different people. In the last chapter I noted that there is structural injustice in the economic, political, cultural, and ecclesiastical spheres — and that each of these can be reinforced by the others. So the person who makes an option for the poor may begin to implement it in any of these areas of life.

In general 'the poor' are the mass of ordinary people who are at or near the bottom of the different 'pyramids of power'. It is very likely that those who are excluded from power in one sphere of life will also be excluded in the other spheres. But there are some exceptions. For instance, there are ethnic minorities in some countries who are socially marginalised and politically vulnerable, but may not be very poor in the strictly economic sense. Again, as I mentioned earlier, all women in a male-dominated society can be called 'poor' in a certain sense; and lay people in the Church are generally 'poor' in being deprived of effective responsibility. It is especially important that Church people who are working to bring justice into society should do all in their power to promote structural justice in the Church itself.

*Solidarity*

I have been describing an option for the poor in terms of the building of alternative structures in society. Now I want to insist that there is another aspect, a more personal, existential one, that is complementary to the structural aspect. An option for the poor by anybody who comes from the more privileged sectors of society has to include personal solidarity with those who are poor and disadvantaged. People who are used to exercising power over others can easily be tempted to continue to do so at the same time as they commit themselves to working for social justice. We may start to devise alternative structures for a new society — but without any personal relationships with those we want to help. The result is paternalism; we may even, at times, end up trying to manipulate the poor to fit in with our plans. So, in addition to working for alternative structures, it is vitally important that we find ways in which we can, in some degree, begin to share the life of 'the poor'.

The crucial thing here is that we endeavour to enter 'the world of the poor'. As Gustavo Gutiérrez points out, this is not just the experience of having little money and not having one's rights respected. To live in this world is to have a particular way of feeling, thinking, suffering, celebrating, having friends, and praying. Anybody from outside who

82

wishes to enter that world must be humble and sensitive. Gutiérrez recalls the words of Jesus, that to enter the Kingdom of Heaven one must become like a little child (Mt 18:3). To be spiritually childlike is the same as being 'poor in spirit'. It is the condition not only for entering the Kingdom of Heaven but also for entering the world of the poor (*Beber en su proprio pozo: en el itinerario espiritual de un pueblo*, CEP, Lima, 1983, 165-73).

There are major barriers of class to be crossed if the privileged are to come into real solidarity with the poor; and barriers of culture to be overcome if people from 'the North' are to become friends with those from 'the South'. The first step is to stop pretending that such barriers do not exist. I recall an incident in a workshop I helped to set up last year. The participants were a mixed group of Nigerians and expatriate missionaries. We were preparing to articulate a joint vision of the kind of society we wanted and the role of the Church in it. All of us in turn were asked to pick out the one big change we would like to see. People spoke movingly of a society where poverty was eliminated, where local cultures were respected, where women were given an equal place. One white priest was strangely silent. Urged to speak, he eventually took his courage in his hands and said simply: 'What I want above all is just to have some real Nigerian friends . . .' For me that was a high point of the workshop. It reminded me that structural change is of little value unless it is linked to better interpersonal relationships; and it encouraged me to take risks in seeking to cross the barriers.

It can be more difficult to cross the class barriers between the rich and the poor than to cross the barriers of culture. How it is to be done in practice will vary from person to person. For some it may involve a major change in lifestyle — perhaps a decision to live with poor people or to give up a privileged job. But at a minimum it calls for some relinquishment of power and privilege. This effort to come into solidarity with those who are disadvantaged is important for a number of reasons. Firstly, it is difficult to see how poor people can really trust us unless we share their life to some extent. Secondly, only practical experience can teach us what it is like to be powerless. Thirdly, the effort has a certain symbolic meaning for ourselves — it reminds us of our commitment and helps us to be more authentic in sympathising with the poor.

It is interesting to recall the experience of Moses (Exodus Ch 2). Here is a man who was educated away from his own people and given a privileged position in the empire (v. 10). He was already an adult when he woke up to the oppression that his people were suffering (v. 11). His first reaction was a violent one: he killed the Egyptian whom he saw beating a Jew (v. 12). Obviously he thought this made him a leader of his people. But he got a rude shock when one of them turned to him: '"Who made you a prince and leader over us? Are you going to kill me as you killed the Egyptian?"' (v. 14). Moses then lost his privileged position and had to go on the run (v. 15). In this way he experienced for himself what it is like to be one of 'the poor'. God prepared him for his role of leadership by allowing him to live as a refugee for a number of years.

The parallels with our own situation are obvious. One day we wake up and realise that we have been given a privileged place in a society that is exploiting our people. We seek an instant solution, frequently in anger. Like Moses we naïvely assume that the oppressed people will hail us as saviours. Like him we are shocked to find that they don't trust us, and may even turn on us in resentment. It may take us years — and a good deal of suffering — to acquire the sensitivity and humility we need in order to be accepted by poor people.

*Why opt for the poor?*

People like us have a fair amount of security and comfort in life. We eat quite well, we generally have congenial work, we have a respectable place in society, and we exercise power and responsibility in various ways. To make a preferential option for the poor is to put all these things at risk. It is to recognise that our privileges are bound up with systems that are unjust. The economic, political, cultural, and ecclesiastical systems that favour us may be depriving others of basic rights. To opt for the poor is to commit ourselves to replacing these systems. That means being willing to relinquish our privileges.

But that is not all; it also means running the risk of serious disruption of society. For it is unlikely that major structural change can come easily. It is quite possible that the effort to bring change will lead to serious breakdowns in the organisation of society. In that case, everybody may suffer for quite some time before a new order emerges. There cannot even be any guarantee that the new systems will prove to be much better than the old ones. We can plan to make them so, and do our best to implement the plans, and even to improve on them; but the future remains unpredictable.

Why then should any of us in the upper or middle sectors of the 'pyramids of power' choose to put at risk not only our own privileges but even the stability of the world? There are pragmatic reasons and idealistic reasons for doing so. The main pragmatic reason is the realisation that our present systems are creaking under many strains, and are liable to collapse:

— The enormous debts of the poor countries — and of the most powerful country in the world — have reached a point where the economic order of the world is in danger of breaking down; and the soaring unemployment rates all over the world are adding to the strain.

— Our political systems are leaving more and more people alienated and powerless; or rather, not quite powerless, for they have an increasing power to disrupt society. Life is becoming more and more insecure for many people; and in the interests of security, people are being deprived of basic rights.

— Competition between the major powers has led to an arms race that threatens to wipe out the human race.

Perhaps then it would be wise to choose to work for radical change, rather than wait for a total breakdown or an eruption. By doing so we might be able to play a more effective role in shaping the future.

The pragmatic argument for making an option for the poor is unlikely to succeed. Pragmatists generally prefer to try to shore up the existing system, making changes only piecemeal and when they are unavoidable. Those who hold power in our world are unwilling to take any kind of effective action to change the power structures — even when the practical arguments in favour of doing so are very strong. That is evident from the reaction — or lack of reaction — to the two reports of the Brandt Commission (*North-South: A Programme for Survival*, 1980; *Common Crisis: North-South: Cooperation for World Recovery*, 1983).

If the pragmatic arguments are insufficient, what about the idealistic ones? They are arguments that depend on a moral sensitivity to the plight of the poor. Moral commitment on its own is not enough, for it does not tell us what needs to be done. But if our moral concern is related to a 'hard-nosed' assessment of the situation we may be willing to commit ourselves to radical action. This is particularly the case if we are Christians; for then our morality is closely linked to a religious system in which the poor have a very special role and in which option for the poor is linked to the following of Christ. These are the topics I wish to explore in the next chapter.

# 6

# Option for the Poor:
# its Biblical basis

*In the Old Testament*

The God who reveals himself to the Jewish people in the Old Testament is above all a God who cares for the poor. The foundational event in Jewish history is God's call of Moses to lead his people out of slavery: 'I have heard the cry of my people and I see how they are being oppressed . . .' (Ex 3:9). His people were politically enslaved, economically exploited, and crushed in spirit. Moses was sent to challenge this injustice and to lead his people into freedom: 'Go to Pharaoh and tell him that the Lord says, "Let my people go . . ." ' (Ex 8:1). God is not merely concerned to set them free from slavery; he wants Moses to lead them into a land of their own where they can live a fully human life — 'a good and broad land, a land flowing with milk and honey' (Ex 3:8). So the liberation that they are given is not just a release from slavery of a number of individuals; it is a historical and political reality — the emergence of a new nation, a people called to live in freedom.

It is particularly significant that the very name 'Yahweh' is linked to the revelation of God's determination to set his people free. Moses asks who this God is who has called him. God's reply is a mysterious phrase which is best translated as 'I am the one who will be with you' — implying that he is the one who will be leading them out of slavery into freedom, the one they will come to know through the history of their liberation. There are two important points to note here. Firstly, God reveals himself as a liberating God. Secondly, this liberation is accomplished through the process of human history, using human agents like Moses: 'I will be *with* you . . .' — accompanying you on your journey to freedom.

87

The plagues in Egypt are usually presented as the way the Pharaoh was forced to let God's people go. But perhaps more important than their effect on the Egyptian emperor was their effect on the Jews. By these marvels Moses was able to convince a group of broken-spirited slaves that by God's power they could challenge the empire and win their freedom. Once they were convinced of God's power and of the fact that he was on their side, they were willing to take the risk of marching out into the desert in search of freedom.

So far it could be argued that God's preference was not for the poor as such but simply for the Jewish people. There can be no doubt that the Old Testament presents Yahweh as the God of Abraham, of Isaac, of Jacob — and therefore of the Jewish people as a whole. But we have to make distinctions when this people moves into their own land and come to have their own kings. The crucial point that emerges from the whole prophetic strand in the Bible is that Yahweh is not just an 'ethnic' God but an 'ethical' God. The gods of the surrounding empires supported those in power and in this way they helped to ensure stability in society. But the Jewish prophets were called by a God who values justice far more highly than stability. He is a God who is concerned about injustice not merely when it is inflicted on the Jews by foreign powers; he is equally or even more outraged by injustice practised by the kings and ruling classes of the Jews themselves on their own people. So the prophetic tradition makes it clear that God is on the side of the victims of injustice.

As a result, the term 'my people' has two overlapping meanings: it refers to the Jewish people in general; and it refers more particularly to the mass of ordinary folk among them who are crushed by poverty inflicted on them either by foreigners or by their own ruling classes. The Old Testament did not go on to the point of identifying the poor all over the world as 'God's people'. But it took an important step in that direction: it insisted that the Jews must have special care for the foreigners who live among them:

Do not ill-treat foreigners who are living in your land. Treat them as you would a fellow-Israelite. . . . Remember that you were once foreigners in the land of Egypt . . .

(Lev 19:33; cf. Ex 22:21)

The Old Testament prophets were not asking the kind of theological questions we have to ask today about the precise sense in which 'the poor' as such are God's people. Their task was more practical: to utter God's condemnation of those who exploited and despised the poor: 'Your houses are full of what you have taken from the poor. You have no right to crush my people and take advantage of the poor.' (Is 3: 14-15). 'They sell into slavery honest people who are unable to pay their debts; poor people are sold for the price of a pair of shoes.' (Amos 2:6; cf. 8:4-8). 'You women . . . who grow fat like well-fed cows, who ill-treat the weak, and oppress the poor . . . the day will come when they will drag you away with hooks . . .' (Amos 4:1).

The prophets spoke out particularly to challenge, in God's name, those who made laws that allowed the poor to be exploited: 'You make unjust laws that oppress my people . . . prevent the poor from having their rights . . .' (Is 10: 1-2; cf. Jer 22:3). This condemnation of unjust legislators is matched by equally strong words against unjust judges: 'You persecute good people, take bribes, and prevent the poor from getting justice in the courts.' (Amos 5:12).

*Structural injustice*

We tend to assume that the outrage of the prophets — and of the God on whose behalf they spoke — was directed simply against the unjust *behaviour* of rich people, or legislators or judges. But the problems in Israel at the time went beyond unjust conduct; there had developed a social order and an economic system that were *structurally* unjust. The rather simple social order of a nomadic people had given way to one which was much more socially stratified. The establishment of the monarchy had played a major part in this change. For it meant that the ordinary people were now forced to support the king, his court, his officials, and his army; and many of them were compelled to work on the large estates of the king: 'Your sons will have to plough his fields, harvest his crops, and make his weapons. . . . Your daughters will have to work as his cooks and bakers. He will take your best fields . . . and a tenth of your corn for his court officers and other officials.' (1 Sam 8:12-15).

Closely related to this change in the political order was a

major economic change. There was the emergence of a large merchant class who were in a position to take advantage of the ordinary peasants. The increase in trading was in turn linked to a gradual change in the pattern of land ownership. When the small farm-owners were unable to pay their debts, the rich were able to take over their land. Many of those who had been owners were now reduced to being hired farm labourers at the mercy of rich property owners. So the gap between rich and poor grew ever wider. It is clear that when the prophets were condemning injustice they were protesting against this whole socio-economic order. The problem was not just a matter of abuses by individuals but a system that encouraged and rewarded those who took advantage of the poor.

Against this background one can appreciate the significance of the Jewish laws governing ownership of property — particularly the 'Jubilee laws'. These were laws which went far beyond the usual purpose of property laws — namely, to protect the rights of owners. They were designed with the specific purpose of ensuring that there would be a certain equality in society. This was to be achieved by setting aside every fiftieth year as a Jubilee year: 'During this year all property that has been sold shall be restored to the original owner or his descendants . . .' (Lev 25:10). This meant that the ownership of land could not be lost permanently. So, in effect, what was being sold, or seized in payment of debts, was not land as such but the number of harvests that remained until the next Jubilee year: '. . . what is being sold is the number of crops the land can produce . . . before the next Year of Restoration.' (Lev 25:15-16). Similar regulations were made to ensure that a person would not remain permanently in slavery (Ex 15:12-15; Lev 25:10).

The Jubilee laws represent a very ingenious attempt to design a legal system that would give at least as much priority to social justice as to justice in individual transactions. It is probable that these laws were never fully put into effect. But they indicate the moral ideal that was part of the Old Testament revelation. Furthermore, they show that such ideals were not intended to be mere theory; rather they were meant to be put into practice in the social order and the legal system. There can be no doubt that any nation or community that committed itself to implementing such a legal system would be making a clear option for the poor.

*Jesus and 'The Poor'*

It is sometimes claimed that the New Testament has a very personal and spiritual concept of salvation, in contrast to the Old Testament where salvation is presented more in social and political terms. This leads on to the conclusion that the New Testament offers little support to those who wish to develop a theology of liberation and of option for the poor. This is a gross over-simplification. It often serves an ideological purpose: it is used to justify a refusal to face up to the challenge of injustice and poverty.

In fact the prophetic mission of Jesus has to be understood as pushing further the mission of the Old Testament prophets, rather than a correction of them. I am not denying that there are differences between the teaching of Jesus and that of the prophets. But to hold that Jesus was not interested in challenging the established order of his time would be a total distortion of all that he stood for. In fact a good deal of the differences between the prophetic figures in the Bible come from the variety of situations in which they found themselves. Moses confronted a foreign emperor. Isaiah was called to challenge the Jews' own kings and ruling classes (e.g. Is 1:23; 3:16), and, since he was himself one of the nobility, he had to break with the people of his own class. Jeremiah found that he had to challenge not only the king but also the priestly caste and the would-be prophets of his time. The situation of Jesus was similar in this respect to that of Jeremiah: the groups that felt themselves most threatened by what he stood for were the religious leaders of the Jews.

It is clear that from beginning to end Jesus made an option for the poor, both in its personal existential sense and in its public or 'political' sense. He grew up as one of 'the common people' in a despised village. In his public ministry he lived poorly, mixed with the ordinary folk, and shocked the 'respectable' people by eating with social outcasts. He acted and spoke in a manner that caused him to be experienced as a serious threat by the various establishment groups in his country. Eventually he was judicially murdered through the collusion of two factions of the religious establishment with the foreign imperial power.

It is true that Jesus spent far more of his time dealing with 'religion' than with 'politics'. But the religion of his time was anything but a private spiritual affair. It was a culture, a way of life, and a set of laws and regulations. It was controlled and used by two overlapping groups, each of whom in a different way was seen as an elite group: the pharisees and the teachers of the Law or theologians (the 'scribes'). These groups exerted oppressive power over the common folk. Jesus was a threat to that power. What he said and did was seen by them — and quite correctly — as an undermining of their authority. He challenged their claim to be the orthodox and privileged interpreters of God's law, ' ". . . you disregard God's command, in order to follow your own teaching" ' (Mt 15:16). For instance, he called in question their right to make rules about the washing of hands (Mt 15:1-5) and to decide the kind of actions that were permissible on the Sabbath (Mk 2:23-3:6). He accused them of being 'blind fools' and 'blind guides'; and he showed how they had distorted God's laws (Mt 23:16-24).

All this concerns what we might call 'the politics of religion' or the exercise of power in the name of religion. The teaching and lifestyle of Jesus are presented in the Gospels as a clear challenge to the power of the religious establishments. He was making a stance, on behalf of the common people, against an oppressive religious-cultural regime. In that sense there can be no doubt that he was making an option for the poor. He was following in the prophetic tradition by attacking the misuse of power. The fact that the establishment he was confronting was exercising power in the name of religion did not make his action any less prophetic; it only made it more difficult. Like Jeremiah, he found that his sharpest confrontations were with those who represented the established religion. (Compare Mt 12:1-14 with Jer 23:11, 14; 26:7-16; 29:31-2.)

Jesus also had some confrontations with political authorities. Luke's Gospel shows him facing Herod and simply refusing to answer him (Lk 23:9); one could hardly imagine a more effective challenge than this eloquent silence. Pilate condemned Jesus to death. His action was not simply the result of a misunderstanding of what Jesus stood for; it was a deliberate choice. This is brought out very clearly in John's

Gospel where Pilate asks Jesus to explain what kind of a Kingdom he was establishing (Jn 18:33-7; 19:8-10). It is in this context that John places the warning of Jesus that the authority of Pilate is not absolute: 'You have authority over me only because it was given to you by God' (Jn 19:11). In John's presentation of the confrontation between Jesus and the Roman governor it would appear that Jesus could have saved his life if he had 'played politics'; but he refused to compromise before this compromising political ruler — just as he had refused to compromise in the face of the religious authorities. All this was part of his option for the poor.

I have been pointing out how Jesus challenged both those who held what I have called 'God power' and those who had political power. I must now add that he also had very harsh things to say about those who had 'money power': 'Woe to you who are rich now' (Lk 6:24); 'It is much harder for a rich person to enter the Kingdom of God than for a camel to go through the eye of a needle.' (Mt 19:24); 'God said [to the rich man], "You fool, this night you must die"' (Lk 12:20); 'The rich man died and . . . he was in great pain in Hades' (Lk 16:22-3); 'Do not store up riches here on earth' (Mt 6:19); 'The love of riches chokes the message' (Mt 13:22); 'You cannot serve both God and money' (Mt 6:24).

What Jesus was looking for above all was 'poverty of spirit' in the sense of awareness of one's need for God. But these various sayings and parables of Jesus make it quite evident that in his view this lack of openness to God was caused by wealth and concern about money. The teaching of Jesus in Matthew's Gospel is that the only way we can experience the treasures of God is to share our earthly possessions with the poor (cf. Michael H. Crosby, *Spirituality of the Beatitudes: Matthew's Challenge for First World Christians*, Orbis, Maryknoll, 1981, p. 56). To share in this way is to give up the security we derive from wealth; and the willingness to sacrifice our security is the crucial element in poverty of spirit. Jesus himself showed the way; he lived a life of dependence on others, having nowhere of his own to lie down and rest (Mt 8:19-20). From all this one must conclude that there is no solid biblical basis for an undue 'spiritualising' of the concept of poverty. It is an ideological distortion of the New Testament to make a sharp contrast between material poverty and spiritual poverty, and to claim that it is alright to be wealthy provided one is 'poor in spirit'.

It may be helpful at this point to summarise briefly the different aspects of the option for the poor made by Jesus:
— He challenged oppressive religious authorities.
— He called in question the assumption of the political rulers (Pilate and Herod) that their power entitled them to impose their will on others.
— By word and example he proclaimed that to be open to God involves being willing to give up one's wealth and share it with the poor; he roundly condemned the rich who were unwilling to do so.
— He had friendly relationships with tax collectors (Lk 5:30) and prostitutes (Lk 7:38); though these were not economically poor they were 'poor' in the sense of being the social and religious outcasts of his society.
— He refused to abide by traditions which led 'respectable' Jewish men to despise or hold aloof from certain categories of people e.g. Samaritans and women (Jn 4:9, 27).
— He insisted that when his own followers exercised authority they should see themselves as servants rather than lords; this is a point to which I shall return in a moment.

## The Kingdom

The presupposition of the following chapters of this book is that to make an option for the poor is to commit oneself to an alternative way of life, an alternative type of society. I have already pointed out that the Jubilee laws of the Old Testament provide a precedent for this approach. But does it also have a basis in the New Testament? Yes, indeed — in the teaching of Jesus about the Kingdom of God. This is in continuity with the Old Testament; for Jesus' proclamation of the Kingdom was a claim that a special time of Jubilee had come and that in him all the highest ideals of the Jubilee were realised: 'He has chosen me to bring good news to the poor, to proclaim liberty to captives, . . . and to announce *the year of grace* given by the Lord.' (Lk 4:18-19).

'The Kingdom of God' is the central symbol in the teaching of Jesus. This one phrase expresses in a compressed way the fundamental core of his message. It would require a major

94

scriptural study to 'unpack' its full meaning. Here I shall simply note some of the more important elements in so far as they bear on the question of option for the poor. When Jesus proclaimed the Kingdom he was first of all announcing God's judgment on the present social order. 'The Kingdom' is the world subject to the rule of God — a point I shall discuss more fully in the next chapter. It is the world as God wants it to be; and that is manifestly different from the world as it actually existed prior to the coming of Jesus. Secondly, the proclamation of the Kingdom by Jesus is an affirmation that things can be changed. Thirdly, it is a claim that the change has already begun to take place. God's power is at work; and it is greater than the forces of evil which have dominated society:

> It is not Beelzebul, but God's Spirit, who gives me the power to drive out demons — which proves that the Kingdom of God has already come upon you.     (Mt 12:28)

Failure to understand what is meant by 'the Kingdom of God' is the main reason why people assume that Jesus corrected and 'spiritualised' the Old Testament concepts of liberation and poverty. Part of the difficulty is purely verbal: because of Jewish reticence in using the name of God, Matthew's Gospel generally speaks of 'the Kingdom of Heaven' rather than 'the Kingdom of God'. When we use this term we already begin to miss the point that what Jesus was speaking of was the reign of God in this world. That verbal mistake is compounded by the assumption that Heaven is a purely other-worldly place or state. Its only connection with this world is thought to be that it is the reward for virtuous behaviour and for putting up with suffering and injustice in this world. Such an understanding of the Kingdom leaves one no room to give full weight to the claim of Jesus that the Kingdom has come upon us (Mt 13:28) and is already present in our midst (Lk 17:21). The result is that one is almost bound to neglect the last and crucial part of what Jesus said when he read out Isaiah's prophecy in the synagogue: 'This passage of scripture *has come true today*, as you heard it being read.' (Lk 4:21).

It is not sufficient to point out how the meaning of the term 'the Kingdom of God' has become distorted; one must also look for the positive meaning of the phrase. A central place to look is in the two accounts of the beatitudes, and the discourses of which they are the kernel (Mt 5:1-7:28; Lk 6:20-46). What emerges is a sustained challenge by Jesus to the whole set of values held by the people of his time. Instead of seeing poverty as a sign of God's displeasure, he says: 'Blessed are you poor; yours is the Kingdom.' He tells the rich that they are the misfortunate ones. He insists that to be persecuted gives one grounds for rejoicing; but that the time to fear the worst is when one is honoured and respected. The radically different values which Jesus proposes here provide the underpinning which enables one to make sense, both intellectually and emotionally, of Christ's own life and death, as well as of the whole body of his teaching. These values are the very opposite of the dominant values in the personal, the interpersonal, and the public aspects of life. Using the language I employed in Chapter 1 of this book, I would say: to live by these 'Kingdom values' is to be religiously, morally, and 'politically' converted.

### The Kingdom and conversion

In the first place, the person whose life is moulded by the Kingdom values which are outlined so starkly in the beatitudes, is a person who is *religiously* converted. In the first chapter I described religious conversion as a vivid sense of God's providence, a conviction that even if a mother should forget her baby at the breast, God will not forget me. This living experience of being in the arms of God is what makes sense of the attitude of 'spiritual childhood'. That is why Jesus could say: 'unless you are converted and become like little children you will never enter the Kingdom of Heaven.' (Mt 18:3). Those who rely utterly on God are the 'poor in spirit' — and they are the ones who belong to the Kingdom (Mt 5:3).

This religious conversion transforms their attitude to *possessions*, to *power*, to social *prestige*, and to their understanding of *religion*:

— They are willing to sell all their *possessions* and give the proceeds to the poor (Mt 19:21) because their hearts are set on God; their treasure is not earthly goods but the values of the Kingdom (Mt 6:19-21).

— They no longer thirst for *power* but are gentle and humble (Mt 5:5) as Jesus himself was (Mt 11:29). 'The greatest in the Kingdom of Heaven is the one who humbles himself' (Mt 18:4).

— Their sense of their own worth does not depend on the *prestige* of being given the first places on public occasions (Lk 14:7-11).

— Perhaps most important of all, they realise that *God's favour* is not to be won with good deeds; they are content to come before God acknowledging their weakness and sin, like the tax collector in Jesus' parable (Lk 18:13).

Secondly, Kingdom people are *morally* converted: their entry into this new world has changed not only the way they relate to God but also the way they relate to those around them. Once again the change can be seen in their attitude to *possessions*, to *power*, to *status*, and to *religion*:

— Instead of hoarding *possessions* they share with others: they are willing to have a common purse (Jn 13:29) and to rely on the hospitality of others, as Jesus did (Mt 8:20); this sharing was evident also in the first Christian communities (Acts 4:34).

— They take seriously the remark of Jesus that the person who wishes to be first must be the *servant* of the others (Mt 20:25-8). They are willing to follow the example set by Jesus himself when he washed the feet of his followers (Jn 13:15).

— They do not seek *precedence* over their companions, but leave it to God to judge who will have the privileged places in the Kingdom (Mt 20:21-3).

— They do not use *religion* to gain power, status, and privilege in the community as the pharisees did:

> They love the best places at feasts and the reserved seats in the synagogues; they love to be greeted with respect . . . and to be called 'Teacher'. You must not be called 'Teacher', because you are all brothers and sisters of one another and have only one Teacher. (Mt 23:6-8; cf. 6:5)

Thirdly, to be a Kingdom person means being 'politically' converted. At first sight this may seem surprising, since the early followers of Christ were so convinced that the end of the world was near that they had little interest in devising a just socio-economic and political order. But the value system of the Kingdom proclaimed and lived by Jesus has obvious implications in the public sphere. These were not fully worked out during the lifetime of Jesus or even in the early Church. But in the teaching and parables of Jesus there are intriguing hints of the radical changes that the Kingdom leads to in the socio-economic and political ordering of society. The Kingdom requires a different approach to *'money* power', *political* power, *'idea* power', and *'God* power':

— We are familiar with the parable of the eleventh hour labourer who was paid as much as those who had worked all day. But we may forget the most important line which is the very first: 'The Kingdom of heaven is like *this'* (Mt 20:1). The parable suggests that the *economic* order of the Kingdom is one where people are paid according to their need rather than according to the amount they have produced. A Kingdom person would not be indignant, as many people in the First World today are, that an unemployed person might on occasion receive as much as somebody who is privileged enough to have a job.

— The *political* aspects of the Kingdom are equally radical. I have already noted that the Kingdom involves a change in the understanding of the meaning of authority: it is understood as service rather than as an exercise of power. This has implications which go far beyond the interpersonal sphere of the relationships among a group of friends. It touches the public or 'political' sphere. 'You know that the rulers of the heathens lord it over them . . . but it shall not be like this with you.' (Mt 20:25-6). The Kingdom way of exercising authority is a clear challenge to the way political power was exercised in Middle Eastern cultures at the time of Jesus (as well as in many other places before and since). In these cultures God was understood to support those who exercised political power. This kind of harnessing of God to buttress the power of some people over others is so common that it hardly surprises us. The shocking thing is that we are *not* shocked that it should take place. Jesus' preaching of the Kingdom of God went clean against this tendency to identify God with the power to dominate others. (cf. Matthew L. Lamb, 'Christian Spirituality and Social Justice' in *Horizons* 10/1, 1983, 44).

98

— The Kingdom proclaimed and lived by Jesus was a challenge to the dominant *ideas* of the society of his time and to those who benefited from promoting them. As I noted earlier, Jesus flouted the traditions that led Jews to despise the Samaritans and that inhibited men from mixing socially with women (Jn 4:9, 27). The full implications of his teaching and practice began to emerge in the early Church: 'There is no difference between Jews and Gentiles, between slaves and free people, between men and women; you are all one in Christ Jesus.' (Gal 3:28). Paul could see that the Kingdom is the antithesis of racism and sexism; but like many Christians up to the present time he partly failed to draw the conclusions for the public or 'political' sphere.

— Perhaps the most radical aspect of the Kingdom is the transformation it brings about in the exercise of *religious* authority. The crucial point is that with the coming of Jesus the time has arrived when those who worship God 'must worship in spirit and in truth' (Jn 4:23-4). This true religion is not localised (v. 21) and therefore cannot be controlled by a coterie of priests; all are called to share in the one priesthood of Christ (I Pet 2:9; Heb 5:5-6). The admonition of Jesus to his followers against being hailed as 'The Teacher' (Mt 23:8) has implications in the public sphere as well as in the interpersonal sphere. If taken seriously it is a safeguard against any attempt to usurp 'God power' — a protection against ancient and modern forms of idolatry and the ways religion is harnessed to support unjust regimes.

### The future is now

In what sense is the Kingdom proclaimed by Jesus a present reality, and in what sense does it still lie in the future? This is the most puzzling question that arises when one tries to understand the New Testament teaching. Scripture scholars have written volumes on the topic; and I shall not try to summarise their conclusions here. I want simply to share an insight which came to me while I was writing this chapter. It is that in trying to answer the above question I had been using the wrong starting point. Without realising it, I had been asking: how can I fit the teaching of Jesus about the Kingdom into our current concepts of 'present' and 'future'? This means that I had been assessing Jesus' teaching in terms of our present categories. What I should have done was to allow my categories and concepts to be challenged by his teaching about the Kingdom. His words — and his whole life — call in question my easy distinction between 'now' and 'future'. For Jesus presents himself and his Kingdom as the future already realised.

There is a real danger that a phrase like 'the future already realised' can be used glibly — as a clever idea with little real meaning. It is only recently that I have been able to see how true it is when applied to Jesus. This is not the truth of logic so much as the truth of action. The way Jesus lived amounted to a re-definition of what it means to be human. His conception of a human life was not based on current standards but on the standards and values of the future Kingdom. By believing in it and acting on it he brought it into existence. He lived as if his Kingdom was already present; and in doing so he made it present — in so far as his personal relationships were concerned.

But the Kingdom is a communal and public reality as well as a personal one. To make it fully present there must be a transformation of communities and of society as a whole. The followers of Jesus are called to 'fill up what is wanting' in the life and death of Christ (cf. Col 1:24) by continuing to live by Kingdom values and in this way continuing to bring the Kingdom into existence. The only way I can truly proclaim my belief in the Kingdom is to live it — in the personal and interpersonal spheres and in the socio-economic and political sphere. Borrowing a phrase from Daniel Berrigan, I can say that what we are called to do is to 'live the future now'. In the following chapters I shall make suggestions about how this can be done in practice.

# 7

# Alternative Values

A lot of people who are deeply concerned about social injustice find themselves rather depressed by the kind of material discussed in the previous chapters. They become aware of the pervasiveness of evil in our world and of the extent to which the structures of society have become distorted and corrupted. The sheer size of the problem leaves them feeling rather helpless. Those who had hoped to change the system become confused — not knowing where to begin. Worst of all is the sense of guilt that comes from awareness of how much one is part of the system, benefiting from it even while wanting to change it.

To break this feeling of powerlessness I can take two courses of action. The first is to tackle some specific aspect of structural injustice, something that is within my reach at this stage. If I succeed, the sense of achievement will encourage me to continue the struggle. The second way of tackling the problem covers a very much broader front for it involves spelling out workable alternatives to the present unjust order. To condemn injustice is relatively easy — and perhaps it is for this reason that we find it discouraging. To propose specific alternatives is much more difficult. We are so dazzled by the present reality that it requires considerable creativity to envisage a society that is structured in a different way. What is in question here is not vague wishful thinking but an attempt to specify concretely the kind of world that could replace our unjust world, in all of its various aspects.

In order to think seriously about alternatives it may be helpful to distinguish three different levels:
— Firstly, we can note certain *values* which should be present in this other and better world.

— It is necessary, secondly, to consider the *institutions* and *structures* which are needed to embody these values in society, replacing the existing unjust structures.

— Just as important as the question of what kind of values and structures we want is the question of how to get from where we are to where we would like to be. So, thirdly, one has to determine what *methods* are appropriate for the introduction and promotion of the alternative values and structures. In this chapter and the next one, I propose to consider the kind of values we are looking for; then in the following two chapters I shall go on to look at the structures and methods.

*Kingdom values*

I have introduced the word 'Kingdom' into the title of this section. The word is used so widely in theological and religious writing that I cannot ignore it. But I am somewhat reluctant to use it because it is a strange and mystifying word for people unused to theological jargon. It seems to be a rather dated word, since the whole notion of a 'Kingdom' comes from another age. An even more serious objection to the word is that many of the people who use it do so in a misleading way. They think 'the Kingdom of God' means simply Heaven, the reward in the afterlife for a life of virtue and suffering in this world. But, as we saw already when considering the teaching of Jesus, this is a serious impoverishment of the biblical concept of the Kingdom.

Certainly, the Kingdom in its full extension is realised only in a future world. But, to borrow a phrase from Roger Garaudy, what is in question is not another world but a different world. This means that what we have to look forward to is not an escape from our world or a total replacement of it. Some people might be inclined to doubt this last statement, feeling that it represents a secularist understanding of the Kingdom. But to be assured of its orthodoxy one has only to recall that when we speak of 'our world' and of 'the Kingdom' what we are referring to above all is people rather than a set of objects; and the people of the Kingdom will of course be people who have lived here on earth. We must therefore conclude that there is a direct continuity between our present world and the Kingdom. When our world is fully renewed, transformed, and fulfilled in accordance with God's plan, then the Kingdom will have come in its fullness.

102

In effect, then, to speak of the 'Kingdom' is to talk about the world as it ought to be and is called to be — the ideal world of the future. Why then bother using the term 'Kingdom' at all? The main reason is that the word is very central in the Scriptures — and especially in Christ's preaching (as we saw in an earlier chapter). Some translators of the Bible prefer to use the phrase 'the reign of God'. This may help people to realise that what is meant above all is our world as God wants it to be rather than some other world. But the word 'reign' fails to bring out something that is implied in the term 'Kingdom': that what is in question is not just a change in moral behaviour by people but a restructuring of human society — one might even say a new system of politics, culture, and economics.

I think the best way to overcome the misconceptions surrounding the term 'Kingdom' is to be as specific as possible — to try to spell out in some detail the kind of alternative world that we are to hope for and work for. The first step is to list a number of what may be called 'Kingdom values' — though they might also be called 'utopian values' or simply 'values of the ideal future'. I shall attempt to do that in this chapter and the next; in subsequent chapters I shall go on to consider the problem of embodying these values in the structures of society.

Everybody will have his or her own pet ideas about what a really ideal world should be like. On what basis, then, should one pick out certain values as pertaining to the Kingdom? I think the best approach is to try to locate the deepest longings of the human spirit — and these in turn may often be discovered where there is the greatest human agony and struggle. For, as St Paul says, the whole creation is groaning as though in childbirth, and we too groan inwardly as we wait to be set free (Rom 8:22). It is to be expected that the very places where the greatest distortions, abuses, and suffering are found, would be the places where the deepest human needs and urges are experienced most strongly.

The Christian — and the Christian Church — are called to promote the Kingdom of God. Of course non-Christians may also be building God's Kingdom. But the Christian is called to do it of set purpose: the primary aim of the Church is not to expand itself but to advance the Kingdom. The first stage in doing this is to recognise where the Kingdom is already coming about in our world. For, if the Kingdom is the completion and fulfilment of the present world, then there are elements in today's world where the Kingdom is already present in an initial or germinal way. It is for Christians, and the Christian Church, to discover such seeds of the Kingdom and to nurture them. That is why the initial step in promoting the Kingdom is discernment. Having discovered where the really significant action is taking place, Christians will know where to direct their energies. They can then set out to cultivate these seeds of the Kingdom both in the secular world and in the institutional and community life of the Church itself.

In the remainder of this chapter I propose to list five urgent needs or aspirations of people today and to show how each of them is linked to a 'Kingdom value'. I shall comment briefly on the present role of the Church in promoting and witnessing to each of these values.

### (1) Unity

One of the most deeply felt needs of people today is the need for unity. People have always experienced it, but in the past the horizons of people generally stopped short at the boundaries of the community, the tribe, or the nation. Nowadays, however, it is clear that nothing less than global unity — the unity of the whole human race — is required. The most obvious reason for this is that global communications and the mass media have made us more aware of each other, and of the oneness of the world.

But there is another and more urgent reason why the aspiration for unity is now a global one: we have in fact become more dependent on each other. Global trade is no longer confined to luxuries; the world has become one market for the most elementary items of food and clothing. I am writing this in a remote rural corner of Africa and a great change is taking place before my eyes. Within the past few years the staple diet of the people has begun to change: much of the food which people now eat is imported from another continent.

Why speak of a need and an urge for global unity as if the world were not *already* unified by the technology of the mass

104

media and by the global economic system? Because these may have *unified* the world but they have not *united* it. It is quite true that Japanese motor cycles and American tinned soups may be bought in the most remote parts of Africa; and that the cocoa grown where I now live may go into the chocolate bought in Europe. But this only shows that there is an economic system which operates on an international level. Some questions must be asked, however. On whose terms does this exchange take place? Is it the kind of trading arrangement that really benefits both sides and could be a foundation for a truly united world? The obvious answer to the latter question is, 'no'.

A truly united world would be one where the people of its different parts would benefit in a fairly equitable way from their links; all the peoples would be the better for their joint activity and cooperation. But that is not the case in our world. The terms of trade are too one-sided. What is called the 'international economic order' is in some respects a kind of disorder. It has arisen out of the colonial exploitation of the past which allowed a few nations of the West to grow strong at the expense of the rest of the world. At present it is firmly controlled by an international financial and banking system which ensures the continued dominance of 'the North' over 'the South' and facilitates a continual expansion of the big multinational companies at the expense of local enterprises. It is clear, then, that the present situation requires that we make the distinction between being unified and being united; the former is a physical or technical matter, while the latter is a moral matter. What people are searching and crying for is a unity in which all are respected, where there is mutual support rather than the exploitation of the weak by the strong.

Unity in that authentic sense must be called a Kingdom value. It is something that the human race needs if we are to become more truly human. It may well be that we need it even to survive. For a world that is technically unified but not united has become extremely vulnerable. A grievance in any part of the world could easily lead to a war that might put an end to human history. On the other hand it is quite obvious that a truly moral unity of all the peoples and classes of the earth would bring great benefits to all.

If we accept that unity is a Kingdom value, this implies that it is of special concern to the Christian and the Christian Church. For, as already pointed out, the role of the Church is to promote the Kingdom in the secular world and in the Church's own life. The first and most crucial step is that of discernment. We have to study the unifying forces at work in the world today. We need to be able to distinguish between two types. On the one hand there are forces and processes which are bringing about a unity that is the imposition of one group on others — for instance of rich countries and powerful groups on the poor and the weak. But we may also discover some movements in our world that are promoting a genuine union between people and peoples. The Churches would be performing a most valuable service if they provided the study and documentation which would help people to distinguish between the different effects of a variety of international agencies. Take for example the section of the United Nations that concerns itself with human rights; and contrast its effects with those of the International Monetary Fund. It is fairly obvious that the former is helping to unify people with respect for all, while the latter operates as an instrument of domination by wealthy countries over those burdened by debt. The issues are by no means so clear-cut in the case of other international agencies — and that is why there is need for careful documentation of their effects.

What about the witness of the Church in its own life to the Kingdom value of unity? I think it has scored some notable successes but is also guilty of some signal failures. I shall give just one example of each. During the time I've been in Africa I've been very impressed by the way in which a shared faith and common membership of a Church inspires many Africans to transcend ethnic or tribal differences. During the disturbances preceding the civil war in Nigeria there were some remarkable instances of a compassion which was quite heroic, when people running for their lives were given shelter by fellow-Christians of a different tribe. Such actions give one grounds for believing that the Church could play a major role in bringing about a genuine community of people and of peoples. Then what is signified, anticipated, and celebrated in 'Holy Communion' would be on the way to becoming a reality, and the Kingdom value of unity would be realised more fully in our world.

106

On the other hand there is one aspect of Church life which I feel I must in conscience mention, since it seems to me to give a counter-witness to Kingdom unity. It is the continued imposition in Third World countries of a rigid uniformity in the institutional and legal life of the Catholic Church. The irony is that it is being done in the interests of maintaining the unity of the Church. This is one place where it is especially urgent to make the distinction between being unified and being truly united. Those who wish to witness to genuine unity — to unity as a Kingdom value — must take the risk of allowing for diversity of culture and tradition.

## (2) Security

Another fundamental human need that is particularly pressing today is the need for security. A few years ago, towards the end of Nigeria's first period of military rule, I was reading essays by adult students on the topic: 'Return to Civilian Rule?' People from various parts of the country were strongly in favour of having a civilian government again. All except those who came from a part of the country where the military take-over had put an end to a period of near anarchy; these people were still in favour of military rule, despite the abuses of the regime. This brought home to me the vital need for a modicum of security — and how much we take it for granted, until it is no longer present. I saw then why Abraham Maslow, in his well-known 'hierarchy of human needs' lists security immediately next to the basic body needs of food and shelter.

Our trouble today is that the human need for security has in many places developed into a kind of group paranoia. In the name of security against would-be foreign aggressors there is an increasing militarisation of society. This leads to a massive waste of resources and human energy; the time and money that ought to be devoted to meeting many other pressing needs are being spent on weapons and armies. In the name of security against subversion from within the State itself, more and more power is given to the 'security forces' — and this can lead to repression, denial of fundamental rights, and torture. The apparatus of the National Security State is being justified by an ideology of National Security, that subordinates all the human rights of the individual to the defence of the State — which in practice, means the government that is in power. Countries of East and West, of 'North' and 'South' have become infected with this frantic defence of 'security'.

At the local and personal levels there are similar attempts to ensure security. I've lived in some Third World cities where more people are employed by private 'security companies' than by industry. In one city the grounds of the Cathedral are used each evening as a marshalling yard for a private army of night-watchmen, who then march off with their weapons and dogs to protect the homes of the rich.

To seek security in these violent ways gets one into a spiral of force. This is obvious in the case of the arms race where the source of the insecurity on each side is the amount of weaponry which the other side deems necessary for its own security. But the same trap operates in the case of internal State security and private security. More and more resources are spent on providing 'security' — and less and less is available to meet the basic needs of the deprived people whose deprivation makes them a threat to security. Those who can afford it have become 'hooked' on security. Meanwhile the excluded ones have less and less to lose.

Despite the oppression carried out in its name, security must nevertheless be called a Kingdom value. In fact the very lengths to which people go in order to protect themselves show what a fundamental human need security is. The question is whether there is any alternative to the self-defeating attempt to ensure safety through violent means. For an answer, one does not have to go into the realms of theory; even a quick look at the way people live in various parts of the world is enough to show that in some communities security needs have been met without relying on undue repression. This happens in societies where there is a tradition of mutual trust and respect. By 'tradition' I mean something more than simply the pattern of respect that characterises people in their relationships with one another; equally important is the way that trust and respect are fostered by the institutions and structures at every level — political, economic, social, cultural, and religious.

The basis on which this kind of security is built is a fair measure of contentment by people with what they have and with their place in society. And the best foundation for such contentment is social justice. For people can generally trust each other to respect a system which benefits all. Of course there are other ways besides the provision of social justice in which people can be persuaded to accept their lot. A really effective caste system or feudal system scarcely allows people to envisage any alternative; and religion may be used to justify such a rigid and unjust stratification of society. The weakness of such systems is that once a crack comes, the whole structure may quickly shatter. In the long run the safest foundation for contentment and mutual trust is social justice.

When the Kingdom comes in its fullness the human need for security will be met not by repression but by trust. The Christian who wishes to promote the Kingdom value of security will want to lessen distrust and to eliminate as far as possible the conditions and structures that give rise to it. This means trying to ensure that people do not have the experience of alienation — either the alienation of those who are so marginalised that they have a sense of being excluded from the benefits of society, or the alienation of the rich who feel they must defend what they have against the masses.

The Christian Church must not only work in society for security based on trust, but must also bear witness to it in its own corporate life. One can at times find striking examples of such a witness. For instance I myself was able to live for two years in a slum on the edge of a Third World city, a place that was so dangerous that people called it 'the jungle'. I could live there in relative security because of the reputation for service and trust built up over the years by those who went before me. On the other hand, I am aware of many ways in which we 'Church people' ensure our own security by failing to share authority with others. Recently, a priest said to me: 'I encouraged the parish council to challenge me; but when they did so I found I couldn't take it.' This very remark indicated that in fact he was beginning to cope with the challenge; but how few there are who would even allow the problem to arise. So often we seek security by holding on to power rather than allowing ourselves to be vulnerable and trusting others.

## (3) Justice

Another Kingdom value is justice. Perhaps more than ever before, people today all over the world are crying out for social justice — and struggling and suffering for it too. In a previous chapter we saw how the problems of injustice in society have become greatly exacerbated by the process called 'development'; and earlier in this chapter I referred to the way in which the world has become 'unified but not united' through the unjust pattern of world trade. Corresponding to this internationalisation of economic injustice, the struggle for justice has also become world-wide. It is becoming ever more evident that a truly human world must be one where justice prevails at all levels — international, national, and local. But though the aspiration for justice has never been so strong and widespread, the extent of injustice is perhaps greater than ever before. Demands for justice have been ignored. Non-violent campaigns for justice have been met with violence by those who hold power. And when oppressed groups have finally resorted to violence, this has provoked oppression on a massive scale.

The problems of social justice are best articulated in terms of fundamental human rights. When one speaks of such rights, what first springs to mind are political rights such as a say in the decision-making machinery of society, and the more elementary right of protection against arbitary arrest and torture. But increasingly there has been talk of basic rights in the economic sphere as well: for individuals and families, the right to work, to a living wage, to free schooling; and, for the poorer countries, the right to a fair price on the world market for their products, and the right of access to markets in the richer countries — as well as the right to the technology which is often monopolised by the 'developed' countries. Somewhere on the boundary between political and economic rights lies the right claimed by the countries of 'the South' to a more effective voice in determining the policy of the international banking system.

In recent years cultural rights are also coming to be seen as especially important. These include the rights of minorities within States. There is also the right of smaller countries to protection against a form of 'cultural imperialism'; for a small number of Western news agencies and TV or film companies dominate the mass media in most of the world – and especially in the Third World.

Within the past twenty years the Churches have consciously set out to study what is happening in the world with a view to discerning where the Kingdom is coming into being. This process has sometimes been called, 'reading the signs of the times'. Individual Christians and Church authorities have come to see that one of the most important of these 'signs of the times' is the struggle for fundamental human rights. This has led to a major change of emphasis by most of the Churches in their moral teaching. Instead of focusing almost exclusively on matters of purely personal or interpersonal morality, they are now concentrating on the whole question of structural justice and on human rights. In my book *Option for the Poor: A Hundred Years of Vatican Social Teaching* I tried to document this major change of emphasis in the teaching of the highest authorities of the Catholic Church; a similar pattern can be found in most of the Protestant Churches. In a later chapter I shall say something more about the change of outlook or 'mindset' that underlies this change of emphasis in teaching.

There seem to me to be two major contributions that have been made at the level of teaching by the Christian Churches in regard to the Kingdom value of justice. One is the clear spelling out of what a truly just society would look like – in other words, the naming of the different elements that go to make up social justice. Perhaps the best and most succinct formula is that used by the World Council of Churches: what the world needs is 'a just, participative, and sustainable' society. This phrasing has the advantage of ensuring that justice will not be thought of purely in terms of the fair distribution of material goods. Equally important – if not more so – is the active participation of ordinary people in making the decisions that affect their lives. Furthermore, justice requires also that we be just to the people of future generations, by not squandering the irreplaceable resources of the earth.

The second important teaching contribution of the Church is the concept of an option for the poor. What is most significant here is the recognition that we can be misled by the idea of 'equality of opportunity for all'. For the rich

111

and powerful can use this formula to justify their taking advantage of others. If there is to be any hope of achieving social justice, it is necessary that the authorities set out to give special protection to the poor; this has to be done in the political and cultural spheres as well as in economic affairs. Theologians have helped to bring this home to Church leaders and to Christian citizens. They have also provided solid biblical and theological arguments why the Church itself should be making an option for the poor.

So much for the *teaching* of the Church; but what of its *practice*? How effective has it been in working for justice? The answer varies from place to place. But it must be said first of all that, compared with the situation of fifty or a hundred years ago, there has been a truly remarkable improvement. The Churches have in many places become the outspoken champions of the poor in their demand for social justice and fundamental human rights. So much so, that in many countries the Church has been subjected to a wave of persecution — precisely because those in power see that it has ceased to legitimate their position; they see that the Church is no longer content just to minister to the victims of society but seeks now to help them overcome their victimisation. The results have been amply documented in regard to the Latin American countries by Penny Lernoux in her book, *Cry of the People* (2nd ed. Doubleday and Penguin, 1982). In South Africa and the Philippines the Church is beginning to take the same kind of uncompromising stand in favour of the oppressed.

Unfortunately, there are still many places — both in the Third World and in the richer countries — where the stance of the Church is less clearcut. Towards the end of Chapter 3, which was concerned with Third World theology, I made some comments on this point; and it will come up again in a later chapter. So at this point I shall leave the question of the role of the Church in working for justice in secular society. Instead, I shall move on to make some brief comments about the question of justice within the institutional Church itself.

Unless the Church is seen to be truly just in its own organisation, its work for justice in society is severely compromised. What is particularly important is that there should be a witness to what may be called institutional or 'political' justice in the Church — that is, that no individual or group should be allowed a monopoly of power, or be in a position to make arbitrary decisions. It must be admitted that in this regard the Catholic Church had little to boast of in the past. In the past twenty years, however, a major change has begun to take place. This is most notable in the way in which authority is exercised in religious orders and congregations of women and men. In other areas of Church life, changes have come more slowly. But at least there are grounds for hope.

On the other hand there are two outstanding instances of institutional injustice which have to be mentioned. They are sexism and clericalism. It is a sad fact that, by and large, the Churches (some more than others) have failed to correct the imbalance and injustice built into patriarchal society. Women as a group are still treated as second-class members of the Church. Furthermore, this treatment is supported by a theology that can only be called an ideological defence of male dominance. A crucial question is the right of women to become ministers in the Church. But even if one prescinds from this issue, one is still confronted by the failure of male authorities to allow women adequate involvement in decision-making. How can we really be a witness to the Kingdom when the life of the Church is marred in this way? If we want to build an alternative world, this is one of the many places where we can start.

Closely related to the question of sexism is that of clericalism. Once again, the crucial issue is one's understanding of the nature of ministry. But no respectable theology of authority could be invoked to justify the failure by clergy to relinquish to lay people the responsibilities that are theirs as Christians. This is one way in which the Church gives a counter-witness to the Kingdom value of justice. To conclude this section it may be remarked that what has emerged is some remarkable instances of a commitment by the Church to justice, and at the same time some striking examples of institutional injustices which need to be corrected in the Church itself.

## (4) Work

Perhaps it seems surprising at first to list work as a Kingdom value. But the soul-destroying effects of unemployment give some indication of the extent to which work is fundamental to human life. Not the endless toil which is the lot of so many peasants who struggle to survive in the poorer countries. Nor the dehumanising routine of an assembly-line where people are treated as robots — and eventually replaced by robots. What is meant by work as a Kingdom value is the exercise of the human power of making, shaping, inventing, creating; of coming into touch with and tapping the life-giving powers of the earth; of cooperating with others in the tasks involved in building a more human world. It is the human experience of putting oneself into some great project — or some minor one which becomes significant because it embodies a person's labour. This 'Kingdom work' includes many of the features that we now associate with leisure.

When we look at the reality of work in our world, the contrast between it and 'Kingdom work' is glaring. For most people, life is dominated by one of three patterns, each one of which makes a mockery of what work ought to be. For some it is the drudgery of endless back-breaking physical work. For others it is the drudgery of mindless repetitive work at a machine. For a third group — whose numbers are ever-increasing — it is being unemployed. The human community has failed notably to put machines at the service of people, to use them to humanise work; instead, they are being used either to dehumanise people by turning them into tenders of machines, or else to put people out of work. Meanwhile, the privileged minority of people, who are in a position to benefit both from machines and from the work of others, have developed a lifestyle that is hardly more success-ful. Those whose work is some kind of 'management' find themselves harassed by the tensions arising from dealing with an alienated work-force; and their lives are dominated by a ruthless competitive spirit. On the other hand, those who live a life of so-called leisure frequently become apathetic; find-ing life empty of the challenge of work, they seek distraction in drink, drugs, or frivolity.

Many centuries ago the Christian Church addressed itself to some aspects of the problem of work. The great monasteries went some way towards integrating both physical work (farming and building) and intellectual work (copying manu-scripts) into a fully human life. In more recent times there

114

have been some communities of Christians who have tried to pioneer a different style of life. But this has seemed to be somewhat marginal to the main interests of the Churches, and of Christians as a whole. The time has come for more sustained and urgent action by the Church directed towards the promoting of work as a Kingdom value.

Church leaders could give more encouragement to those individuals or communities who are trying to develop alternative styles of living: those who are trying to use simpler technologies, and those who live on a diet that is both more healthy and less wasteful of scarce resources. The Chinese expect their managers and intellectuals to spend time working on the farms. They are trying in this way to lessen the gap between different categories of workers and to break down 'elitism'. Should this not be seen by Christians as one of 'the signs of the times'? And if so, should we not be trying to do something similar ourselves? To do so could create a bond of solidarity between people who now have little in common except their Christian faith; it could also provide a better balance of different kinds of work in the lives of the individuals involved. It would be a great inspiration to people if a significant number of Church leaders were to follow the example of the very few who have adopted an alternative lifestyle. I am thinking of people like Bishop Mwoleka of Tanzania who belongs to an Ujamaa village and spends time each week doing communal farm work. I shall return to these points in a later chapter when I am dealing with alternative institutions.

## (5) Progress

Few words are so bandied about today as the word 'progress'. It is taken for granted in local communities, in nations, in countries, and in the world as a whole, that things can change for the better. By this is not meant just the turn of the wheel of fate, with changes for better or worse alternating. What people are looking for today is a lasting improvement, a development that will not be reversed. It may well be that this is a typically modern notion, not shared by the people of the past or even by those who still live according to a traditional pattern. Nevertheless, the belief in the advancement and improvement of the world is now so widespread — and so much in tune with the Christian faith — that one must conclude that progress is a Kingdom value.

When we look at the actual situation in the world today we are forced to conclude that, for most people, 'progress' has proved to be a myth. I am here using the word 'myth' in its worst sense; for there has been, not just a failure to live up to the promise of lasting improvement, but a cruel deception of people. In the name of progress, millions of people in the Third World have been required to give up much of their former way of life, in exchange for benefits which have proved illusory for most of them.

They lost many of their traditional social structures which had provided safeguards for the weak, the old, and the poor — and which generally ensured some measure of equity (if not equality) in society. The older patterns of authority were undermined. The generation gap is now a culture gap as well. So, parents and elders are no longer in a position to educate the young. The result is that the moral fabric of society has been damaged almost irreparably. Traditional values are rapidly disappearing, with nothing to take their place except opportunism. Officials and office-holders abuse their power; they display indifference and arrogance towards those they are supposed to serve. Corruption is rampant. Not merely the kind of bribery that 'greases the machine' to get things done; but the kind of 'competitive bribery' that eliminates any connection between true worth and success — in business, in politics, and even in education.

Such 'progress' as has come has been confined, in most Third World countries, to a relatively small privileged group. For them there are many material benefits and an enormous increase in power. For the masses the good effects have been quite limited. There has been a lowering of the rate of infant mortality. And Western medicine has undoubtedly helped many sick people. But even these benefits have been spread unevenly. Furthermore they have not been integrated into a coherent pattern of human welfare. For instance, the lowering of the rate of infant mortality has not been linked to appropriate changes in the system of social welfare; the large family is still the basic form of social security; and the result is a population explosion which leaves countries in greater poverty than ever.

Furthermore, the introduction of Western medicine has widened the gap between the privileged and the underprivileged, and introduced almost unlimited opportunities for abuse and corruption. As for Western schooling, my personal experience in Africa is that frequently it does not merit the title 'education'. It offers certificates to a privileged group, formed increasingly of the children of people who themselves already hold a relatively privileged place in society. These certificates are used to designate an 'elite' class who monopolise most of the resources of the nation.

In the 'modernised' countries of 'the North' the benefits of 'progress' are, of course, much more obvious. And many of these benefits have reached the majority of the population. But the real cost of 'progress' is beginning to emerge. For one thing, there is a sizeable proportion of the population in Western countries which is excluded. It is becoming clearer that these people can no longer be seen as 'the ones whom the benefits of the system have *not yet* reached'; rather they must be seen as 'the casualties of the system', the ones who pay the price for the benefits of the majority. (Of course they are not the only ones who pay the price for our 'progress'; the main casualties of the system are the poor of the Third World, the vast majority of the human race.) In the Communist countries the basic principles of the system include a commitment to a more even spread of the material benefits of 'progress'. But the price of this has generally been great restrictions on human rights and freedom, and the creation of a power elite, who often have economic privileges as well.

In both East and West many of the benefits of 'progress' have come from the cashing of cheques on the future. By that I mean two things:
— first, the running up of huge debts;
— and secondly, the squandering of irreplaceable resources (e.g. clean water, minerals, forests, oil).
We are asking future generations to pay for our benefits. Closely linked to this is the ecological price paid for both industrial and agricultural 'progress'. This is a point to which I shall return.

In recent years Church leaders have begun to wake up to the myths of progress. One crucial aspect of this awakening has been the realisation of the importance of 'sustainability'. As I noted earlier, the World Council of Churches included this concept in its definition of justice. A second important aspect is the realisation that what most of the poor of the world need is not so much 'development' as liberation from oppression. Latin American Church leaders have played a most important role in pointing out the problems that arise as a result of so-called development. In the Roman Catholic Church the Synod of Bishops in Rome in 1971 was greatly influenced by this Latin American thinking. It pointed out the myths of development; and Pope John Paul II has been emphatic in speaking out against such a dehumanising 'progress'. Recent conferences of the WCC have been equally firm in rejecting this kind of 'development'.

The Churches have been much less articulate in proposing alternative forms of development — ones that would be genuinely human. No doubt this has been partly due to a desire to avoid giving the impression that the Church has a blueprint for the ideal society. But I am afraid it may also be due to an unwillingness to be too critical of the Western model of development, and so perhaps seem to give encouragement to those who opt for a Marxist alternative. Would it not be better for Church leaders to stop looking over their shoulders in this way and instead to lend support to those who are working for a truly radical alternative to both the consumerism and injustice of the West and the bureaucracy and repression of the East? At present, many Church people seem to spend more time pining for the past than building a truly human future. What is required is some way to link the social and political values of progress, work, justice, security, and unity, with the more obviously religious and personal values which are generally associated with the Christian faith. In the next chapter I shall examine some of the latter kind of values and see how they link up with the more public Kingdom values which I have been looking at up to now.

# 8

# Personal and Interpersonal Values

In the last chapter I looked at five Kingdom values, all of which are very much concerned with the public sphere of secular life. I suggested that the Christian community must be involved in promoting and witnessing to these values; for the primary purpose of the Church is, not to advance itself, but to serve the Kingdom.

In Chapter 9 I shall consider how such values can best be embodied in society in alternative structures, and through the use of alternative methods. But before going on to that question I want in this chapter to examine some other Kingdom values. These will be values that are generally associated with the personal and interpersonal spheres of life rather than the public sphere. For this reason they are more easily seen as having 'religious' implications, in contrast to the more 'secular' values considered in the last chapter. I shall select four of these values — relationships, roots, harmony, and hope. I want to see how these can be related to the more worldly values dealt with already.

## (1) Relationships

There is a very keen awareness today that, if people are to flourish they need deep and authentic human relationships with others. Much of modern literature centres on this search for interpersonal relationships; and there is a spate of popular psychology which offers to help people in their search.

Unfortuantely the gap between aspiration and achievement is very wide indeed. The 'modern' lifestyle of the West is quite destructive of human relationships. It gives a central role to competitiveness; and this 'value' has come to pervade the interpersonal sphere as well as business life. Not only in the West but also in the East and 'the South', people are becoming so concerned with efficiency and productivity that there is little scope for depth and tenderness. On the other hand, the urgency of our search for authentic relationships suggests that these have priority in the Kingdom.

Christian teaching and practice have always put a lot of stress on the importance of deep human relationships. It is true that until recently there were notable weaknesses in the theology of marriage; and the theology of community was also marred by an inadequate understanding of authority. But these inadequacies are being corrected. The modern theology of marriage and of community returns to an older stratum of the Christian heritage; it has a solid base in the Scriptures. There has been a great deal of experimentation with different forms of Christian community right down from New Testament times. Recently, there has been a particular emphasis on 'basic Christian communities'. It is important to note that the communities envisaged here are mainly those of people at the bottom of society — the poor and the marginalised. So, in the concept of the basic community there is a linking of interpersonal values with such public values as justice and true progress. It is significant that this approach has been successful in areas where there is great poverty and where the Church has taken an option for the poor. In other places, where the stance of the Church is more ambivalent, the notion of the basic Christian community is frequently misunderstood or thought of as just an interesting idea.

## (2) Roots

'Rootedness' is a Kingdom value. By that I mean that human individuals and communities, if they are to flourish, must have a sense of identity, and of their own history. This is what is given to people by their culture. But, sadly, the way the world is developing deprives individuals and whole nations of their culture, their roots. In the industrialised countries the 'massification' of people and the mechanisation of life have combined with consumerism to undermine the sense of identity that people had in the past. More and more people are feeling 'lost', rootless. The search for cultural and historical roots has recently become something of a fad in the USA; but the need is a genuine one.

The Third World is being subjected to a massive cultural domination: Western ways of acting, thinking, and feeling are being imposed on people all over the world. In the process, traditional cultures and ways of life are being wiped out. Ivan Illich claims that fifty languages die each year (*The Right to Useful Unemployment — and Its Professional Enemies*, London, Marion Boyars, 1978, p. 24). There is a sustained attack on traditional ways of making a livelihood, of exercising authority, of recreation and celebration, of ensuring social security for the old, the handicapped, and those who are mentally ill; and Western-type schooling has almost replaced traditional forms of education. Traditional methods of healing are by no means eliminated — but they have been misrepresented and under-valued. As for the sphere of religion: it would appear that traditional religion in the Third World is still thought of as 'paganism'.

The Church is in an excellent position to recognise cultural rootedness as a Kingdom value. For Christians today are vividly aware that the faith is not to be identified with any single culture. One has to go back to the time of St Paul to find any parallel for this sense of the universality of the Christian faith. The crucial point is that universality is not to be confused with uniformity: it is precisely because Christianity can be pluriform that it can be truly universal. It is this conviction which makes Christians aware of the importance of a sympathetic understanding of all cultures — and of the vital need for dialogue with other religions. The Churches, then, have no reason to condone cultural imperialism; on the contrary, the official stance of the main Churches is strongly in favour of recognising, preserving, and developing the riches of every human culture.

So much for the theory. In practice, however, it must be noted that most of the Churches have in the past contributed to the undermining of traditional cultures and ways of life. There is now a much greater sensitivity to traditional values and practices. But this does not mean that all is well, either in the Third World or in the industrialised countries. In the latter, the modern style of life — in work, recreation, and communications — is leaving people 'lost' and rootless. So

121

Christians must be exploring alternative ways of living. I shall say more about this in the next chapter.

The cultural problem in the Third World stems from two sources. Firstly, many Western or Westernised Church authorities are still inclined to impose Western laws, institutions, and practices on the young Churches. One of the main reasons for this is a continued failure to respect traditional religions. The new awareness among Christians of the importance of dialogue among the religions has had little effect on the attitude of Western-educated people towards the 'primal' religion of traditional cults. During my years in Africa I have only met one person who proudly acknowledged that he was a traditional believer — and that was in Oshogbo in Nigeria where the Austrian artist, Susanne Wenger, has given people new confidence in their traditional cults, by herself becoming an active participant in the traditional forms of religion.

A second cause of cultural difficulty in the Third World is that there is often an inconsistency in the way in which the Church operates there. In the strictly ecclesiastical sphere it may be promoting local culture in some important ways — for instance, by adapting its public worship. But the activity of the Church in society at large may still be undermining people's culture and sense of identity. For over a century, the Church has been one of the major agencies promoting change in the Third World, mainly through the introduction of Western-type schooling and medical services — as well, of course, as a Westernised religion. Church leaders today must take more account of the disruptive effects of this promotion of Western systems. Here is one more instance of the need for the Church to see the close links that exist between those Kingdom values that are obviously 'religious' and those that have to do with the public sphere which we think of as secular. Church leaders need to be concerned with more than just 'religious' values; it is a matter of urgency that they promote a whole alternative way of living — one that anticipates the Kingdom.

*(3) Harmony*

I have not listed peace as one of the Kingdom values examined in this chapter. The reason is that peace, as a Kingdom value, is something much broader and deeper than the absence of violence and strife. It includes most of the values which I have already listed — notably: security, justice, and deep interpersonal relationships. But there is a further dimension to peace, one that is so important that it has to be listed separately. It is personal harmony, the gift of inner peace.

There are two slightly different aspects to this inner peace. One is a certain integration of the personality, an ability to be 'at home' with all the facets of oneself. The second is a sense of being in harmony with the world. On the basis of my contact with people in Africa I would say that their traditional way of life promoted both of these aspects of peace. Those who still live according to this pattern seem to be more accepting of themselves than I am; they do not appear to be as ashamed of their inadequacies. Most of the people I meet are less restless than me — not only more tolerant of themselves but far more patient with others. They live more closely in touch with the forces of nature: they get up with the sun and stop working when it gets dark; their work is determined by the coming of the rains; and the children celebrate half the night long when the moon is full. Yesterday I attended a funeral; the man was buried outside his front door; so in a sense he was still there to take part in the community celebration which followed the burial.

'Modern' life tends to undermine all this. In industrialised countries we work and play according to an order based on the 'convenience' of machines. We force our biological rhythms to adapt to these mechanical patterns. For a long time the more sensitive people have been aware that we pay a high price for doing this violence to ourselves. But until very recently anybody who pointed this out was derided as unrealistic and an enemy of 'progress'. Furthermore, the technologies used in Western industry, agriculture, and medicine are very 'violent'. This was the word used to describe them by Fritz Schumacher, author of the now famous book, *Small is Beautiful*, in a speech which he gave on the day before he died, in 1977 (for the text see George McRobie, *Small is Possible*, London, Abacus, 1981, p. 10). This built-in violence in relation to nature tends to make us violent and exploitative towards others, and restless in ourselves.

Some people are seeking a remedy for inner restlessness by the use of meditation techniques or a return to prayer.

This certainly helps people to survive and cope. But it is not sufficient to rely on a temporary escape from the stresses of a way of life that has become destructive of life. A more radical approach is required — and is being sought by an increasing number of people. There is now a significant minority who are trying to find an alternative pattern of life, one that is more in harmony with the biological and climatic rhythms of nature. These individuals and groups are generally aware that many of the values they are looking for can be found through a selective return to some of the elements of the culture and way of life of the past. It is particularly sad, then, to see that, while this is happening in the West, most of the dominant people in the Third World are busily trying to adopt the Western way of life without adverting to the damage it can do. It is hard to appreciate what one has until it has been lost.

The Churches should have no hesitation in recognising that harmony — within oneself and with the world — is a Kingdom value. In fact Christians have always stressed this virtue, recalling the texts in St John's Gospel where Christ promises his own peace, a peace that the world cannot give, a peace that overcomes anxiety and fear (Jn 14:27). The inadequacy in the traditional Christian approach does not lie in any playing down of this gift. Rather, it comes from seeing it in a context that can be too exclusively personal or private. A good deal of the older spirituality encouraged one to seek inner peace as an *escape from* social injustice. A more authentically Christian approach is to seek inner peace *in the midst of* the struggle for justice. So once again what is most important is to link this 'religious' value with the more obviously worldly values such as justice and security. Can we find a way to combine a contemplative approach to life with a commitment to social justice? Can we be fully engaged in the struggle for human liberation in the public sphere while maintaining and nourishing our inner freedom and peace?

*(4) Hope*

Hope is perhaps the most basic Kingdom value of all, for it is hope that gives meaning to the very idea of the Kingdom. The best way to understand what is meant by 'the Kingdom' is to see it as the object of the deepest and most authentic human hopes. The basis for the various Kingdom values I have been listing has been the fundamental hopes that people cling to in spite of every disappointment. But we live in a world where not merely is it very hard to have our deepest hopes realised but where our hope itself is becoming problematical.

Long ago in school we learned that the sins against hope are despair and presumption. Looking at the situation around me, I would prefer now to speak more concretely and say: Many people have almost lost hope, while many others cling to false hopes. In the industrialised world the loss of hope frequently takes the form of alienation. People look for a 'job'; but few of those who find employment have any real sense of involvement in their work. Again, people have little sense of responsibility for the life of the community; public services are something to be provided by 'them', the authorities, who are not part of 'us'. The problem of alienation is particularly severe for those who are unemployed, or homeless, or marginalised in some other way. Vandalism may be seen as a violent rejection of society by people who find that society no longer offers them any fulfilment of their hopes – or even anything to hope for, except its destruction. Others, including some of the 'respectable' people, find other forms of escape from their loss of hope: drugs, alcoholism, or gambling.

In the Third World the loss of hope can take the form of fatalism: people may be immersed in a 'culture of silence' – so crushed by poverty and the daily struggle to survive that they never think that they themselves could have the power to change things. Those who live immersed in this 'culture of silence' are not necessarily despondent all the time. Undoubtedly, some of them are completely crushed in spirit; they can no longer cope so they allow themselves to become apathetic. That is the kind of thing that is meant when Christians in this part of Africa speak of becoming 'sad', and consider it to be a sin. But for the most part, people struggle on, in the daily grind of living. They experience the joys and sorrows of everyday life. What they are deprived of is the *deeper* hope that can envisage – and strive for – a totally different world, one that allows them to live in a fully human way.

I see very little evidence that the Churches in Africa have

succeeded in offering to people that kind of hope. This is partly because they have not tried very hard to do so; the version of Christian hope that has been presented has been mainly other-worldly in its orientation. However, I have worked in some places where a determined effort is being made to convey to people a more authentic Christian hope, one that emphasises the relationship between the present world and the future Kingdom. The most difficult thing is to make the initial breakthrough, to help people break out of the culture of silence and see through the false hopes which they have been using as an escape or a safety-valve.

I suspect that my own difficulty at present may be fairly typical. In the parish where I work a lot of young people are quite involved in Church work — prayer-groups, religious education, and above all the choir. But this activity is very 'churchy'. There is little awareness of the role of the Christian community in transforming the world. In other words, few Christians have an adequate understanding of Christian hope. My guess is that this is one reason why very many people who take part enthusiastically in a two or three-year catechumenate, nevertheless give up active involvement in Church life not long after they have been baptised. Only a certain type of person retains interest in a Church which has the virtues of a good organisation but has very little to say to many aspects of 'secular' life or to many of the deep needs and hopes of people.

I said that we are confronted with a twofold problem about hope: some have almost lost hope, while others cling to false hopes. What are these false hopes? They can be purely secular or even materialistic hopes; or they can be an escapist version of 'spiritual' hope. Here in the Third World these abberations are seen most starkly. A lot of people have opted for all that is worst in Western materialism and competitiveness; there is ruthless exploitation of the weak and poor. Meanwhile, quite a lot of those who are the victims of society cling to the hope of winning a big prize in the pools, or becoming successful through great good luck, brought on by some religious or quasi-magical power. The more spiritual version of distorted hope is generally based on some apocalyptic notion of the Second Coming — the New Jerusalem will descend from the sky on those who await it.

The persistence of such distorted conceptions of the Kingdom is evidence of the sheer strength of the human urge to hope, even in hopeless situations. It also helps one to take account of an aspect of hope that could easily be overlooked — the fact that it is a gift. Some years ago, when I first began to work in the slums of a Third World city I came up against problems that were beyond belief — enough to make anybody despair. Yet I was astonished to find that very many of the people who lived there were bubbling with life and hope. It was then that I came to realise that hope is a gift. In the last analysis, if I am hopeful it is not because I have calculated the odds and concluded that my action is likely to succeed. Rather, hope is that most fundamental drive in me which, in the most impossible situations, enables me to take action to change the odds.

I do not think it is quite accurate to say that it is the task of the Church to give people hope or even to restore their hope. I think hope is a primordial gift from God which, in a sense, has to precede any Church activity. What the Christian community can do is perhaps to encourage people to get more in touch with the hope that is in them. And it can offer them a fitting object of hope, to replace or correct the idols or distorted ideals in which so many put their hope. Not that Christians can be very specific about the exact nature of the Kingdom in which we hope; in fact a most crucial task of religious education is to help people to avoid a fundamentalist reading of the Bible. We must learn to appreciate the importance of the symbolic accounts of the Kingdom given in the Old and New Testaments. But we must not look to the Bible for a geography of the Kingdom.

If we want to be specific about what we are hoping for, then we have to go through the rather elaborate process in which I am now engaged: first we must try to discern the main Kingdom *values* (which I have been attempting to do in the previous chapter and this one); then we have to envisage *institutions* in which these values can be embodied, and *methods* by which our present structures can be replaced by the new ones (the subject of the two following chapters). But all of this will be a rather abstract and futile exercise if we attempt to work it out first in theory before putting it into practice. The process of discerning Kingdom values and of working out appropriate structures and methods has to be guided by practical experience.

The word 'praxis' is frequently used to indicate the particular combination of thought and action that is required. It is not simply theory interspersed with practical application; that way of expressing it seems to give priority in time and importance to theory. But what is called for is 'reflective action' – activity that is constantly being evaluated and corrected in the light of its results.

My only problem with the word 'praxis' (apart from the fact that many people are simply mystified by the word) is that it fails entirely to indicate one major feature of the action/reflection of the Christian, namely, the place given in it to Christ. If I really want to partake in building the Kingdom of God as lived and taught by Christ, then it is important, but not sufficient, for me to explore the deepest human needs of today's world. I must also spend a lot of time reflecting on Christ's life and words, allowing them to seep into my own life through prayer. In this way I begin 'to put on the mind of Christ'. As my ways of thinking and feeling gradually come to be more in harmony with those of Christ, I can begin to sense, 'from the inside', the true nature of the Kingdom.

However, it is important to note that this prayerful reflection on the life and words of Christ is not to take place in some separate 'religious' department of my life. Rather it will be constantly impinging on my practical efforts to discover and promote Kingdom values. My reflection on my action will be deeply affected by my prayer centred on Christ. This does not lead to a facile comparison between Christ's actions and mine; for I must take account of the great differences between his situation and my own. At times, certainly, my action can be directly modelled on his. But, even where that is not appropriate, my discernment and my action can be truly Christlike. This means that they will be inspired by his Spirit. My relationships with others will be governed by the kind of compassion and courage shown by Christ. Furthermore, Christlike action is action that is permeated with his sense of the constant care of the mysterious and provident one whom he dared to call 'Abba'. It is action that springs from the same kind of radical integrity and commitment to the values of the Kingdom that Christ himself constantly

showed. And if my action is to be Christlike it must above all
be animated by his unwavering hope in the coming Kingdom
— and his conviction that it is coming into being here and
now (cf. Luke 4:21).

*Conclusion*

To draw to a conclusion this long study of Kingdom values
I want to note some of the important points that have emerged.
The first is that the study indicates how utterly misleading
it is to try to divide values into just two categories — the
spiritual and the temporal. The truth is that all values have a
temporal or secular aspect and a spiritual or transcendent
aspect. Some of the most urgent problems facing Christians
today arise from an undue concentration by the Church in
the past (and even still) on supposedly 'spiritual' matters. It
is clear that the way forward is for the Church — and for
Christian groups and individuals — to pay much more attention to such apparently secular values as justice, cultural
rootedness, and meaningful work. However, there must be
no playing down of those values — such as hope and inner
peace — which have traditionally been associated with
religion. There is need for action on different fronts; but
it should all be inspired by an integral vision. Perhaps it would
be more accurate to speak not so much of an integral vision
as of an integral hope. What we hope for is a Kingdom for
which we have no blue-print. But with the help of Christ's
Spirit we can recognise where it is coming into existence;
and we can promote it, give witness to it, and in this sense
anticipate it.

The second point to note is that there has been a coherent
pattern in the way each of the nine Kingdom values has been
treated. In each case we found that our world is pining and
groping for the value in question; the value responds to a
fundamental human need. But in each case we found that
there was a gulf between our aspiration and our achievement. The sinfulness of our world is evident in the way it has
either thwarted or distorted these basic values. Indeed the
most appalling abuses of human dignity are to be found in
the way people try to meet these needs for themselves and
prevent others from doing so. The more eagerly people seek
to meet their deepest needs, the more sin pervades and mars

the results. Clearly we cannot be saved merely through human efforts. If our world is to be rescued it must be 'through grace' (cf. Eph 2:8). All that is taken into account when we say that the world is in need of 'salvation', 'redemption', or 'liberation'.

The need for liberation and new hope is the opening for the Church. As I have said, the task of the Christian community is to discern where the Kingdom is coming into being in our world. Then we are called to promote its coming. One way in which this is to be done is by direct action in the world. Another way is for the Christian community itself to give a living witness of the value in question, whether it be justice or security, unity or harmony. In this way the Church is called to anticipate the Kingdom: by making it evident to people what the Kingdom will really be like, the Christian community can hasten its coming.

Unfortunately, we saw that the need for redemption is not confined to the world outside the Church. The Church's own institutional and community life is itself seriously marred by aberrations and distortions of the Kingdom values to which it is called to give witness. This is a source of embarrassment and shame — but not of despair. For as Christians we believe that, though we are called to promote the Kingdom and witness to it, nevertheless the work is ultimately not ours but God's. Even our weakness and failure can be used by God: 'For we know that in all things God works for good with those who love him.' (Rom 8:28).

# 9

# Alternative Economics and Lifestyle

How are the values of the Kingdom to be realised effectively in our world? It would be a serious mistake to assume that our main aim should be to bring about the moral conversion of as many individuals as possible, so that they would then give priority to Kingdom values. Something more than personal conversion is required. There must also be transformation of the structures and institutions of society. This is not a substitute for personal conversion, but it is required to encourage and sustain such change. In practice, we need to put a lot of thought and effort into trying to change the structures. Otherwise we are likely to end up moaning and moralising about the evil conduct of people. Alternatively, we may become like the people who have got completely wrapped up in 'Bible Crusades'; they often seem to live in a very restricted world, believing their own propaganda, mixing mostly with like-minded people, and seeing everybody else as a candidate for conversion.

An option for the poor means a commitment to working to overcome structural injustice. So it means attempting to get rid of the institutions and structures which deprive people of their rights and leave them voiceless. But it is not simply a matter of dismantling such institutions. It is naïve to imagine that we can live without structures of any kind. What needs to be done is to overhaul drastically many of our present structures and to replace entirely those which are so oppressive or inadequate that it is not worthwhile trying to adapt them.

We need to envisage an alternative world, one where Kingdom values are embodied not only in the political and economic structures of society but also in the whole tradition and way of life. The institutions and traditions of any group of people are embodiments of certain values. Some of them have been designed with the specific purpose of getting people to act in certain ways; others have taken shape over many years without conscious planning but in a way that encourages certain patterns of behaviour. This means that the nature or purpose of such institutions is to make sure that we respect certain values, or at least act upon them. For example, a central purpose of a trade union is to ensure that its members are adequately paid, that they are not dismissed arbitrarily, and that they are protected from, or compensated for, dangers in their work. So the union is, at its best, an institution which promotes the Kingdom value of justice. Unfortunately, a trade union, as well as employers' organisations and other such protective agencies, may at times sacrifice justice in society as a whole in order to pursue the sectional interests of its own members. So we need not merely to opt for the Kingdom value of justice, but also to examine the effectiveness of existing institutions in embodying and promoting that value.

Instead of doing this in an abstract and utopian way it seems better to approach the question concretely. To do so we can look at past and present institutions and structures of various kinds, to see their positive and negative aspects. This is a major task; it involves looking beyond our own history and culture to study features of other civilisations, other ways of protecting and fostering human values. For instance, it would be particularly helpful today to examine how people in non-Western cultures have worked out a balance between the 'accelerator' mechanisms that promote change in society and the 'brake' mechanisms that inhibit change from becoming so rapid that people can no longer cope with it. Again, it could be useful to see how other civilisations have offered rewards for initiative and hard work, while at the same time not allowing too wide a gap to open up between the 'successful' ones and the others. Above all, we could benefit from looking at the various ways in which people down the ages have tried to ensure that goods and responsibilities are shared out fairly, and that the weaker sections of the community are protected from exploitation.

There are so many alternative institutions and structures

to study that it would be easy to get bogged down in endless detail. One way of lessening this danger is to have a systematic framework as a guideline for the examination. I want to propose such a framework, and to offer some illustrations of the different elements that could fit into it. The framework is based on the one I outlined in Chapter Four. There I suggested that a 'power pyramid' tends to develop in each of four overlapping areas of life — the economic, the political, the cultural, and the ecclesiastical. Power in these areas is monopolised by a small minority. These can 'trade off' favours with one another. Meanwhile, those at the bottom of each pyramid are left powerless and voiceless. Now that we are beginning to envisage an alternative world, we can use this same framework. We can examine alternative institutions and approaches in each of these four areas, and take account also of how these alternatives may support one another in somewhat the same way as the oppressive structures do.

In this chapter I propose to discuss the question of alternative economic structures and approaches. I shall be looking at the alternatives to what I called the 'money power' pyramid, which represents the present unjust economic order. In the next chapter I shall go on to consider alternative structures and approaches in the areas which I called 'political power', 'idea power', and 'God power'. The treatment of the economic issues will be longer than that of the other topics. That is because once a certain economic system is chosen, this determines to a considerable extent the structures that will develop in the political and cultural spheres — and even in the ecclesiastical sphere. The inhumanity of the present world order in the economic sphere makes it extremely difficult to have human structures in the other spheres. If we want to change the present systems in politics or education or even in the Church, we need to envisage an alternative order in the economic sphere.

## Question the Basic Principles

In the economic sphere the world is dominated by a banking and trading system that has divided it geographically into the wealthy and powerful 'North' and the poor and debt-ridden 'South'. It has also stratified individual countries into different classes; and has left those in the lower classes marginalised and increasingly trapped in a cycle of poverty. Time and again Church authorities have spoken out to insist that this whole economic order is radically unjust. The United Nations, too, has accepted that it should be replaced by 'a new international economic order'. At the national level social justice can only be realised by equally drastic changes which would give the poor a chance.

But what kind of alternative structures ought to replace the present economic system? The kind of proposals made by the Brandt Commission, or even those put forward by 'the group of 77' (poorer countries) at the United Nations Conference on Trade and Development (UNCTAD) are essentially compromises which are thought to be 'reasonable' enough to be accepted by the wealthy nations. While they would go some way towards meeting short-term difficulties they do not take a sufficiently radical look at the underlying problems. Because they are trying to be 'realistic' they propose only relatively minor changes in the present system; they do not question its presuppositions; and so they fail to face up to the real issues.

At least three of the basic principles of the present economic system need to be questioned:
— (1) the determination to advance through economic 'growth';
— (2) the commitment to use ever higher technology;
— (3) the practice of making trade more and more international.
Between them, these three elements in the present system lead to the following problems:
— Resources are used up more rapidly than they can be replaced. This is an injustice inflicted on future generations. It also causes problems in the present. It gives rise to undue competition for the available resources. This provides an economic reason for war and the arms race, which in turn waste vast resources.
— More and more people are put out of work.
— Communities and nations become less and less self-sufficient. They are more and more dependent on imports — and therefore more locked into the present unjust economic order.
— The strong take advantage of those in a weak bargaining

position, so the gap between rich and poor is widened even further. For instance, the poorer countries which are trapped in heavy debt now find that, in the regulation of their economies, they are forced to adopt as the central guiding principle the servicing of their foreign debts rather than the welfare of their people.

## Alternative principles

A truly radical alternative will have to reject the three principles I have just listed. So, firstly, the world as a whole, and particularly the 'developed' nations, will have to plan a pattern of human development that does not require ever greater 'production' and consumption. I have put the word 'production' in inverted commas because it is a misleading term. What is called 'production' really means, for the most part, either extracting from the ground such resources as minerals or oil; or else consuming resources by giving them a different shape e.g. turning petro-chemicals into clothes or plastic bags. The use of the word 'production' creates a kind of myth: it disguises the fact that we are wasting precious resources; and it gives the impression that we are doing something praiseworthy — 'creating wealth', as it is called.

We have to learn to do with less of this kind of expensive production. That means adopting living patterns that make us partners of nature rather than its exploiters. We need to make use of what are called 'soft energy paths' (in contrast to 'hard energy paths'). This means that we would use such renewable energy sources as solar power, wind and wave power, and biomass; and that we put much more emphasis on the conservation of energy. (Cf. Duane Elgin, *Voluntary Simplicity: An Ecological Lifestyle that Promotes Personal and Social Renewal*, Bantam, New York, 1982, p. 147).

Closely linked to this questioning of a 'growth'-oriented model of development is a second point: we need to challenge the present tendency to introduce ever higher technology. This does not mean that we should always opt for a low-level, labour-intensive technology. What is crucial is that whatever equipment we are using should be appropriate for the work, in the particular situation. In choosing to employ a particular kind of equipment we need to take account of all the factors that are involved. At present, the owner of a factory or a large farm may choose to install mass-production equipment simply on the grounds that this makes more profit. One of the myths common in our society is the assumption that 'efficiency' of this kind is good for society as a whole. It is because of this mistaken belief that governments frequently offer subsidies to industrialists or farmers to install labour-saving equipment. But what is seldom taken into account is the full cost of such action:

— People are put out of work and may have to be supported by society for the rest of their lives; a spin-off effect is that many of the young generation cannot find work, so they grow up alienated and may become vandals or drug-addicts.

— The high-level technology almost always requires more energy and uses up scarce resources. But this long-term cost is not taken into account, because it does not at present affect the one who is, as they say, 'investing' in the higher technology.

— The ecological cost of the new approach is often very high. The water, air, and ground of the locality may be polluted by industrial wastes. The food chain may become poisoned when farmers use large amounts of strong pesticides or add dangerous drugs to animal feed. It is quite likely that these costs are ignored or grossly underestimated. So the 'efficiency' which justifies such investment is a misnomer. It may cut the costs of the owner of the industry or farm, but this is largely by passing on some of the real costs to the community at large or to future generations. Why then is it encouraged by governments? Because each country is competing with others to widen its markets by cutting costs. The hidden or indirect costs are not fully taken into account. The assumption is that they can be paid for by the future generations who will have benefited by present 'development'. This assumption is proving to be totally unjustified; it is part of the myth I mentioned above that 'high technology' is more efficient and is better for all.

So far I have mentioned two basic principles that must characterise an alternative economic system: it must not rely on continued growth of 'production' and consumption; and it must not use high-level technology unless this can be shown to be appropriate in terms of the total real cost. A third principle must now be added: far more emphasis has to be put on local self-sufficiency, as against ever-increasing dependence on international trade. One reason for this is that in a single world market some are far more dependent than others; and those countries or groups that depend on a single crop or product are frequently exploited. Another reason is that the turning of the world into a single integrated market-place has been part of the model of development that uses ever higher technology and calls for ever increased growth in production and consumption. For the future, the ideal must be much greater self-sufficiency among local communities in the production of basic foodstuffs and everyday necessities. Where a necessary item is not available locally it should normally be got from some nearby community. International trade would concentrate on the exchange of materials and products that are both really needed and would be genuinely inefficient to produce locally.

## Unrealistic?

Could we really have an economic order in the world that would be based on the three principles I have just outlined? To those who think it is impossible or unrealistic, the simplest reply is to recall the past. The economic system of most human societies during most of the history of the world was governed by these principles. That was not a matter of choice but was simply how things were. What happened before can happen again. In fact the real danger is that the human race may have such a situation thrust upon it in a most harsh and unplanned way. Our society is heading for a break-down, either a sudden one through all-out war or a more gradual running down of the system through a convergence of factors:

— shortage of resources combined with massive waste through the arms race;
— increasing unemployment and alienation;
— ever greater bureaucracy, inefficiency, and corruption;
— ever greater pressure on poor and debt-ridden countries, groups, and individuals.

If we do not set out consciously to devise a world that is based on the kind of principles I have outlined, we are very likely to be thrown back into a very primitive form of economic organisation with few of the benefits of modern technology.

137

We tend to forget that civilisations have broken down before. The marvellous Roman roads and aqueducts fell into disuse as people went back to living in little communities which squabbled with each other for local resources. Even today there are countries where something similar has taken place. I was in Uganda towards the end of Idi Amin's rule. I found that people had reverted to a subsistence economy. What mattered was not the mighty Jinja dam which supplied electricity even for export, but the banana tree in the garden which provided food for the day. I doubt if things are much better there at present. Fifteen years ago there were phones in the area in which I am living at present; but we now survive without a telephone within a hundred miles. That kind of thing is happening increasingly in the Third World; and even in the wealthy countries there are significant breakdowns in the system.

I am not proposing that we go back to living just as our ancestors did. For we now have the possibility of choice. We can continue to make use of the benefits of modern science wherever it is appropriate – in protecting our health, in communicating with people who are far away, in the use of labour-saving devices that are genuinely efficient, in opting for more wholesome forms of food. But we need to look closely at traditional societies to see where their patterns of living were better than the modern lifestyle. It is essential that our choices should be based not solely on the narrow criteria of short-term profitability for individuals, but on the long-term effects. These long-term considerations are not purely economic, if that term is taken in a restricted sense; they include such wider human values as contentment and creativity – values on which it is difficult to put an exact economic price.

## Signs of Hope

I am concerned lest what I have been saying may sound like 'pie in the sky' – a lot of idealistic notions that have no chance of being taken seriously. So it is worthwhile mentioning that there are strong and growing movements in both the First World and the Third World that would give support to a good deal of the approach outlined here. Surely, one of the 'signs of the times' must be the remarkable growth of the

138

'ecological movement'. It can no longer be dismissed as a 'crank' affair; for it is beginning to offer to Western society a truly radical alternative – a style of development that challenges the assumptions of the present system.

In the area of technology there has been an equally remarkable change. It can be dated from 1965. It was then that Fritz Schumacher and some friends formed the Intermediate Technology Development Group; and in the same year he first found a wide audience for his 'Small is Beautiful' approach (– see George McRobie, *Small is Possible*, Abacus, London, 1982, pp. 24-25). By adopting a strategy of 'appropriate technology', Third World countries could show the rest of the world that there is a viable alternative to the present model of development. But I must add that I do not believe that the ruling elites in most Third World countries have any serious intention of opting for such an approach – any more than do those of the wealthy countries. It simply suits them to play at being interested. However, circumstances are changing rapidly. In many Third World countries the present plans for 'development' are becoming totally inoperable – and obviously so. As this happens, the real growth sectors in the economies of many countries may well be the places where appropriate technology is being effectively applied. But this hope cannot be realised so long as the development of these countries is left in the hands of local 'elites', allied to multinational companies, who have a vested interest in ensuring that the use of simple local technology does not develop.

At this point economics intersects with politics. Changes in the economic structures must be linked to major political change in the international order and within both the wealthy and the poorer countries. In the next chapter I shall have something to say about such changes. But first there are other aspects of the economic question to be dealt with.

## An alternative lifestyle

In speaking about alternative economic structures I have concentrated so far on two closely related issues:
– production, where I've stressed the need for appropriate technology;
– and distribution or trade, where I've emphasised the importance of local self-sufficiency.

139

There remains another issue, namely, *consumption*. An alternative world will be one where the patterns of consumption are radically different from those of the so-called 'developed' world — and of the privileged minority in the Third World. It will be a world whose inhabitants live a life of 'voluntary simplicity'. (See the book of this title by Duane Elgin, referred to above, p. 135.)

There are several converging reasons why we need to change our lifestyle towards more simple living:
— it is essential that we do so, if the poor are to have a fair share of the limited resources of the earth;
— from an ecological point of view it is urgent that we do so;
— it is highly to be recommended in the interests of bodily health;
— it offers us the possibility of a considerable reduction in stress, leading to greater tranquillity of spirit and peace of mind;
— it is the only course of action that offers a likelihood of full employment, and satisfying work for all;
— it would allow nations and communities to develop an environment in which young people could have an education that was neither unrealistic nor alienating.

What would it mean to adopt a lifestyle of voluntary simplicity? Above all it would involve the elimination of waste and of the incentives to waste that are so dominant in modern life. Economic growth is linked at present to greater consumption; so it is 'good' that advertisements encourage us to buy useless things and to discard many useful items as no longer in fashion. In a society committed to voluntary simplicity, usefulness and durability would be the key economic values; and the culture would foster such values. This implies notable changes in our styles of housing, travelling, and eating. For instance, every effort would be made to ensure that public transport was of such a quality that there would be little need for private cars.

Food has such a central role in any economy — and in particular in the present international economic order — that it is worthwhile looking at the situation which has developed over the past generation and comparing it with an alternative food policy based on 'voluntary simplicity'. In the West, a great deal of the protein we eat comes to us in the form of meat. This is a very wasteful way to produce protein – especially when the meat is produced by feeding grain to animals. The grain that is fed to animals for slaughter in Western countries would be more than sufficient to provide enough good food for everybody in the world – if we were satisfied to take more of our protein from vegetable sources rather than in the form of steaks, pork, and poultry. This change in eating habits – and the resultant change in agriculture – is one major element in the adoption of a lifestyle of voluntary simplicity. Those who have made the change vouch for the fact that it does not involve a tremendous sacrifice. Imaginative cooking can ensure that meals are as satisfying as ever. The change can be a very pleasant one if it goes hand in hand with a change in attitude towards cooking; this in turn is linked to a change in our understanding of sex-roles – boys, as well as girls, need to be taught to cook well and to see it as an enjoyable activity.

In Western countries, farming has evolved into 'agribusiness' – a method of food production which is very wasteful. It uses high technology, provides little employment, and is very costly from an ecological point of view. Agriculture has come to depend very heavily on the use of chemicals and drugs to deal with pests and crops disease. Control of the whole food industry has fallen increasingly into the hands of a small number of very large corporations. What is especially alarming is that these few companies are gaining a monopoly control of food seeds; and the variety of seeds is greatly reduced.

Meanwhile, many Third World countries find that their economies are almost totally dependent on the production and export of one or two 'cash crops' (e.g. tea, coffee, cocoa, sugar-cane, tobacco, bananas). The price of these products is kept very low, because the market is controlled by Western-based multinational companies. Peasant farmers who once produced food for themselves and their neighbours are being squeezed out; their land is being taken over for the production of cash crops for export. Fortunes are made by international financiers who buy and sell 'futures' – food crops that have not as yet even been harvested. In this way the livelihood of Third World workers and their families have become the object of speculation in the great Western money markets.

An alternative policy would be to encourage much greater

141

self-sufficiency in food at every level — from the family up to the nation. The use of appropriate technology would make small-scale production of food profitable, easy, and interesting. There would be much less reliance on chemical and biological means of increasing yields and controlling crop disease; organic methods would be used instead. Small-scale trading would ensure that people had a sufficient variety of food. Massive international trading in food would be the exception rather than the rule. Such an approach would notably curtail the opportunities for injustice at the international and national levels. It would lay the foundation for a food economy that would be far more just, sustainable, and healthy than the one we now have.

What I have written here on the issue of food is just a brief introduction to a topic that should be of the greatest concern to Christians — or indeed to anybody who is interested in the future of our world. The whole topic has been explored in considerable detail, and the results have been presented in a very readable form, with a wealth of documentation, by Frances Moore Lappé in two paperback books — *Diet for a Small Planet: Revised Tenth Anniversary Edition* (Ballantine, New York, 1982) and, *Food First: Beyond the Myth of Scarcity* (co-author, Joseph Collins, Ballantine, New York, 1979). These are books that have changed many people's lives.

### Spirituality of simplicity

Since very early Christian times the Church has had a theology and spirituality of poverty. The choice of voluntary poverty was closely linked to penance and self-denial; and the emphasis was on attaining personal freedom of spirit, through detachment from the things of this world. The call to voluntary poverty was seen as one for a relatively small number of specially chosen people. There is still need today for individuals who embrace voluntary poverty — though the emphasis nowadays will have to be much more on being in solidarity with those who have no choice about being poor and deprived. However, such a renewed theology of poverty is not what I want to discuss here. What is required even more urgently is a spirituality and theology of frugality or voluntary simplicity.

The emphasis in such a spirituality is not on personal

mortification and penance, but on finding a way of life that would allow everybody to have a reasonably fulfilled life of frugal comfort. The following passage from Duane Elgin's book brings out this point:

> A conscious simplicity . . . is not self-denying but life-affirming. Voluntary simplicity is not an 'ascetic simplicity' (of strict austerity). Rather, it is an 'aesthetic simplicity' (where each person considers whether his or her level and pattern of consumption fits with grace and integrity into the practical art of daily living on this planet).
>
> (*Voluntary Simplicity*, p. 134)

Such a spirituality differs from a spirituality of poverty above all in the fact that it is appropriate not just for a select few but for everybody. Of course one can expect that it may be a long time before most people are willing to adopt such an outlook. A relatively small number of people will have to be the pioneers both of the new lifestyle of which I have been speaking, and of the spirituality which articulates, supports, and inspires it. But essentially what is in question is an outlook that one could reasonably expect the whole human race to adopt.

To speak of a spirituality of voluntary simplicity is not to open up a whole new agenda, over and above the changes of lifestyle outlined in the previous section. What a spirituality adds is not new content — new things to be done — but a vision that can inspire one to work for such changes, and a sense of tranquillity and deep joy in living a life that is not wasteful and not cluttered with unnecessary possessions. To adopt such an outlook is to call in question the basic driving force of modern 'development'. For, as Schumacher remarks:

> . . . what is the great bulk of advertising other than the stimulation of greed, envy, and avarice? It cannot be denied that industrialism, certainly in its capitalist form, openly employs these human failings — at least three of the seven deadly sins — as its motive force.
>
> (*Good Work*, Abacus, London, 1980, p. 26)

Surely it is eminently Christian to challenge a model of development that appeals to greed and envy? Anybody who wishes to be a Christian must take seriously the Kingdom values outlined in the two previous chapters — and this means trying to ensure that these values are embodied in society. But the only hope of doing that lies in changing the 'modern' patterns of production, distribution, and consumption, by the promotion of a more simple and frugal way of life. Indeed it can be argued that to do so would enable us to bring Christ's Sermon on the Mount back into the centre of daily Christian living. At present the ideals of the Beatitudes seem so unreal that they tend to be reserved for specially called people; and the reason why it is so hard to relate them to real life is that the structures of our society embody values that are the very opposite of Kingdom values. But those who are working to build a simple frugal society find that the Beatitudes can come alive for them: blessed are the poor, the gentle, the single-minded, the merciful, the peacemakers.

One of the most moving appeals I have ever heard was made by Xavier Gorostiaga in a short talk given to the Trócaire Conference in June 1983. This Jesuit economist, who works in the planning department of the government of Nicaragua, pleaded for 'a civilisation of simplicity', a civilisation designed to meet the needs of the masses. He showed that such a change of structures is quite realisable — provided we really want it. He also pointed out that the Church is in a position to give legitimacy to such an approach. It was clear that his 'civilisation of simplicity' is something more comprehensive than just a new economic and political order. It includes a new set of values and attitudes — a new spirituality. Some years ago, Father Arrupe, then head of the Jesuit order, distinguished clearly between a spirituality of poverty in the strict sense, and a spirituality centred on frugality. While recognising the need for a certain number of committed Christians to embrace radical poverty, he insisted that the challenge for most is to work out a way of life that is truly frugal. Reflecting on Gorostiaga's talk, I recalled Father Arrupe's words; and I concluded that in working for 'a civilisation of simplicity', and proposing it to others, Gorostiaga was following Arrupe's inspiration and showing how it could be put into practice.

People who want to make an option for the poor and to build a more just world — a world of Kingdom values — often feel frustrated and paralysed because they do not know where to begin. One advantage of becoming aware of the movement for 'voluntary simplicity' is that it offers a starting-point to such people. To change one's eating habits might seem a rather futile way of trying to change the world. But changes of lifestyle can have a powerful effect. They symbolise one's commitment to radical change and are a constant reminder to oneself of the need for, and the possibility of, an alternative world. They can also affect other people, making them question themselves about their values and way of life. However, even if very large numbers of people were to change their style of eating, travelling, and living, this would not be enough. There is need also for radical changes in the political, cultural, and ecclesiastical spheres. These will be the subject of the next chapter.

# 10

# Alternatives in Politics, Culture, and the Church

Changes in economic structures have little hope of success unless they are accompanied by an equally radical transformation of political structures. What is needed is cooperative and participative structures at every level of society. At present, people have very little opportunity to share effectively in the making of the decisions that most affect them: workers can lose their jobs through the decisions of anonymous boards of directors; and planning decisions are often made by bureaucrats who remain faceless to those whose lives may be disrupted by these decisions. A legal system that supports an unjust status quo must be changed to ensure that the law protects the poor and the weak. At present, the task of security forces is to stifle and repress any opposition to the existing unjust order; what is required instead is a system that provides security for all, not just for those who are rich and powerful.

But how are these high ideals to be attained? In alternative political structures, as in economic ones, a most important element will be the 'small is beautiful' approach. If most industries and farms are relatively small in scale, then the workers have a better chance of formulating policy. Cooperatives — of workers and of consumers — should be encouraged and facilitated by the legal and educational systems. In the area of politics (in the strict sense of the word) there is need for a policy of decentralisation: decisions should be made at the level of the local community as far as possible, so as to achieve maximum participation of people. If such a policy is to work it must be accompanied by a great deal of realistic community education. The ordinary people could also become much more involved in ensuring their own security, instead of leaving the task to professionals.

Indeed the role of 'professionals' in society needs to be questioned. Ivan Illich argues very strongly that we have allowed various professional groups — such as lawyers, doctors, social scientists, architects, and teachers — to deprive us of our fundamental right to look after ourselves. The members of these professions claim a monopoly of 'special, incommunicable knowledge' in the spheres they have carved out for themselves; and 'gain legal power to create the need that, by law, they alone will be allowed to serve' (*The Right to Useful Unemployment — and its Professional Enemies*, Boyars, London, 1978, p. 78). They foster the illusion that those outside the profession are ignorant and helpless, quite unable to look after themselves on a do-it-yourself basis; so, ordinary people allow power to pass into the hands of 'a self-accrediting elite' (ibid. pp. 55, 67).

Illich presents his case in language so extravagant and rhetorical that it inclines one to dispute what he is saying; but it can scarcely be denied that one effect of the development of the professions has been a considerable reduction in self-help. Within the context of the present social order a case can be made for professional monopolies of various kinds. But in an alternative world — one that sets a high priority on participation, on self-help, on variety of approach, and on smallness of scale — there could be a much better balance between amateurs and experts.

Health care is an area of life in which the dominance of professionals has created serious problems. Firstly, doctors are credited with such a high degree of scientific knowledge and expertise that ordinary people are inhibited from being actively involved in caring for the sick and promoting health. They have passed over an extraordinary amount of their responsibility to the 'experts' of the medical profession and to pharmacists. Secondly, the problem is compounded by the way in which this professional group make use of their dominant position.

The medical profession ought to give priority to community health care. So they should ensure that most of the available resources (including their own time and energy) are devoted to health education and services to promote good health and prevent illness. But instead they allow the vast bulk of the resources to be spent on curative medicine. Even within this

147

overall approach there are further serious imbalances. A disproportionate amount of money and expertise is allocated to the building and running of general and psychiatric hospitals; and within the hospital system an undue amount of the resources is spent on highly specialised forms of surgery. One of the most serious problems of all is the excessive reliance by doctors and their patients on the use of drugs; independent observers frequently express alarm at the extent to which certain drugs, such as tranquillisers, are over-prescribed. But drug companies continue to make inordinate profits by pushing their products through the medical profession.

In the Third World all these abuses and imbalances are far more serious because there is less control on the abuse of power. I have seen at first hand how the inhabitants of slum areas on the fringes of African cities are ruthlessly exploited by doctors – and by the pharmaceutical industry at every level, from the local unlicenced peddler of medicines up to the multinational drug companies which delude people with elaborate advertising campaigns. It is very sad to see parents incur massive debt to buy what they are led to believe is the best medical care for their sick child – and to know that their almost magical belief in the wonders of Western science and medicine is being used to 'con' them.

What is required is a radical reversal of policies so that health education is given a far higher priority – and is closely linked to other aspects of adult education. This requires that medical people should cooperate much more closely with educationalists and community leaders – and that they be willing to relinquish the almost sacred aura of the medical 'expert'. I believe that in order to bring this about it is important that interested medical people become trained in the use of a 'psycho-social' approach such as I shall describe a few pages further on. This can go a long way towards a change of attitudes and approach. But I think it is likely that the power groups will do all they can to block changes that would reduce their dominance and their profits. At that point there will be need for decisive political action to bring about the necessary changes at the structural level.

## The Role of the Poor

From all that has been said in previous chapters it is evident that major changes in the international order are urgently required. I want now to consider how these are likely to come about. Poor countries ought to have the opportunity to be masters of their own destiny in economic matters. But from whom can we expect action to come — from the wealthy countries or from the poor ones? One would have to be very naïve to imagine that a new and more just world order will be established through the action of the very countries and groups who benefit most from the present unjust structures. That is why it makes political sense — as well as religious sense — to speak of salvation coming through the poor. Concluding an address to the World Council of Christian Education, Ivan Illich spoke in words that are at once realistic and prophetic:

> In the liberation of the world from the idols of progress, development, efficiency . . . the Third World has a crucial responsibility. Its masses are not yet totally addicted and dependent on consumption. . . . Most people still heal, house and teach one another, and could do it better if they had slightly better tools. The Third World could lead the rest in the search for an environment which would be both modern and humane.
>
> ('Lima Discourse' in *Learning for Living* 13, Jan 1974, p.89)

Illich went on to claim that the empires of East and West 'can be saved from the tyranny of their idols only by those who have renounced the fleshpots of Egypt'. However, he was well aware that many in the Third World have no desire to play such a role:

> But by no means are all those who wander in the desert members of the People of God. Some . . . establish outposts of the empires in the middle of the wilderness. Others . . . return into the slavery which their fathers left . . .    (ibid.)

It is easy to see why most Third World countries do not lead the way. They are usually governed by a small privileged group who have little to gain and much to lose by a change of the structures. There are, however, a few exceptions — a few Third World countries which have tried an alternative way. For some years China closed its frontiers and tried to become self-sufficient, relying on its own resources, of which the greatest was its people. Tanzania has been trying to work out its own model of equitable and viable development. More recently Nicaragua has had some remarkable success in enabling its people to meet the urgent need for simple housing. But unfortunately these experiments have had to be carried out by very poor countries with little support from the international community – and even in the face of pressure from powerful countries whose governments want the experiments to fail.

At this point one is led on from political questions in the strict sense to wider issues of education and the ways in which people's beliefs and commitments are formed. For it is clear that radical political changes – at every level, international, national, and local – won't just happen of their own accord. They will take place only when people organise themselves to bring them about. So it is essential to consider the kind of alternatives that are required – and are possible – in the area of what I have called 'idea power'.

## Psycho-social approach

In a previous chapter I noted how pyramids of power have developed not only in the economic and political spheres but also in the sector of society that concerns itself with the formation of people's beliefs and values. Power in this 'cultural' sphere tends to go hand in hand with power in the other spheres; and there are many instances of a trade-off between, say, newspaper owners and politicians or businesspeople. It is obvious, then, that an alternative to our present unjust world must include new structures in this 'cultural' sphere. Mao Tse Tung was quite right to stress the importance of a 'cultural revolution' – that is, a radical change in the ideas and attitudes of people. If this is to take place it will have to be fostered and supported by major structural changes.

Rather than giving a theoretical account of the changes that are required in this sphere of beliefs and commitments, I prefer to describe briefly a practical attempt to establish alternative structures and approaches. In doing so I shall be speaking from first-hand experience since I have been involved, myself, over the past seven years in trying to use this approach in a number of different countries. It is generally called 'the psycho-social method' – though a number of us who have

150

been involved have reservations about the use of the word 'method'. It might suggest that what is in question is simply a technique; therefore we prefer to speak of 'the psycho-social approach'. This approach is one that seeks to change both individuals and society. Its aim might be said to transform both the 'mental structures' of participants in the programme and the structures of society. In describing it here I am not at all setting it up as a model for others; I am too well aware of its inadequacies. But it may be taken as one example of an attempt to work towards alternatives in an area of 'culture' which touches on politics and religion.

The 'psycho-social method' is a form of adult education which is designed above all to help those who are trying to make an option for the poor. It was first worked out as a training for community workers, people working at the grass-roots, with the poor in the Third World. But it has been found very helpful by people in a wide range of work — doctors, economists, seminary teachers, agricultural advisers, people engaged in pastoral ministry — as well as people involved in all kinds of social and community work. One of its great strengths is that it is inter-disciplinary in approach. In fact, it challenges the usual categories of specialisation, while making use of insights from various sciences. The training is not intended simply to help people to be more effective in carrying out the tasks assigned them by an unjust society (e.g. how to be a 'good' teacher in a school for the children of the rich, or how to be a better nurse in a hospital that uses up so many resources that little is left for community health). Rather it helps participants to articulate the uneasiness they are experiencing in such situations and animates them to initiate alternative systems. It is a method that tries to encourage change, that seeks for radical, structural solutions to problems of poverty and injustice.

It was designed as a leadership training programme. But those who are most deeply involved in it have come to be more and more hesitant about using this word 'leadership'. The kind of leadership which interests them is almost the direct opposite of what the word means to most people. The training is not designed to give leaders the ability to get people to follow them blindly. Rather the aim is to help people discover for themselves their real needs, and to

151

enable them to make their own decisions and initiate their own action. It aims to help *everybody* to have a share in leadership.

Training in the psycho-social method is taking place in several parts of the Third World. I myself have been associated with the programme in four African countries, as well as trying to use the method in workshops which I have conducted in Ireland and elsewhere. There is nothing rigid about the format, so the pattern has developed differently in various countries, depending on the situation and the people. I am writing this in Nigeria so I shall outline what we are attempting here. The story of what has been happening in eastern and southern Africa is a more exciting one; I was privileged to have some little involvement in those areas — but their story is not mine to tell. We are still at an early stage here so what I shall describe is as much a set of hopes and aspirations as an achievement. But at least we have got beyond the paralysis stage — the point where people are quite disenchanted with many of the existing systems and approaches but have not yet been able to find, or initiate, an alternative.

*Elements in the method*

Many of the elements in our programme can be found also in other training programmes. What gives the psycho-social approach its distinctive character is the particular combination and emphasis in the use of these elements. The first point to note is that we believe there is little point in training people for community leadership unless this is combined with a thorough-going programme of 'development education'. This means that we want to train leaders in something more than the skills of working with groups and helping them to initiate action. We want to help them discover the root causes of poverty and apathy. Therefore the training programme puts a good deal of emphasis on social analysis, with a view to helping participants to locate the structural causes of the social problems they are meeting every day.

This analysis of society is to be done by the participants themselves. What the facilitators can give is mainly a framework which suggests the aspects that need to be looked into. Resource people can also help the participants to look at the problems from a sufficiently broad perspective. Many local

152

problems cannot be solved unless there are changes at the national level. Similarly, many of the national problems — particularly of Third World countries — have to be understood as being the result of the international order. The training programme sets out to help participants to understand the relationships between local, national, and international causes of problems.

Perhaps the most central principle of the psycho-social method is the conviction that the agents of human development must be the people themselves. In referring here to 'the people' I mean above all the grassroots people, who so frequently are left powerless and voiceless in society. Since we are committed to this principle we have to ensure that we do not contradict it in the way we run our training programme. So the main element in the training is a series of 'workshops', in which the participants themselves reflect on their own experiences, and decide themselves what they want to learn, rather than listening passively to lectures on topics chosen by others. The format of the workshops is one that can be used by the trainee leaders in their own work with grassroots groups.

The training programme is designed to ensure that there is a rhythm of action, followed by reflection, followed by further action and reflection. This is achieved by having a 'phased' series of workshops. The basic programme includes an introductory workshop, followed (for those who are interested) by a series of three further workshops. Later on, there can be other, more advanced workshops; so that the training continues and nobody claims to have 'learned it all'. In our situation we find it necessary to leave an interval of six months after each of the four 'phases'. (In some other countries the interval is about three months.) Each of the workshops in the phased programme lasts for six very full days. The first part of each workshop is devoted to a review of the period since the previous one; participants reflect on their attempts to implement the plans they made there. The last part of each workshop is given over to making concrete plans for action to be undertaken in the coming months.

The main part of each workshop is a blend of different exercises, drawn from a variety of sources, and some designed for the occasion. All of them require the active involvement

153

of the participants. Quite often the individuals are asked to work out something on their own, then to share the results first in small groups and then in the whole group. In all of this there is as much emphasis on the process as on the content: there is a training in facilitation, in working for consensus, and in the techniques of planning.

The material dealt with in the various exercises covers a very broad spectrum. A typical day might begin with a reflection on a passage of Scripture. This might be followed by some 'listening exercises' in which the participants learn to be more attentive and respectful to others. Then a couple of hours might be devoted to an exercise in cooperation. This could be a task of immediate concern to the group, such as working out a joint plan of action. Alternatively, it might be a 'simulation', that is, a type of game which brings up in an obvious way the kind of problems people meet in real life. For instance, the exercise might be to find the correct pattern in which to put together various pieces of paper; this apparently simple task could show up the tendency of some to be very pushy and task-centred, of others to be apathetic, and so on. Reflecting on what happened in the 'game', people learn a great deal about how to cope with problems of cooperation in real life.

Later in the day the participants might move on to reflect on the sources of poverty in their particular areas. Once again this might be done by the use of a simulation, or a film, or a playlet, as a means of helping them to locate significant elements in their own experience. This could lead to a request for some 'input' — perhaps a talk on how the international economic order affects the local situation, given by one of the resource people on the organising team, or by one of the participants themselves. The workshop approach does not exclude the use of occasional lectures; but such input would come not at a fixed time but only when it answers a clear need experienced by the group. (In the course of a six-day workshop there might be two lectures and a couple of very short talks.) Late in the evening the day's work is frequently rounded off by a time for personal prayer, followed by a liturgy in which the insights and joys, the frustrations and commitments of the workshop find expression.

This account may indicate how the training programme

seeks to help the participants to take account of three important spheres where they need to grow:

— the public sphere of economic, political, cultural, and ecclesiastical activity;

— the interpersonal sphere where the participants learn to work better with groups, and to cooperate better with each other;

— and the personal sphere where each of us is called by God to grow in depth, in tranquillity, and in a fuller awareness of the presence of God in his or her life.

*Generative themes*

The word 'social' in the term 'the psycho-social method' hardly requires explanation. But why add 'psycho' to it? The reason is that there is a psychological element as well as a social element in the training. The participants are helped not merely to look at the social structures but to look especially for those issues which arouse strong feelings in the ordinary people. The reason for this is that we are convinced that many development projects fail simply because the problems they are trying to deal with are not experienced, by the people they are supposed to help, as their most pressing problems. If people are to be the principal agents in their own development, then obviously the work must begin at a point where they themselves are deeply concerned; action will come only when people feel strongly about an issue.

The most distinctive feature of the psycho-social method is the particular attention it gives to training would-be leaders to discover the issues that are of greatest concern to the grass-roots people. These issues are called 'generative themes' by Paulo Freire, whose ideas are a major source of inspiration for those who developed the training programme. The psycho-social method offers help in the careful study required to discover the 'generative themes' of a community. It also trains leaders to find effective ways of bringing up such issues with groups, making use of playlets, pictures, simulations, or even passages from the Bible, to raise the key issues.

The 'generative themes' are different in different places; in one area the need to learn to read and write may be felt to be very urgent; in another place the people may be far more concerned about the pattern of land ownership. Leaders find that it is well worth while sacrificing their own agenda and priorities in order to concentrate on the issues that are perceived as important by the local people. By doing so they ensure that the people themselves will really 'own' whatever programme or action emerges. The key to success lies in the effort to discover the 'generative themes' of the community. These are generative in the sense of giving rise to effective action by the people. They are also generative in another sense: once people begin to tackle these issues they tend to be led on to discover further important needs and problems that they can deal with. For instance literacy programmes frequently lead on to awareness by the people of the importance of community health, or of better ways of farming.

*New emphases*

The psycho-social method is not something that is fully worked out and unchangeable. From the beginning it has been adapted and expanded. In Kenya, where the method was developed, there were at first two main elements in it:

(a) the Freire-inspired search for generative themes; and group reflection on these themes, sparked off by the use of 'codes' (pictures, playlets, etc);

(b) group work and human relations training, based largely on work in this field in North America.

Later on, the need was felt for much more emphasis on organisational planning, and management skills. Then the advanced people asked for more sophisticated schemas to guide their study of the economic structures of society. Later again there has been a lot of emphasis on techniques of evaluation — especially 'participative evaluation' where the participants learn to assess objectively the effects of their own work. So all these new elements have been incorporated into the psycho-social method.

Here in Nigeria we are still at a fairly early stage, not yet ready for the more advanced elements. However, we have from the beginning emphasised one element which we feel may be our distinctive contribution to the method: we give a very central place to what we call 'faith-sharing'. It involves building into each workshop a lot of time for personal reflection on selected passages from the Bible; and then sharing — in small groups and in the whole group — the ways in which

156

we were moved by the text. We have found this a very powerful way of bonding the group together — more effective, and more 'real', than some of the human relations exercises designed for this purpose.

Some of us involved in the Nigerian programme would like to add another distinctive element to the training: we introduced an exercise which we call 'deep listening'. One might call it 'the honours course' in listening. The aim is to enable people to cope better with strong feelings of hurt, anger, inadequacy, etc, by providing them with a totally attentive, non-judgmental listener. (We borrowed the technique from the Co-counselling movement.) We feel that this 'deep listening' offers participants a most effective way to grow, and blossom, and be healed, in the personal and interpersonal spheres. It also has important implications in the public or wider society sphere. For it is a means which can help people to avoid the kind of 'burnout' that so often afflicts those engaged in social work; provided, of course, that they feel quite free about using it only to whatever extent they choose. Furthermore, it can help grassroots people to cope more effectively with destructive emotions, and to decide more freely where they want to focus their righteous anger. It is much too early to say that this kind of 'deep listening' has become an integral part of the programme here. It will take time before people can discover whether it really appeals to them. If it does not 'catch on', then we must not try to impose it just because we think it important.

Working in a cross-cultural situation on the delicate matters of strong emotion and deep hurt, it has been interesting for us to discover the extent to which somewhat similar techniques were used in traditional African cultures. Indeed those who follow the psycho-social approach have, from the beginning, stressed the importance of respecting people's traditions, and making use of techniques based on local culture. The psycho-social training includes a careful study of the way of life of the people of the area. This has revealed that an integral part of the tradition was the use of very valuable techniques of communication and decision-making.

In Africa, for instance, people find it easy to take part in short spontaneous plays, because that has been part of the tradition. So those who are conducting psycho-social workshops can use such playlets to spark off group discussion. Another example: during an extended advanced-level workshop in East Africa I discovered that the people of three different tribes there give a special role to a person whom they call 'the listener'. When they want to reach a joint decision on some important matter, 'the listener' is present but remains silent throughout the discussion. Towards the end, 'the listener' speaks for the first time, summing up the points on which there is general agreement. In a Western-style discussion this is left to the chairperson, who, having several other tasks to do, can scarcely be expected to do so well in the task of listening and summarising. Traditional techniques like this can be rediscovered and incorporated into the psycho-social training programme. It is vitally important that people be helped to appreciate their own culture. For without a culture people are aimless, rootless, and virtually deprived of the framework in which moral values carry conviction. When considering the concept of 'progress' in Chapter 7, I noted how the undermining of traditional culture in the Third World has led to gross corruption and exploitation.

## An alternative Model of Church

I have been describing a practical attempt to develop an alternative system of education. Obviously it is much more than education in the sense of schooling. It is intended for adults, not children. And it is not primarily concerned with giving people information and ideas; rather it aims to help them to understand their situation better and to take action to improve it. It is a form of what I called 'idea power' that is very closely related to political power and to economic power. Furthermore — and this is the point I wish to consider next — it touches very much on religious and ecclesiastical questions — the area I called 'God power'.

The psycho-social training programme as it has developed in different countries is a Church programme. However, it is anything but 'churchy' in its orientation. Its primary purpose is to help people in promoting the Kingdom of God. In fact, it is the most effective means I have found for rescuing Church leaders and keen Christians from the tendency to put most of their energy into building up Church institutions while taking insufficient account of the wider human society. It helps them address themselves to the urgent need of people everywhere for justice and respect for their human dignity and rights. In this way it helps the Church to recover — or discover — its true purpose.

Closely related to this is the commitment of those using the method to ecumenical action. The aim is to train leaders or facilitators for different Churches and Church agencies — as well as for a variety of other agencies concerned with human welfare and development. The hope is that these leaders will ensure that the Churches cooperate and share to a much greater extent than in the past. The organisers of the training programme do not want to set up any large institutions themselves, but rather to operate in and through the existing ones — helping to adapt them where necessary.

One very significant change which the use of the method can bring about in the Church is a change in the relationships between those who hold authority and the grassroots people. The participative style of leadership which it promotes can be a great help to Church ministers in making them see that they do not have to stand on their authority and hide within their roles. The psycho-social approach is ideal for those who are trying to build up basic Christian communities. For it combines a strong emphasis on working for justice and participation in public life, with an approach that ensures that justice and human rights are respected in the Church community itself; and its training in joint planning and in cooperative activities helps to ensure that all the members really share in the exercise of ministries of various kinds. I still remember vividly the final liturgy of a workshop we held in Nigeria a few years ago. During the week the clergy and the laity had come to a much deeper appreciation of each other. The text that emerged in the liturgy as summing up the new relationship was: 'I no longer call you servants, but friends.'

An East African bishop who took part in a workshop and became an enthusiastic supporter of the psycho-social method described it as 'an education in how to be a bishop'. There is an urgent need for such an education: the way in which the role of a bishop is understood at present has effects that are truly disastrous. Let me illustrate this by referring to the situation in two dioceses which I know. The first is in a

159

remote area of East Africa. The Catholic bishop there is a missionary from Europe. He will soon be handing over to a local person — and the new bishop is almost certain to be one of two fine African priests who were classmates and are more or less equally qualified for the task. The one who is chosen will become a millionaire overnight, for he will be the legal owner of all the Catholic buildings and institutions in this large diocese. He will have almost unlimited power to dispose of these resources as he sees fit; the Vatican would be most reluctant to remove him unless he is guilty of flagrant mismanagement over a long period of time. His power will include the right to appoint his one-time classmate (who might have been chosen as bishop) to the poorest parish in the diocese. He will have advisers — but he may refuse to heed them. Over the years he may well become more and more cut off from his fellow-priests, not to mention the laity.

The second diocese is in a remote and rather poor part of East Africa. The bishop there is a local man who took over from a European five years ago. Since then he has lived fairly simply. But now he feels that his position as a bishop requires that he should live as more of 'a big man'; in the local culture a chief must live like a chief. So he has built an enormous house, lavishly furnished; and he is now levying the parishes to pay for its upkeep and for a large secretarial and domestic staff. Meanwhile several of his fellow African priests are struggling to survive in remote and unviable parishes. Even the lucky ones, who have been favoured by him with the 'plums' have a vastly lower standard of living — and the insecurity of knowing that they may be transferred if they fall from favour. Is it any wonder, then, that they want to go overseas to gain doctorates in something or other that will enable them to get a respectable job in an institute of higher learning?

## Change of attitudes and structures

The examples just given show that the problem of excessive episcopal authority is particularly acute in the Third World. In other parts of the Church there are more safeguards against abuse; but bishops still find themselves rather cut off from their priests and people by the fact that they have undue power. The situation calls for two kinds of change — a change

160

in people's attitudes and a change of structures. Firstly, there is need for a change in attitudes. Bishops have to learn to let go of much of their power, to share responsibility willingly, to allow themselves to be challenged. Those who work with bishops have to learn to combine a courageous expression of their views with respect for both the person and the office of the bishop; they have to avoid flattery and the currying of favour, while still offering the loyal support and affirmation which is so important for those in authority.

I know a small number of dioceses in Africa and Latin America where things have changed very much for the better. Almost invariably the changes have come through the use of some form of participative techniques, such as the psycho-social method. The crucial thing is that these methods allow the authorities to learn gradually and in practice that the relinquishment of power does not lead to anarchy. They find out — not from books or theory but through actual experience — that people are willing to take on heavy responsibilities and that they can be trusted. But I must add that changes of this kind will remain fragile so long as the structures are not changed. We need changes in the way the role of the bishop is defined in law and in practice. There will have to be much clearer definition of the limits of episcopal authority and of the rights of those subject to it.

This brings us, secondly, to the need for a change in the structures. The Church must find ways of ensuring that the authority of bishops is not so absolute. That should not be too difficult, since the Catholic Church already has — in its religious orders, congregations, and societies — a very large number of people whose exercise of authority is carefully hedged around with safeguards. For instance, as a member of a missionary society I live subject to the authority of a man who has the office of 'superior general'. My relationship with him is vastly different to that of a diocesan priest towards his bishop. Despite his imposing title, I think of him mainly as somebody whom we have asked to do a difficult task. I sympathise with him and try to cooperate with him and help him. I do not feel that I am at his mercy. If we had a difference of opinion he would not have very much opportunity to victimise me, since our structures allow for various forms of protection and mediation; and of course we both know that he cannot hold his office for more than a maximum of twelve years. The authority of bishops needs to be restricted in somewhat similar ways.

How can such changes in structure take place? The Vatican authorities have already taken some steps, by making laws about the need for each bishop to have finance councils and so on. But in the Third World these regulations do not go far enough; and some of them can easily become a dead letter. Rome could be much more insistent on the sharing of responsibility — especially since bishops in the Third World are generally dependent on grants from the Holy See. But the Vatican authorities are themselves reluctant to relinquish power; and they do not seem to consider it to be a very high priority in bishops. The foreign missionaries who work under the authority of a local bishop are not in a good position to demand that he relinquish power or change his lifestyle. For it was the missionaries who, in their original zeal, did not bother to build safeguards into the Church structures. They allowed the bishop (who was normally, at first, one of themselves) to exercise a power that was almost absolute. Now that the bishop is a local man, it would seem racist to demand a different structure. So they content themselves with protecting their own members — leaving the local priests, religious, and laity more defenceless than ever.

I believe that this is one of the greatest weaknesses of the Catholic Church in the Third World. I have described it in terms of inadequacies in attitudes and in structures. But in the long run both of these are attributable to inadequacies in our spirituality. The spirituality in which we were brought up — and which we passed on to others and embodied in the way the Church is organised — did not give a high priority to structural justice in the Church itself. There was a great deal of emphasis on obedience, on the willing sacrifice of oneself for Christ and the Church. As a result, anybody who was concerned about the rights of those subject to Church authority seemed to be somehow disloyal or at least ungenerous. Holy people were not expected to be concerned with such matters. In fact any particular interest in one's rights within the Church would have been felt to be inimical to authentic spirituality.

On the basis of my own experience I would say that a

good deal of this spirituality lingers on, even in people who have liberated themselves from the poor theology which underpinned it. In recent years, of course, very many Christians in the Western world have questioned the old spirituality and have adopted a much more confrontational approach. But I am not at all sure that they have succeeded very well. Their insecurity — combined with the individualism that mars much of Western life and attitudes — has led many of them to be strident, angry, and divisive in their approach. I doubt whether present-day Western theology and spirituality have the resources to overcome this major problem. One must look rather to Third World theology and its associated spirituality for the way forward. I have already devoted a chapter of this book to an account of this alternative theology. It now seems appropriate to devote another chapter to a more extended treatment of this topic.

# 11
# Alternative Theology

In the foregoing chapters I have been considering alternative approaches to economics, lifestyle, politics, education, and to Church life. Now I want to go on to deal with the question of alternative approaches to theology. There are two sections in this chapter. In the first part I shall examine various currents in Third World theology. This will lead on to the second part where I shall attempt to work out an alternative theology rooted in the situation of Ireland, a small country on the fringe of the First World.

## Section One: Emerging and
## Merging Currents in Third World Theology

Already in Chapter 3, I gave a general outline of Third World theology. In this first section of the present chapter I shall give a more detailed account of this alternative approach to theology. I shall consider whether, or in what sense, one is really entitled to speak of Third World theology as such. This will involve an examination of the different theological currents which are now converging in the Third World, and some account of the deliberate attempts being made to promote dialogue and interaction between them. I shall conclude this section with a brief account of the different reactions of theologians in the First World to the challenge of this alternative approach to theology; that will lead on to the second section of the chapter.

Let me begin by recalling some of the main themes of Third World theology. As I noted in Chapter 3, they are the themes that permeate the prayerful reflection of Mary on the work of God in her life, as recounted in Luke's Gospel:

164

— an emphasis on the personal and communal experience of the saving power of God in human history;
— a sense that there is a struggle between those who respect the true God and those who would compel us to worship idols of various kinds;
— awareness that the poor and the oppressed have a privileged role as agents of liberation;
— a vivid consciousness that God is working marvels through, and on behalf of, these lowly ones who, in their weakness, rely on him;
— an insistence that the lifting up of the poor implies the breaking of the power of those who are oppressing them;
— and, finally, a strong sense of hope, based on the promise of God to protect his people.

The features I have just listed are characteristic of liberation theology. But on what grounds can one attribute them to Third World theology in general — and how do these two relate to each other? It is only in very recent years that one could begin to speak of Third World theology as such. Prior to that there were various efforts to do theology in the context of different continents. The Ecumenical Association of Third World Theologians (EATWOT) was established in 1976 and since then it has promoted interaction, challenge, and convergence between leading theologians in different corners of the Third World. There is no question of looking for a totally unified Third World theology. But within a relatively short time something new has emerged. It is theology with a different style and a different agenda. One of the more important currents feeding into this emerging Third World theology has been the liberation theology which began in Latin America and has now spread to such places as the Philippines; but there are several other currents as well. I propose to give a short account of a number of the more important currents or strands which are converging to offer a strong challenge to the dominant Western theology.

## Asia

'The common denominator between Asia and the rest of the Third World is its overwhelming poverty; the specific character which defines Asia within the other poor countries is its multifaceted religiosity.' That is how the Sri Lankan theologian, Aloysius Pieris, described the context in which theology must be done in Asia. For some years it was assumed that the major contribution of Asian theologians lay in the attempt to establish a dialogue between Christianity and the other great world religions. In most Asian countries Christians are just a small minority, living in a culture moulded by rich religious traditions, some of them much older than Christianity itself. In such a context, theologians were forced to raise questions about even the most taken-for-granted assumptions of all previous theology — questions about the unique role given to the Jewish and Christian scriptures (as distinct from the scriptures of Asian religions) and even about the centrality of Christ.

Exciting as these issues may be, it has now become clear that they are not the only ones that face those who wish to reflect on the relevance of Christian faith in the Asian context. In fact the attempt to establish dialogue with other religions could even distract theologians from the need to face up to the other crucial aspect of the Asian reality — the overwhelming poverty of most if its inhabitants. One of the major achievements of EATWOT has been the extent to which it has succeeded in preventing a sharp polarisation of Asian theologians into those who give priority to a theology of dialogue and those who are committed instead to political and economic liberation.

It is now widely accepted that both aspects are crucial. Dialogue without commitment to liberation could mean a dialogue among a privileged elite in the different religions — and a continuing indifference to the plight of the masses. On the other hand, it would betray a peculiar kind of blindness if one were to seek liberation in the economic and political spheres while taking little account of the religious traditions which are basic to the Asian way of life. As a result of the convergence between the two different approaches there is now a keen awareness of the various ways in which religious beliefs and values intersect with the social reality. It has become clear that there are liberative elements in all the religions; and also that they all contain elements that support apathy and can be used to give legitimacy to social inequality and injustice. The emergent Asian theology is making a major contribution to Third World theology.

## Africa

Africa, too, has its own particular contribution to make to Third World theology. Most of the new generation of African theologians have been deeply concerned about the traditional cultures of their peoples. They have been insisting that it is not sufficient to have a superficial process of 'adaptation' to make the Christian faith more acceptable to Africans; Christianity must really 'take flesh' in the various cultures. Therefore, these theologians call for an 'incarnation' of the faith in Africa. More recently, however, liberation theology has begun to have an influence among African Christians. There was the danger of a polarisation among African theologians as there was among the Asians.

Interchange and dialogue under the auspices of EATWOT have helped to lessen this danger. The result has been the emergence of the concept of 'anthropological poverty'. By this is meant the disruption of the traditional life of African peoples, the destruction of the social fabric of their societies, and the loss of their values, cultures, and religious beliefs. It is a form of impoverishment caused by colonialism and, more recently, by economic and cultural neo-colonialism. African theologians are now calling for liberation of a particular kind — from the imposition on African peoples of a Western understanding of human nature — with the emphasis on individualism, competition, and the struggle for power. In this way the theology of 'inculturation' and 'incarnation' have come to be linked to the theology of liberation; there is a keener awareness of the connection between culture and religion on the one hand and politics and economics on the other.

## Latin America

I have mentioned already that a major current in Third World theology is liberation theology. I want now to note that in fact there are at least three different theologies which are liberationist in their origin and purpose. The one we normally associate with the term 'liberation theology' is the one that came to the fore some years ago in Latin America. It emphasises the various elements I mentioned in Chapter 3

167

when I was examining Mary's prayer in Luke's Gospel. But the approach of the liberation theologians of Latin America is distinguished by one other point: their theology follows on, and is closely linked to 'social analysis'. The influence of Marxist theory is very evident in the way in which they explain the structures of society. For many of them, 'class analysis' is the key to understanding — and overcoming — injustice and oppression.

Theologians from other parts of the Third World often felt misunderstood and pressured by the liberation theologians of Latin America. In particular they felt that different forms of oppression which were experienced very keenly by them — e.g. racism, sexism, cultural and religious imperialism — were all being 'explained' by the Latin Americans in terms of a class analysis. The result, they felt, was the imposition of a notion of liberation which was too univocal, too limited — one that put the emphasis almost exclusively on political and economic issues. However, the various conferences sponsored by EATWOT have provided a forum in which this dissatisfaction could be expressed and the Latin Americans could be challenged. The result has been a significant widening and deepening of the theology of liberation. In the final statement of the most recent of the EATWOT conferences it is admitted that the various forms of oppression 'cannot be subordinated one to another' (Sixth EATWOT Conference: 'Doing Theology in a Divided World', Geneva, January 1983, Section 11). But it is noted also that they cannot simply be listed one after another as though they were separate, isolated issues; for they 'are linked in the working of a single world system of domination'. The Latin Americans are now much more ready to take seriously the views of those who have approached the question of liberation from a different starting-point.

## Black theology

'Black theology' is a form of liberation theology that has come from a rather different experience to that of most of the Latin American theologians. There are two strands in it — the North American and the South African. I shall begin with the former. It has come to the fore only in recent years; one might see it to some extent as a Christian reflection on the 'Black Power' movement. But its roots go much further back — to the experience of slavery and exile of the Blacks of North America, and their deep Christian hope for liberation. Indeed, one of the most notable features of this theology is the way in which it tunes in to the cry of a whole people for freedom. For generations the Christian hope of the Blacks has been expressed in the rich biblical imagery of the Old Testament. Black theology is liberationist above all in its attempt to ensure that the hope of the people is not directed solely towards the next life; it insists that they have to hope and work for freedom and justice even in *this* world.

The second distinctive feature of Black theology is its emphasis on racism as a particularly obnoxious form of oppression. Originally, the Black theologians were not particularly interested in the kind of class analysis propounded by many of the Latin Americans. Indeed they reacted strongly against what they saw as an attempt by the mainly white theologians of Latin America to 'explain' racism in purely class terms. In very recent times there has been a considerable convergence between the views of the two groups — facilitated largely by EATWOT which has brought them into dialogue with each other.

Black theologians are well aware that economic factors have played a major role in the genesis of racism; after all, the slave trade flourished for economic reasons. As a consequence of dialogue with the Latin Americans, they are now more keenly aware of how racial prejudice is still underpinned by economic factors. However, the Black theologians insist that once racism comes into existence it tends to take on a life of its own, which defies purely rational analysis. Black people are not just discriminated against because they are poor, but are also impoverished because of racial prejudice. Therefore racial prejudice is now not merely an effect of economic injustice but a cause of it as well. The liberation theologians of Latin America have recognised that they must take more explicit account of the evil of racism. They have been forcefully reminded by Blacks and Asians that racial and cultural oppression are rampant in their own part of the world. They are trying to listen to the challenge and to be vigilant in ensuring that they do not play down these realities.

The second strand of Black theology is particularly interesting. It has a good deal in common with the Black theology of North America — above all its challenge to racism. But it also has distinctive features. Perhaps the most notable of these is that it sets out to contest the basic 'myth' of the white Afrikaners. These are descendants of Dutch settlers who were themselves oppressed by the British. To escape this, many of them took part in a 'great trek' northwards, a journey in which they fought for life and territory against the local population. There are obvious similarities between their history and that of the Israelites who escaped from Egypt and conquered the Promised Land. It is understandable then that they borrowed much of the Old Testament concept of 'the Chosen People' and used it to construct a religious justification for their identity, their history and their present attitudes and way of life. Furthermore, most white South Africans (English-speakers as well as Afrikaners) seem to have 'swallowed' another myth — that the regime is a bastion of defence for civilisation and Christianity against communism, terrorism, and anarchy.

The Black theology of South Africa has to show how these two myths are used by the whites to justify massive injustice and oppression of the people of other races. The situation shows what a dangerous weapon a theology of liberation can be. For here is a people who experience themselves as rescued by God from oppression and as still battling to preserve their way of life; and their sense of being a special, chosen people blinds them to the racialism and injustice for which they are now responsible. In South Africa, perhaps more obviously than anywhere else, there is 'a battle of the gods', a struggle about the 'ownership' of such basic religious symbols as 'chosen people', 'exodus', 'promised land', and even the word 'liberation' itself. This situation shows how important it is to ensure that such symbols remain in real contact with the kind of realities in which they are rooted historically. Otherwise what can happen is that a privileged and relatively wealthy group of people, such as the white Afrikaners, may come to own and use powerful religious symbols which ought to be proper to a poor and marginalised people.

A second point to note about the Black theology of South Africa is that it is in a very good position to mediate between liberation theology and the main theological concerns of the rest of Black Africa. The South Africans share with other African theologians a concern about 'cultural impoverishment'. They can, however, easily link this with their concern about other forms of impoverishment. For the situation in which they are living is one where there is a very obvious connection between injustice in the different spheres — political, economic, social and cultural.

The South African policy of setting up 'homelands' (or Bantustans) is causing massive disruption of social and family life for millions of people. The official justification for this policy is to ensure the preservation of traditional African cultures and ways of life. But what in fact is happening is that the lowest category of workers and the unemployed are being banished to barren and remote 'homelands'. At the whim of the South African government migrant labourers from these impoverished Bantustans will be allowed into 'white' areas. But they will have no guarantee of employment and few guaranteed human rights. For the 'homelands' are not even considered to be part of South Africa; therefore the wealthy part of the country will take no responsibility for the appalling social and economic problems of these 'foreign countries'.

I have already pointed out how the Afrikaners have adopted a distorted version of the biblical notion of liberation to underpin their oppression of the Blacks. We find now that in the sphere of culture there is a similar kind of distortion, one that borders on the hypocritical. Under the guise of preserving the cultural identity of the African peoples, the government is in fact setting up what have been called 'rural slums'. Needless to say, the forced migration of millions of black people is doing immense damage to the fabric of social life and therefore to the culture of the people. The theory of the 'homelands' is nothing more than an ideology which is used as a mask to cover political and economic injustice. In challenging it, Black theology is helping to bring out the close links uniting different kinds of liberation in all spheres of life.

### Feminist theology

A third form of liberation theology – and one that is very influential – is feminist theology. It emerged mainly in the First World as part of the wider movement for women's liberation. At first there was no evident link between feminist theology and Third World theology. But in very recent years a dialogue has been going on between some of the best-known feminist theologians and leading Third World theologians; and once again EATWOT has played a major role in this process. The relationship between the two groups has not always been an easy one; but both sides have benefited considerably from the contact.

Feminist theologians from the First World have to make a choice. On the one hand they may make common cause with other categories of oppressed people, while seeking to ensure that the experience and the voice of women are not ignored in the overall struggle for a more just world. On the other hand they may make the question of the liberation of women *the* fundamental theological issue; then they would consider other liberation struggles to be of significance only to the extent to which they can be used to help the feminist cause. At the dialogue between First World and Third World theologians, organised by EATWOT in Geneva in 1983, it was clear that several of the feminist theologians had taken the first of these options; but one or two others seemed rather more ambivalent.

There are very good grounds for seeing a close connection between different forms of oppression. For there can be little doubt that sexism is not merely a psychological and cultural reality. A major element in it is economic: in almost every part of the world women are expected to do more work for less pay than men; and a good deal of the labour of women goes unpaid. Dialogue between feminist theology and the Latin American type of liberation theology helps to broaden the outlook of those on both sides. The feminists can teach the others to take more account of the patriarchal structures of society – and also to advert to the sexism and *machismo* that is so common in Latin America. At the same time the women can learn from the kind of social and structural analysis favoured by the liberation theologians.

Third World women theologians are in a position to play

a very important role. They can speak for their Third World sisters who find themselves doubly oppressed — as women, and as people living in the disadvantaged part of the world. But they often find themselves pulled in two different directions, neither of which is the one in which they want to go. On the one hand they feel that they are being asked to take up the issue of women's rights, as defined by First World feminists. On the other hand they feel that male theologians in the Third World too easily assume that the issue of women's rights arises only for privileged women of the First World. As the final document of the Geneva dialogue makes clear, Third World women believe that sexism has to be faced up to. However, this is to be done not in isolation, but rather 'within the context of the total struggle for liberation in their countries'. Furthermore, the document notes that: 'Neither Third World men or First World women can determine the Third World women's agenda.' (Section 27)

One particularly interesting point has emerged from the kind of dialogue promoted by EATWOT. It is that neither the feminists nor the Asians are as willing as the Latin Americans and the Black theologians to accept uncritically the Exodus story as the fundamental model for liberation. Indeed both groups feel compelled to ask awkward questions about large parts of the Judaeo-Christian Bible.

The women find in the Bible a very deep-rooted patriarchalism — assumptions of male dominance that are incompatible with an authentic Christian faith today. It is true that Christians already tacitly 'edit out' various items in the Bible which no longer seem acceptable (e.g. the suggestion that in a holy war, God approves of the slaughter of men, women, and children). But to edit out of the Bible the patriarchal outlook that is so central to it, would mean that the Bible would no longer be the book we now know. Meanwhile the Asians (or at least some of them) also have difficulties with the Bible. It seems to give so privileged a place to Jewish history that the religious history of Asia is not taken sufficiently seriously. So they suggest that to have a fruitful dialogue with the world religions Christians may need to put more stress on the God of Creation than on the God of History.

173

## Dialogue with the First World?

I have been examining some of the different currents that have come together to form Third World theology. One significant point that has emerged in the process is that dialogue between different marginalised groups is very fruitful and relatively easy. Much more difficult, and not nearly so fruitful, is any attempt at consensus – or even dialogue and mutual understanding – between 'establishment' theologians and any group who seek to challenge their dominance. Does this mean that Third World theology cannot seriously hope to be heard in the First World? Not really; for the First World is not as monolithic as some Third World theologians have assumed. There is a wide range of options open to theologians from Europe and North America. I would hope that one good result of the kind of dialogue organised by EATWOT in Geneva in early 1983 would be a more nuanced understanding by Third World people of the different stances and approaches to theology that can now be found in the First World.

Without trying to categorise these different options too rigidly I think it may be helpful to list four different approaches, and to comment on how they relate to Third World theology and the work of EATWOT:

(1) First of all there is the majority of establishment theologians in Europe and North America – most of the professors and those who aspire to be their successors. As I noted in Chapter 3, they appear to be complacent in the face of the present unjust world order, not accepting any particular responsibility to set about changing it. EATWOT people would dearly love to challenge such theologians face-to-face. But unfortunately the professors and would-be professors are too preoccupied with other matters to find time for such dialogue; there are lectures to be given, exams to be corrected, books to be written – even books about liberation theology! Some of 'the professors' are quite willing to invite distinguished theologians from the Third World to come and take part in their conferences or to be visiting lecturers in their universities. But a number of the most committed of the Third World theologians concluded that this is a dialogue carried out on First World terms – and it can be

a way of patronising the alternative theologians and domesticating their theology. One reason for the formation of EATWOT was to ensure that, when the time came for dialogue between Third World and First World theology, it would be conducted on more equal terms. I believe this is extremely important — and that is why I have paid so much attention to the work of EATWOT in preference to other attempts to bring about interaction between the two theologies.

(2) There is one group of theologians who are very willing to take account of what is being said by Third World theologians. This is the small number of scholars to which I have already referred in Chapter 3, the group who have set out to attack liberation theology and to provide an ideological-theological defence for a world order in which Western countries are dominant. EATWOT cannot hope for a very fruitful dialogue with them, for the lines of confrontation have been drawn very clearly. But Third World theologians may find it helpful that these opponents are articulating quite openly the option they have taken, rather than allowing it to remain implicit.

(3) Among First World theologians there is a third group: scholars who have established a certain reputation as 'liberals' or rebels against the establishment, particularly against Church authorities. Contrary to what might have been expected, Third World theologians do not always find it easy to discover common ground with these non-conformists. In fact, from a Third World perspective, it sometimes appears that they are fighting the wrong battles — or even that some of them are more concerned about their own 'academic freedom' than about the gross deprivation of human freedom inflicted unjustly on the poor of our world.

(4) There is a fourth group of theologians in Europe and North America. They form part of the growing groundswell of religious opposition to the present world order, and of challenge to the complacency or complicity of large sectors of the Church in the face of the injustice and poverty which stem from the system. This small but significant number of theologians live in the heart of the First World — or on its

periphery – but they have much in common with Third World theologians. They do not really form a group in the proper sense, since they come from a very wide variety of situations. Some have opted to live with the poor; others continue to function within the established system of higher education. One of the most eloquent is the German poet-theologian, Dorothee Sölle. She sees herself as living 'within the belly of the Beast', but refusing as far as possible to be part of it. She feels the system she is rejecting is so all-embracing, so difficult to overcome, that she would not claim to be proposing a theology of liberation. She speaks instead of 'a theology of resistance', on the analogy of the resistance fighters of World War II. The 'first act' of such theologians is one of commitment to exposing the evil of a system which brings about the impoverishment and exploitation of millions of people both in the Third World and, to a lesser extent, within the wealthy countries.

When EATWOT organised a dialogue between Third World and First World theologians it was only natural that in Europe and North America it was this last-mentioned group of theologians who were most interested in taking part. During the meeting in Geneva there were difficult moments. Some of the 'alternative theologians' from the First World were hurt: they felt they were being turned into scapegoats and 'whipping boys' for the sins of the First World – and this by some Third World theologians who, they felt, were perhaps more secure and affluent than themselves. They felt that a purely geographical division of the earth into First World and Third World is far too simple; for there can be privileged theologians in poor countries and poor ones in wealthy countries. On the other hand, many Third World theologians felt that even the more committed and 'converted' of the First World theologians were still too complacent – even about their own resistance – and too slow in taking the kind of radical action that is required. The Geneva dialogue went some way towards resolving these tensions, as the final document indicates. The participants from different areas were able to discover who were their real allies and who were their opponents. This is likely to lead to greater solidarity and more fruitful dialogue in the future.

## Alternative First World theology

Living in the heartland of industrial Europe, Dorothee Sölle has tried to articulate what it means to opt for justice in that situation. One aspect is solidarity with people from the Third World (including migrant 'guest-workers'). But for her it also involves support for the peace movement, and for feminist and ecological movements in the First World.

Those who opt for an alternative theology in North America are in a rather different situation. Ethnic minorities of all kinds — including Blacks, Hispanics, and indigenous peoples — have already been working for some time to develop their own theologies. The 'Theology in the Americas' programme has played an important part in promoting this work. Indeed I suspect that it was because this programme pre-dates that of EATWOT and was at first closely associated with it, that EATWOT considers such minorities to be part of the Third World. So an immediate item on the agenda of theologians whose roots are in the dominant culture of North America is to work out their relationship with those who represent the minorities.

It would be impertinent of me to attempt to prescribe the kind of approach that is appropriate for those in North America or Central Europe who wish to do theology in an alternative manner. What I can do, however, is to look more closely at the situation where I have lived for most of my life — a small country on the fringe of Europe. The bulk of its inhabitants belong to what I would call 'the little peoples' of Europe. They are people who have not been guilty of colonial expansion but have rather been among its first victims; but they now benefit to some extent from being part of the First World. In the next section I shall consider what it might mean to do theology out of such a situation.

### Section Two
### On the Margin of the First World

Remarkably little account has been taken of the situation of countries or cultural groups that exist on the fringes of the First World — places like Greece, Portugal, Sicily, the Basque territories, and Ireland. Perhaps the fact that all the places I have just mentioned lie on the edge of Europe is what makes them distinct. They are 'on the periphery' — and not merely in a geographical sense. I believe that the peoples of these areas have a great deal in common with each other, and are quite different from the people at the centre, in each of the different spheres of human living — economic, political, cultural, and even religious. Perhaps the people of these areas are living 'in the belly of the Beast' (to use Dorothee Sölle's phrase); but if so it is because they have very recently been swallowed by 'the Beast'; and they remain rather indigestible morsels.

I think it is important that some effort be made to articulate a theology that is rooted in such situations. For what would emerge would be neither a Third World theology nor a First World theology in the usual senses of these terms, but something different. It could be a theology that would be significant not merely for the peoples of the periphery but for the world as a whole. Though the different places I have mentioned have much in common, I think it is better to be as specific as possible. Therefore I propose to concentrate on the situation I know best — the Irish one. At a later stage it might be possible to work out a more general 'theology of the periphery', taking account of the elements common to the different places.

In many respects the situation in Ireland has a good deal in common with much of the Third World. Indeed it is not too much to claim that until about twenty-five years ago Ireland was, for all practical purposes, a Third World country (though the term was not in use at the time). In the late 1950s the Irish government launched a major effort to bring Ireland into what would now be called the First World; and this effort seemed to have succeeded when in 1973 Ireland was finally accepted as part of the European Economic Community. But a closer look at the situation shows that what has emerged is a country with an odd mixture of Third World and First World characteristics.

From the point of view of its political history, Ireland has very much in common with most Third World countries. Like them, it has been the victim of colonialism; and much of its present troubles, North and South, stem from this colonial history. Like many African, Asian, and Latin American countries, Ireland struggled against an imperial power; and most of the island was eventually granted a precarious political independence. Equally precarious is the political neutrality which it has succeeded in maintaining, despite pressure from Western powers. Its commitment to neutrality means that in international affairs it can at times take a stand that leans towards the Third World viewpoint; and it can play a peace-keeping role in some troubled parts of the world.

Ireland is quite untypical of the First World in having a high birth-rate – and this accentuates its problem of providing work for all of its people. Its efforts to promote economic development have been similar to those adopted in many Third world countries – and have had a similar very limited degree of success. At first it tried to gain some economic independence and build up local industry by adopting a policy of protectionism and import substitution. This policy failed to provide employment for the growing population, so in the second half of the 1950s the government made a radical change in its economic strategy; it opted for 'export-led growth' by providing very attractive incentives to multinational companies to invest in Irish industry.

The problems arising from this policy are quite similar to those of some of the better-off countries of the Third World. Control of the economy has passed more and more into the hands of the transnational corporations, leaving the country very vulnerable to massive unemployment. Ireland finds itself competing with countries like South Korea or the Philippines for investment by multinationals. This makes it very difficult for the government to insist on adequate safeguards for workers and for the environment.

The pattern of agriculture in Ireland was until recently a Third World one: subsistence farming on the one hand and, on the other hand, heavy dependence on the export of one cash product – in this case live cattle. Since Ireland joined the EEC this pattern has changed considerably. Subsistence farming has been practically eliminated, except in small-holdings in poor parts of the country. The number of people employed in agriculture has been drastically cut. Ireland now has the problems of over-production of expensive food which has to be put into 'subvention' storage and eventually sold off at a subsidised price.

179

In this respect Ireland shares the problems of the First World rather than the Third World. Joining the EEC has led to a significant change in the way food is produced — or has at least accelerated the change. There has been an increase in the use of imported grain (such as soya beans) to feed livestock; so Ireland is becoming more tied into an unjust and ecologically damaging pattern of First World agriculture. Furthermore, discrimination against Third World agricultural products is a necessary element in keeping up the income of agricultural producers. In other words, Ireland has moved quickly from being a *victim* of the world's unjust trading pattern to being a *beneficiary* of it.

With the recent rapid growth in unemployment, there are now up to 30% of the Irish population who are living below the poverty line or are seriously deprived. This is very high by comparison with the wealthier countries, but it is of course much better than in the Third World, where the proportions of rich and poor would be reversed, with up to 70% of the population living in poverty. In recent years, the attempt to 'modernise' the economy has resulted in a widening of the gap between rich and poor; both the rural and the urban poor have become more and more marginalised. A 'new rich' class has arisen; and they do not hesitate to use their economic power to influence the political authorities for their own benefit. Moreover, the members of this class are becoming more and more the agents and instruments of foreign (multinational) capital.

Culturally, Ireland has a good deal in common with Third World countries. Indeed I find that the closer I can get to my own roots in the west of Ireland, the better I can relate to the African people among whom I am living at present. In regard to attitudes to time-keeping and to technical matters, the Irish seem to be about half-way between the mid-European and the African approach. When I am tempted to join other Europeans in finding fault with African people for failing to look after machinery properly, I recall an incident that occurred in my own village in Ireland when I was a boy. A local man was selling a very ancient motor car. The prospective buyer asked: 'Does she burn oil?' The owner replied very honestly: 'Well now, I suppose she would if she got it.' . . .

Like the Third World countries, Ireland is suffering from a

massive cultural invasion. Its weak and open economy leaves it without the resources needed to promote its own culture. There is also a strong reaction against the narrow puritanism that marked its earlier efforts to protect its traditional values. Its colonial history has also left it with a major problem of cultural identity. More than half of the population of Northern Ireland, and a small but significant minority in the South, do not identify with the traditional Gaelic and 'Catholic' culture. So those who are searching realistically for a way out of the present violence and tension have to work for some kind of cultural pluralism.

## The religious situation

From a religious point of view Ireland has at least as much in common with the Third World as with the First World. Most of the population has not been secularised. They still have a strong religious sense. Indeed, Christianity functions as a kind of 'folk religion' in a somewhat similar way to that of Latin America. But this situation is changing rapidly. Economic changes are giving rise to a new and more urbanised pattern of social life; and the young people living in this new situation are much more secularised than the older generation.

The Gaelic cultural and religious heritage is so rich and powerful that there is keen competition between different groups who wish to use it to legitimate their positions. The far-out Republicans — the people who want to 'unite' Ireland by using terrorist tactics — believe they are the true heirs of the past. So they make blatant use of traditional cultural and religious symbols to give legitimacy to their campaign of violence which they present as a liberation struggle.

Many of the mainline politicians in the South also present themselves as the inheritors and upholders of the tradition. They 'domesticate' the cultural and religious heritage for their advantage. Quite a lot of them also use the tradition of armed force Republicanism in the same rhetorical way, while rejecting the present violence. They know that it is only in a very qualified sense that the conflict in Northern Ireland can be seen as a struggle for liberation against foreign oppression; for the kernel of the problem is the unwillingness of the Northern Unionists to share power with 'the Catholics' or

181

to make any concession to their aspirations. But these politicians still use the rhetoric of the Republican struggle, linking it uncritically with the Gaelic and Catholic heritage.

Catholic Church leaders are alarmed at the rapid loss of traditional moral values and practices. They see a close connection between this morality and the cultural-religious heritage. They would like to preserve both together; and they believe that the best way to do so is for them to retain as much control as possible over the educational system. They believe that they need to maintain a strong influence in the schools in order to ensure that 'the faith' will be handed on to the next generation. This idea of 'handing on the faith' is the unquestioned model used by Church leaders when they think of the promotion of Christian values. It has led to a struggle between Church and State for the control of the 'cultural apparatus' of society — particularly the educational system. The Church leaders seem unwilling to trust politicians or government officials, or the leaders of other Churches — or even the community at large.

In practice what has emerged is a rather uneasy compromise and alliance between the establishments of Church and State about the 'ownership' and control of the cultural heritage. It is particularly disturbing that many of those who see themselves as protecting the legacy of the past are in reality using it to protect themselves and to retain their power. For that reason many people experience the heritage of the past as deadening rather than life-giving, a weight that presses down on them rather than a liberating power.

Members of the other Churches feel in danger of being 'swamped' by the Catholic religious and cultural tradition; so their leaders struggle to preserve occasional 'islands' where their own distinctive tradition is dominant. As a result there is not only a struggle between Church and State in cultural affairs; there is also a muted and not fully acknowledged struggle between the Churches. Ecumenical relationships are formally correct. But one is left with the impression that the occasional common prayers are undertaken more because they will look good, and will indicate a common rejection of violence, than out of any deep urge for unity.

Church leaders remain obviously part of their own ethnic-cultural groups, sharing their aspirations and imprisoned within their prejudices. They have not succeeded in giving the kind of generous and imaginative leadership that would help people break down the barriers of suspicion and competition. In recent years I have been in fairly close contact with some Irish Catholic theologians and leaders. I must confess that I have been shocked at the extent of their indifference to ecumenical concerns and at the intransigence and suspicion which lie under the surface. Those who show particular interest in ecumenism have been subtly — and sometimes not so subtly — marginalised.

The effect of all this is that religious authorities, while sincerely condemning violence, are reinforcing the divisions in Ireland. They are strengthening the links between religious affiliation and cultural-political identity. Consequently, they are contributing to the root causes of hostility and suspicion between people of the two traditions. I have no doubt that some of them are troubled about this. But leaders of the Catholic Church feel an obligation to defend their heritage and to enshrine as much as possible of its values in public life. They insist that what looks like Catholic intransigence is in reality simply a defence of public morality and order, based on 'natural law'. Others reply that these concepts themselves are a Catholic imposition.

### Part of the Establishment

In order to understand the role of the institutional Church in Irish society one must ask, what is its purpose, and how does it seek to achieve its goals? It seems fairly clear that the aim of the Catholic leaders is to ensure that Christian beliefs and values permeate the way of life of the people. What they envisage is not simply a very general 'Christian presence'; they want the distinctive symbols and doctrines of the Catholic Church to be embodied in public life. They are to find expression on public occasions, and in education, the media, the law, and the administration — as well as in the way people relate to one another.

In order to achieve this permeation of the culture, the leaders consider it necessary for the Church to be deeply involved in many key social, cultural, and economic structures in society — e.g. controlling and staffing schools, hospitals, and various social services; and playing an active role in advisory councils to government, and in voluntary associations of all kinds. This inevitably means that 'the Church' is deeply involved in politics in the broad sense.

Clearly, then, the institutional Church is — and wants to be — an integral and major part of the present 'system'. This does not mean that the Church is quite content with the present order of society. But Church leaders want to be in a position to be a voice of conscience in the nation. They believe that the most effective way in which they can do so is by ensuring that the institutional Church is deeply involved in the various parts of the system. In that way they can uphold morality not merely by exhortation and example but also by the exercise of control or influence in the places where the crucial decisions are made. The problem with this approach is that it makes it very difficult for the Church to exercise a truly prophetic role in society. For the institutional Church is very much part of 'the establishment'. Church leaders are 'respectable'; they sit at the top tables with those who hold power; the newspaper photographs show them presiding over the weddings of the rich.

It would be quite wrong to conclude that the Church is cut off from the poor. For it provides relatively low-cost educational and medical services, and it plays a major role in the social services. It began by filling gaps in the State services and providing for the casualties of an unjust social and economic order. More recently it has found itself struggling to maintain its influence in the educational, health, and social welfare systems. This struggle to be a major part of 'the system' takes place at the very time when it should perhaps be questioning the whole system. For it is becoming clearer that the economic and social structures are widening rather than narrowing the gap between the rich and the poor.

A revealing incident occurred a couple of years ago while I was working in Maynooth College, the ecclesiastical centre of Ireland. A fund-raising spokesman for the College was reported as saying that leading Irish businessmen (two of whom he mentioned by name) expect Maynooth to be a centre of stability in Irish society. This remark led to a controversy: a prominent ecclesiastic claimed that discipline in the seminary had gone so lax that Maynooth could not be a centre of order and stability; others rushed to defend the college. What amazed me was that nobody took up the issue of whether the function of the national seminary is to provide the kind of stability that suits our new business tycoons!

One of the more striking features of the Irish economy is the very large profits made by the banks in recent years. I believe this has played a significant part in damaging the economy. For the bank employees have demanded a larger 'slice of the cake' in the form of higher salaries. This has given rise to a spiral of wage demands by other middle-class people — and in this way it has resulted in higher inflation and increasing unemployment. One might have expected the Church to have called for restraint by the banks — or for the government to exercise greater control over them. But it would be difficult for Church leaders to speak out in this way. For the banks have become financial patrons of the Church. They made generous contributions at the time of the visit of the pope to Ireland; and they have become benefactors of the national seminary. Such an 'investment in good will' is perfectly acceptable within the existing system; but I would say that the banks get very good value for their money.

## An alternative approach

I have outlined a complex of problems faced by Ireland in the political, social, economic, cultural, and religious fields. For I believe that any serious attempt to 'do theology' from an Irish perspective must be a response to the actual situation and that it will depend very much on how one interprets that situation. I believe that there is need for an alternative approach in each of the various spheres that I have been considering. I have been examining the role of the Church in the past few pages so I shall begin this outline of alternatives by noting what I consider to be the crucial contribution to be made at the religious and theological level. It is simply to help the Irish people to believe that we really have a choice. In this we differ from most Third World countries, for they have become almost entirely trapped in the present system. In Ireland we are still free to choose our future.

Most of our economists and politicians are trying to convince us that our range of choice is extremely limited. They are correct — but only if we intend to retain the model of development, and of society, chosen for us some years ago by the politicians, on the advice of some 'modern' economists. Within that system the way forward is to insert ourselves more and more thoroughly into the club of the rich nations. This means trying to deal with our economic difficulties by looking for a bigger share in the benefits of the First World — privileges that come, in one way or another, at the cost of loss to poor people and poor countries.

By making such choices we would become more inextricably tied to the Western model of development; and we would distance ourselves more and more from the poorer countries. We would lose contact with our roots and our own historical struggle for liberation. In making such a decision we would be allowing the ownership of most of our industry — and perhaps later much of our land — to pass into the hands of foreign companies or individuals. We would be approving a so-called rationalisation in agriculture and industry that would create permanent high unemployment. We would be deciding — not overtly but in practice — to allow continued callous discrimination against the deprived groups in our own society. We would be abandoning any serious effort to maintain a distinct cultural identity. What it all adds up to is the embracing of the structures, the attitudes, and the ideology of the First World.

But we do not have to choose this path. There is an alternative way. Our human and material resources are sufficient to make this alternative a realistic option for us. We have a lot of fertile land, thinly populated; we have significant mineral resources, as well as energy resources (especially. renewable ones); the seas around us are rich in food and minerals. The Irish are quite well educated and well disposed. We have not yet lost our sense of community and our willingness to help others, especially the weak. We have a capacity to enjoy life and to appreciate what life is really about. As a people we are still inspired by the Christian faith and its values.

All this equips us to choose an alternative way. Instead of inserting ourselves ever more deeply into the rich people's club, we may choose to live out our destiny as a small but truly independent country, working in partnership with all who have a similar vision. This would mean opting for:

186

— much greater self-sufficiency in the economic field; this might include the upgrading of traditional forms of mixed farming, instead of single-minded specialisation in agriculture; the return to more part-time farming; and, in industry, a stress on locally-required products and small-scale operations;
— a commitment to a model of socio-economic development that relies on renewable energy sources and appropriate technology; one that encourages decentralisation and the flourishing of local communities, while promoting social equality and participation by all in decision-making;
— a strengthening of our political independence in solidarity with other neutral nations;
— determined efforts to preserve our own culture and the best of our own traditions — not in a fossilised form but in a way that accepts the diversity we have and is open to others;
— the living out of our Christian faith in small communities where people can share with each other at every level; where all have a part in decision-making and in the exercise of a wide variety of ministries; where the Christian community witnesses to Kingdom values in its own life; and where it promotes these values in society by positive support where that is appropriate and by challenge where that is called for.

I have suggested that the crucial contribution that is needed at the religious-theological level is the belief that we are not trapped in the present system but that change is possible. Without being pretentious and rhetorical one can compare our situation to that of the Jewish people in the time of Moses. Like them we have been driven by economic necessity into the 'Empire'. Like them we find ourselves near the bottom of that affluent society and unable to envisage a life of independence. The task which God gave to Moses was to convince his people that an alternative life was possible; and his call to committed Irish Christians today is similar. Liberation for us, as for the Jews, must have political, economic, social, and cultural aspects. But prior to all that, for us as for them, is an aspect that is religious in the broadest sense: the realisation that *it is not inevitable that we remain subject to the gods of the Empire*. Like the Jews we have a God who does not want us to live in dependence, a God who calls us out of Egypt into true freedom in our own land — and by a route that involves the risks of the desert.

187

## Widen the choices

What is to be done in practice by those who wish, like Moses, to call their people into an alternative way of life? I think their first aim should be to open up to the people a wider choice. This widening must be of two kinds; for it has to do both with the range of options open to us and with the type and number of people who are to make the choice. Firstly, then, we need to be convinced that the choices are not as restricted as we are constantly being told. At present there is very little difference in policy between the major political parties in the Irish Republic on economic, political, social, or cultural affairs. So they offer us little choice.

There is, however, a certain polarisation in society on cultural-religious issues — though it is one that cuts right across party loyalties. On the one hand there are those who wish to preserve what they see as the traditional religious and cultural values by embodying them in the educational system, the health and social services, and the constitution of the State. These are opposed by the liberal 'modernisers', who tend to be somewhat indifferent to the heritage of the past and want Ireland to become more and more like the secularised countries of northern Europe. Neither group seem to be very aware of the fact that, in the long run, our cultural and religious values will be determined largely by the choices we make in relation to economic matters. Unless people choose a model of economic development which is significantly different from the present one, it is almost inevitable that the traditional cultural and religious values will lose their relevance to Irish society.

At present we are in a strange situation. We are spending our energies squabbling about cultural-religious values as though these were quite unaffected by our choices in economic matters. Meanwhile we are being offered little real choice on the crucial economic issues. It is time our people were helped to see that the options are not so limited. We can learn from what has happened in West Germany. There, a relatively small group of committed people — the ecological 'Green Party' — succeeded in opening up wider options for the people. Their activities led to important changes in the policies of the major parties. In much the same way a small but effective 'ginger group' could open up for the Irish people the possibility of a truly alternative approach to development. This would not have to be isolationist in the usual sense of the term; it could be done in cooperation with similar movements in other parts of the world — and particularly in the smaller countries of Europe. The activity of such a group would not be subversive; they could operate in a peaceful and democratic manner, while still challenging many of the taken-for-granted assumptions of our present society. Indeed they could lead us to a much deeper conception of democracy.

This brings me to the second way in which the choices of the Irish people need to be widened. It is the matter of *who* makes the key decisions about our future. At present they are made by a small number of senior civil servants, who give advice to the politicians, by the directors of the banks and of multinational companies, and by the policy-makers of the Church. Those who are looking for significant changes in Irish society can easily be tempted to spend their time and energy in trying to influence this elite group of decision-makers. But the most important change that needs to be made is to enable the powerless and even the alienated to participate in shaping our society. If the Irish Church were to commit itself to promoting this goal, that would be a truly worthwhile and challenging ideal.

Committed Christians who really tried to work for the poor — not 'from above' but in real solidarity with them — would be in a position to rediscover the roots of authentic religion; for the task would require, and evoke, conversion in its three aspects — personal, interpersonal, and political. Instead of jockeying for cultural-political power in an attempt to stem the drift towards secularism, the institutional Church would be acting in a more obviously Christlike way. It would be truly bringing 'good news' to the poor, and in this way promoting the Kingdom of God. It should claim no monopoly in this task; Church people would have to be willing to work alongside other dedicated individuals and groups. If 'the Church' devoted its resources and energies to enfranchising the poor, it would be less tempted to confuse the promotion of the Kingdom with the maintenance and extension of the power of the Church.

The kind of activity which I have in mind would include the following:

— community development work, of a type that gives the initiative to local people and does not simply domesticate the poor by defusing their frustration;

— adult education and consciousness-raising to enable people to discover their gifts and develop a sense of their own worth;

— helping in citizens' advice centres where people from deprived areas could be enabled to discover their rights and air their grievances constructively;

— the building up of basic Christian communities, and the provision of training programmes for the leaders and ministers of such communities;

— involvement in tenants' organisations, homeless people's groups, and prisoners' rights organisations, as well as various local groupings of people living in deprived situations.

Action of this kind should not be initiated and organised from the top down. To be effective it would have to emerge from the deprived people themselves, through the use of the kind of approach I outlined in Chapter 10, when I was describing 'the psycho-social method'.

There is need for more friendly contact between Church people and the small number of activists who are now working on behalf of deprived groups. This requires both structural and attitudinal changes. From a structural point of view the institutional Church must become less obviously part of the Establishment and more an agency which challenges the system. If this takes place it will contribute to a change in the attitudes of Church people. And if the Church itself succeeds in adopting a more collaborative style in its own organisation and community life, this will help Church people to be less institutional and formal in their approach.

It seems to me that the Irish Church has now reached a turning-point, a moment of decision. For the first time that I can remember a number of clergy and religious have been arrested for siding with the most deprived sector of Irish society ('the Travellers') in their confrontation with the 'respectable' people and security forces. What will be the reaction of the Church leadership and of the main body of Christians? Will the Church as an institution and as a community take a decisive stance in defence of the poor? Will it overtly or tacitly disown the activists and support 'law and order'? Or will it perhaps try to ignore the issue by main-

190

taining an embarrassed silence? It is unlikely that the Church will be able to speak with a totally united voice. The test for its leadership will be whether they are ready to take the risk of coming out strongly in favour of the poor, despite the risk of meeting formidable opposition from some of their own members. My hope and prayer is that the Church — leaders and members — will seize this opportunity to look again at their priorities and make a decisive option for the poor.

## Reorientation and Renewal

Obviously, all this would require a re-allocation of resources by the institutional Church from some of the present areas of concentration. It would also necessitate a major reorientation of attitudes and priorities — as well as considerable retraining of personnel. Already, some of this has begun to take place. A number of Irish dioceses have held assemblies of all their priests. Using a very participative approach (called the Berger methodology), they have looked closely at their present situation and have clarified their ideals for the future; then they set out to plan for the realisation of their ideals. These assemblies have been very enriching experiences for those who took part in them. Great credit must go to those bishops who took the risk of sponsoring the assemblies; for it involved a relinquishing of power and a sharing of responsibility with their priests. The big issue now, of course, is whether the priests will be willing to make a similar act of letting go of *their* power; will they use this kind of methodology to break out of their isolation and share responsibility with the religious and laity?

In the past few years, several religious orders and congregations have been coming to realise that major changes may be necessary if they are to be true to their original inspiration and charism; most of these institutes were founded to provide alternatives to 'the System' rather than to be among the more powerful and 'respectable' interest-groups in the educational, social welfare, and medical establishments. Painful heart-searching is being done by these communities about what would be involved for them in making an option for the poor. Some are still reluctant to accept that such an option has 'political' implications. Others have moved on to

191

a point where they sense the radicality and difficulty of what is called for; but they feel paralysed about where to start. I know a number of congregations of sisters who have been crying out for theological guidance — and religious inspiration — from theologians and Church leaders. The response so far has been quite inadequate. The reason is that many of the 'experts' are themselves confused — if not actually in flight from the challenge and busily rationalising it out of existence.

In recent years I have been asked to help various groups of clergy and religious (and even one group of bishops!) in their 'renewal programmes'; and in general this has been a very heartening experience for me. However, I notice one major difficulty: most of these groups would like to do their agonising and work out their solutions behind closed doors. They are scared of revealing their uncertainties to those outside their own homogeneous groups. As a result, clerics cut themselves off from lay people, men from women, middle-class Church people from those of the poor who have learned to articulate the frustrations of their people.

More and more, I have come to believe that real conversion can take place and fruitful changes can occur more easily if people are prepared to work in mixed groups. But if they refuse to take this risk they are isolating themselves from the very people who could challenge them most effectively. In doing so they are also missing the opportunity of being reassured. For the challenge is most threatening when it remains unarticulated or is expressed by somebody else on behalf of the excluded ones; when it is heard face to face, the threat dissolves and people can begin to move forward together.

### International linkages

Church people who are working for justice in Irish society often feel that they do not receive much support or understanding from Church authorities. This is a source of surprise to development workers from overseas, many of whom have been helped by the Irish Church. The problem is that the Church in Ireland seems to have two faces on issues of justice and human development. On the one hand there is its 'Third World face' as represented above all by Trócaire, the official

192

development agency of the Irish Catholic Church. In the eleven years since it was set up, Trócaire has been remarkably forward-looking – and even at times quite radical – in its approach. Its aim has been to promote a type of development that tackles the root causes of poverty. And it has not been afraid to work for human liberation by lobbying and by campaigning publicly against repressive regimes in Latin America, South Africa, and Asia.

All this contrasts sharply with the other face of the Irish Church on matters of development and justice – the face seen by those who challenge the system and the model of development adopted at home in Ireland. It is true that quite recently Irish Church agencies have issued some out-spoken statements on social issues in Irish society; but when it comes to action, Church people are still working mainly within the existing structures. Few tears were shed by Church leaders when, a couple of years ago, the 'Combat Poverty' agency was closed down by the government of the time. For the efforts of this agency to tackle poverty at the structural level had brought it into conflict not only with politicians but also with some Church authorities.

The contrast between the two 'faces' became particularly obvious at a conference on global development and justice sponsored by Trócaire in Galway in June 1983. At that conference, Nan Joyce, a spokeswoman for 'the Travelling People', the most marginalised and persecuted group in Irish society, asked: 'What is Trocaire doing for us, the Third World in your midst?' This cry from the heart evoked loud applause from the Irish participants, and considerable sympathy from the Third World delegates. But it met with a rather embarrassed silence on the part of the organisers of the conference. The reason is that Trócaire's strength has been in sticking firmly to the specific mandate given to it by the Church authorities.

I do not think one should ask Trócaire to abandon its specific focus, which is global and Third World development, in order to do what ought to be done by other organs of the Irish Church. However, I venture to repeat here a suggestion I made at the Galway conference, one that was well received at the time. It concerns a way in which Trócaire could respond to the plea of people like Nan Joyce, without compromising its own specific purpose. What I suggested is that there should be established within Trócaire a small section which would have the aim of promoting international linkage. This department would work in close association with the two main departments of Trócaire: the Projects Section (through which it supports groups in the Third World) and the Development Education Section (through which it promotes awareness in Ireland of Third World issues).

Through this new department Trócaire would be able to help the Church at home, by making use of the warm personal relationships that have developed between its staff and some of the outstanding development leaders of the Third World. The department might be called 'The International Solidarity Section'. Its specific role would be to promote contacts between Trócaire's Third World friends and those who are working for justice in the Irish situation. Grassroots leaders in Ireland — and those who are supporting them — frequently feel quite isolated. It is a great support to them when they are put in touch with those who are doing similar work in the Third World — people who are respected in Ireland for what they are doing.

Already some missionary and religious institutes in Ireland have begun to promote this kind of linkage. About three years ago I took part in a workshop which brought Third World theologians into contact with representatives of deprived groups in Ireland. It was quite extraordinary to see how well they were able to relate to one another and how much encouragement and religious-theological inspiration came out of that meeting; it could well turn out to have been a turning-point in the life of the Irish Church.

## We all must choose

I have been considering different aspects of how the Church in Ireland could make an effective option for the poor. I want now to change the focus for a moment and look at this issue from below rather than from above. In the previous sections I suggested ways of overcoming the difficulties facing people who have power and prestige in the Church. It is not easy for them to take the risk of relinquishing power and coming into solidarity with the poor. But a point that

194

has come home to me recently is that these are not the only ones who have to take a risk and make a difficult option. Through being involved in a mixed group of people exploring together what it means to work for justice, I realised that the 'option *for* the poor' has to be met with an 'option *by* the poor'. It is crucially important — and very difficult — for many of the poor to reach out in trust and friendship to people whom they have experienced in the past as 'above' them.

Some of my most painful moments have come when I felt that links of friendship which had crossed the social barrier were suddenly undermined by suspicion, distrust, and the temptation to manipulate me. At times like that I experienced the weight of social sin — a force that almost deprives us of our personal freedom. On the other hand, there have been experiences of reconciliation, of restored trust, when I once again dared to hope that an option *with* the poor could become an enduring reality. The very fragility of that hope makes me deeply aware that it can be neither earned nor possessed. It can only be accepted moment by moment as a gift — from other people and from God.

## Conclusion

Reading over what I have written in this treatment of the Irish situation I wonder whether readers will recognise it as an attempt to do *theology* — or will it just be seen as a mishmash of wishful thinking about socio-economic and cultural matters. I believe it is theology — though it is, of course, much more as well. For my interpretation of the Irish economic and cultural situation is grounded in a religious vision. I have been trying to articulate theologically two fundamental religious convictions which are at the heart of the alternative approach which I have proposed. The first is that God has called *all* of his people to live a fully human life; and that God expects the Church to challenge any social order that systematically excludes and impoverishes certain groups. The second conviction is that we are free — not just as individuals in the private sphere but collectively in our socio-economic life. We are not trapped in the present system which in many respects is unjust and inhuman. An alternative way is open to us. We can create something new — under God, the one who 'makes all things new':

> The Lord says: 'I am making a new earth and new heavens. . . . The new Jerusalem I make will be full of joy, and her people will be happy. . . . There will be no weeping there . . . babies will no longer die in infancy and all people will live out their life span. . . . People will build houses and live in them themselves — they will not be used by someone else. . . . They will fully enjoy the things they have worked for. . . . I will bless them and their descendants for all time to come.' (Is 65:17-23)

**Postscript.** As I was correcting the proofs of this book, Father Harry Bohan, Founder/Director of the Rural Resource Organisation, South Boundary Shannon, showed me the draft of a book he has just written under the title *Ireland — Two Thousand Communities: The Future in our Hands.* I was greatly encouraged to find that his analysis of the Irish scene and his proposals for the future are quite similar to my own. Father Bohan writes out of a wealth of practical experience which gives considerable authority and credibility to his views.

# 12

# Evangelisation, Justice, and Development

In previous chapters I have frequently used the words 'development' and 'liberation'. At this point I feel it would be helpful to try to specify more precisely the meaning of these terms and to show how they relate to other theological words such as 'evangelisation', 'mission', and 'justice'. For no area of Church life is so bedevilled by misunderstandings and disputes as the activities associated with justice. Some of the difficulty is verbal: confusion arises because words such as 'evangelisation', 'liberation', 'development', and 'mission' are given a variety of different meanings. But behind this confusion about words lie deeper sources of misunderstanding. In the first section of this chapter I shall examine some of the reasons why this whole topic is so controversial. In later sections I hope to sort out the different meanings given to some of the key words, in order to lessen the verbal confusion. I hope to do this not in a purely theoretical way but rather by drawing on my experience as a person with a foot in two camps: I am now working as a missionary in the Third World, but I have tried to retain as far as possible the links I have had with a home-based development agency. This makes me aware of the tensions that sometimes arise between Church agencies devoted to global development, and missionaries working in the field. I hope that what I say may 'mediate' on some controversial issues and help to bring about better understanding.

## Section One
## Mindsets

Much of the tension that surrounds justice issues stems from the fact that committed Christians may have notably different

197

conceptions of the nature and role of the Church. The particular notion that each of us has of what the Church is all about gives rise to a 'mindset' — a complex of beliefs, values, and attitudes. This mindset colours our interpretation of situations, influences our judgments, and even affects our choice of allies and friends. Each mindset underpins a different spirituality. I want to consider briefly four different conceptions of the nature of the Church. Each of them is associated with a very different mindset and spirituality; and all of them are common in the Church today. In many respects these different outlooks are incompatible with each other; and the fact that the different views are held by different people is a source of controversy and pain.

It is customary nowadays to speak about different 'models of the Church'. There is one important difference between what I want to say here and the usual presentation of such 'models'. I am not talking about a variety of equally valid models, each of which is needed to complement the others since no one of them contains all the truth. Rather I am thinking of a growth in understanding by the Church of its own nature; this advance gives rise to a succession of 'models', where the earlier ones are completed and corrected by the later ones. In the teaching of the Roman Catholic Church this advance took place with extraordinary rapidity. Church documents issued in the ten-year period between 1961 and 1971 reflect the move from the first to the fourth concept of the Church. In the other Churches the process was somewhat more gradual; but it was still so fast that not everybody could keep up with it.

## From Fortress to Pilgrim

The dominant image of the first mindset is the Church as a fortress which stands out against the world in an attitude of defence and offence. It is 'the Church militant'. In view of this military image it is understandable that the associated spirituality puts a lot of emphasis on discipline, and on the more institutional aspects of the Church. If the Church is an army, then the role of the generals and officers is all important. In the Catholic Church the fortress takes the shape of a pyramid, with the pope at the top. Under him are the bishops;

198

then come the priests, and then the religious. At the bottom are the laity, with lay women being even further down than the men. The crucial virtue in the spirituality of the lay 'foot-soldiers' is obedience. No wonder, then, that Church schools were admired for their discipline. At its worst, this spirituality was ghetto-like, individualistic, and escapist. But at its best it gave people a sense of God's transcendence. It also gave people a sense of security; there was little need for agonising, since all knew their place and how they were expected to act.

This was still the dominant conception of the Church in 1961, the year before Vatican II began. Quite a lot of Christians have never left it behind. They may have adapted some of their ideas and practices to take account of more recent developments; but their fundamental outlook and spirituality have not changed significantly. That is why I use the word 'mindset': these people were moulded and shaped a generation ago; and their attitudes are now 'set'. As a result, they find themselves out of sympathy with those whose spirituality is rooted in a different mindset.

An important change took place when a new dominant image of the Church replaced that of the fortress. This new image is that of the pilgrim people of God. The pilgrim, like the soldier, may be marching through the desert; but the attitudes of the pilgrim are quite different. Christians with this outlook think of themselves as the community of believers, gathered by the Spirit, to follow Christ into the Kingdom of God. The emphasis is on the togetherness of the Christian community; there is a fundamental equality among Christians; it is prior to any special role of ministry given to some. The 'ordinary' Christian is no longer seen in negative terms as one who is not a priest or religious.

In the Catholic Church the new dominant image was accepted officially in the first year of Vatican II; and it finds expression in the Council's document on the Church. This recognition of the basic equality of all Christians represents the acceptance by Catholics of one of the great insights of the Reformation. The greatest strength of this outlook is that it is truer to the biblical conception of the Church. It enables lay people to feel they are not second-class Christians. Indeed it calls into question the very use of the phrase 'the

199

laity' and it leaves little room for clericalism. But the new approach also gave rise to difficulties. It led to a type of public worship which, in attempting to be comprehensible and involving for everybody, lost its power of evoking a sense of the sacred. It also pointed up the need for a radical reform of the existing clericalist structures of the Church; so it gave rise to problems about authority in the Church. The questioning of authority, in turn, left many people feeling insecure and lost. A more fundamental problem, I believe, is that the new approach was dependent more on theological theory than on experience. There was a lot of *talk* about Christians being the community of the People of God; but there was little understanding of how best to give people the actual experience of being a real community.

### From Church to World

The third mindset and spirituality springs from a major change of focus. This is a shift from a point of view which starts from the Church to one in which the starting-point is the world. So the dominant image is that of the Christian community at the service of the wider human world. The new insight is that the phrase 'the People of God' must be applied not only to the Church but also to all of humanity. The role of the Christian community as the special people of God is to be within the world and at the service of all God's people. The word 'service' is of crucial importance. The call of committed Christians is not simply to march through the world as pilgrims on the way to the Kingdom. They are also called to serve the world by cooperating with the Lord of History in transforming the world into the Kingdom. This requires a major change in spirituality; there emerges a whole new set of values and attitudes — a spirituality of the world.

This shift of focus took place in the Catholic Church during the last two years of Vatican II. It finds expression in the Council's second great document on the Church — the 'Pastoral Constitution on the Church in the Modern World'. At about the same time the Protestant Churches were experiencing a similar shift of focus. It is doubtful whether the shift has occurred to the same extent in the Orthodox Churches.

200

The great strength of the new approach is that it removes the traditional split between the sacred and the secular. Here we have a spirituality that evokes commitment to every aspect of authentic human living. This is evident in the Council document, which devotes long sections to work, culture, marriage, socio-economic development, and to the search for peace. The biggest weakness of the new outlook is that, in promoting service of the world it can lead to the wrong kind of 'worldliness' or 'conformity to the world'. As I shall point out in a moment, it can be very uncritical of current worldly values.

The new mindset and spirituality has transformed the lives of many Christians. The change of approach has affected religious sisters (who used to be 'nuns') perhaps more than any other group. The many priests, Church officials, and lay people who failed to make the shift of focus from Church to world were mystified and often alarmed. They could not understand why many congregations and individual sisters were changing their apostolates and their lifestyle. The changes were often taken to be part of a process of secularisation, inspired by a spirit of independence, disobedience, and 'women's lib'. This shift of spirituality was much more divisive than the previous one. It remains a major source of controversy and scandal in the Church. People on either side of the great divide are unable to be in sympathy with the values and priorities of those whose mindset is so different from their own.

Perhaps one reason why so many clergy are unsympathetic to the new spirituality is that their own minds were set at the time they studied theology, long before the new approach came to the fore. Many of the sisters, on the other hand (even older ones), came to theology much later — and it was then that their mindsets took shape. It may be important to note this link between the time of theological formation and the dominant mindset of the person. For this could help to explain why some of the people who shocked those of an older outlook are now themselves reluctant or unable to make the further shift that is called for in the Church today.

## Whose World?

The Church's understanding of its nature and role continues to develop. Contrary to the assumption of those who made the great shift of focus from Church to world, this is not the last or greatest shift that is required. Within three years of Vatican II's document on 'The Church in the Modern World' came the Medellín Documents, issued by the Conference of Latin American Bishops. This represents a further major shift of focus — one that is paralleled in the documents of the World Council of Churches. The new question that has emerged as crucial is: 'When you set out to serve the world, whose world are you serving? Is it the world as structured by the rich and powerful, a world built on the dominant values of competition and success at all costs? Or is it the world as God wants it to be, one in which structural poverty and powerlessness are challenged, and the poor are privileged agents of God in bringing about the Kingdom?' The dominant image of the new approach could be the power pyramid described in an earlier chapter. This reminds one that the world as we have it is marred by structural injustice. So the Christian who wishes to serve the world must seek to overcome this built-in evil.

The spirituality represented by this new outlook is one that seeks to retain the best elements in the earlier worldly spirituality. But now people are called not to be so naïve in the way they make their option for the world and for human life. The undue optimism of the earlier approach is called in question. There is a keen awareness of the need for challenge and asceticism, and a recognition of the inevitability of suffering. Consequently this fourth outlook finds a good deal of common ground with the older 'fortress spirituality' — though in other respects it is radically different in approach. I suspect that the major difficulty with what I am calling the 'fortress spirituality' is that many elements in it are just the fossilised relics of an older living spirituality which challenged the world in a way similar to the spirituality of Medellín. Over centuries, much of the spirit behind them was lost; so they became distorted and at times unrecognisable. Hence the need for a 'new' outlook which is largely a rediscovery of what the Church stood for at first — but with certain truly new aspects as well.

One of the crucial insights in this fourth mindset is that the world develops into the Kingdom by a process that has negative and positive aspects. Liberation is the negative aspect: every kind of evil and oppression must be overcome. The poor are called to play a privileged role in this work of liberation; but to do so they need to be animated to believe in themselves, to trust each other, and to resist oppression. The positive aspect of the bringing about of the Kingdom is expressed in several European languages by a word equivalent to the English word 'promotion'. It means genuine human progress — in contrast to the kind of so-called 'development' described in an earlier chapter. I think the best English word to express this positive aspect is 'humanisation'. Its meaning can be brought out by means of such examples as the fostering of a sense of community, or of human rights.

The new spirituality has several important strengths. One of the most important is that it enables us to rediscover one of the central themes of the Bible: God's special concern for the poor and his call to them to overcome oppression. Christians find themselves called to a genuine solidarity with the poor of the world. When this call is answered, Christian faith comes alive. Part of the new spirituality is a realisation of the importance of small Christian communities, especially among the poor. It is above all in such groups that one can have a living experience of what it means to be a member of a community. Like every spirituality, this one has its dangers. A person may become so involved in working for justice in society that personal and interpersonal values are neglected. This could easily lead to the phenomenon known as 'burnout', where the person's emotional and spiritual resources seem to have been entirely used up and the person becomes 'dead' inside. There are also other dangers. A person might become totally politicised, insensitive to other values. One might also have such high ideals that one could be tempted to justify total ruthlessness by a so-called 'liberation movement' in pursuit of these ideals. Or one might become an angry and bitter person because of the failure of others — or of the Church — to live up to one's unrealistic ideals. Hence the need for a balanced spirituality of the kind I described in the first chapter of this book.

A lot of the misunderstanding and controversy associated

with action for justice by Christians, stems from the fact that all four of these spiritualities exist side by side in the Church today. The different mindsets do not result in a healthy pluralism but rather in suspicion and intransigence. To help oneself to understand what has gone wrong one may use the image of a train. The point of departure for the 'Church train' was the 'fortress spirituality'. The train travelled very quickly from this first station to the fourth station — the spirituality I have just described. There were brief stops at the two intervening 'stations'. The departure from each station was so rapid that very many of the passengers were left behind. Some are still stuck at the very first station; others got off at the second or third. The really sad thing is that those who failed to travel all the way do not realise that the train has departed without them. So there are people at each of the earlier stations who assume they have reached the end of the journey. That is a peculiarly intractable source of misunderstanding and controversy. It takes a kind of conversion for anybody to recognise that he or she may have missed the train, or got off at the second-last station!

## Section Two
## Development and Mission

Taking account of the rapid development which has occurred in the Church's understanding of its own role, I would like next to examine how the Christian concepts of development and social justice fit in with the concept of mission. I think the best way to do this is to contrast the outlook of the pre-1960 period with that of the present time. Twenty-five years ago the outreach of the Church was seen as having both temporal and spiritual aspects. The temporal aspect might be summed up under the heading 'service'; and for the spiritual aspect the appropriate word was 'mission'.

Those who felt called to give 'service' on behalf of the Church would see themselves as showing the compassion of Christ to needy people, whether Christian or non-Christian. The aim was to give help to the needy in the 'temporal' (as distinct from the 'spiritual') sphere. Under the heading of 'service' would be included the staffing of schools and hospitals — especially those that catered for poorer people. It also included the providing of special services and assistance for such groups as the poor, the homeless, the handicapped, and youth.

In contrast to this, the focus of interest for those concerned with 'mission' was primarily spiritual and ecclesiastical: their aim was 'to save souls' and 'to build the Church'. At this time the word 'mission' referred above all to the 'foreign missions' — the building up of young Churches in those parts of the world where Christianity had not yet taken root. (However, the word 'mission' had not entirely lost its wider meaning; this was shown by the occasional use of the word in other contexts, e.g. parishes had 'a mission' once every few years, and a priest who left the ministry was said to be 'off the mission'.) Missionary work involved such purely ecclesiastical activities as public worship, preaching, giving religious instruction, and the 'administration' of sacraments. But it might also include the erection and running of schools and hospitals, since such activity could contribute to the building up of the Church. As a result of this way of understanding the work of the Church, many foreign missionaries found that their lives involved a conjunction of 'mission' and 'service'. Neither of these was reduced to being merely a means to the other. The two existed side by side, linked together in practice without any profound theological theory to clarify the relationship between them.

The Church's understanding of its outreach today is much more sophisticated. Indeed an adequate and generally accepted language to describe what is involved has not yet emerged. So, part of what I am doing here is offering a set of terms — a language that can be used consistently to describe different aspects of the Church's work. The meaning of each term is clarified mainly by relating it to the other terms in the set. We can begin by noting that there is a real continuity with the past. The concepts of 'mission' and 'service' are still valid. But we have to be more nuanced in the way we use them. We can no longer be content with the simple distinction between 'the spiritual' and 'the temporal' spheres. For it is clear now that the distinction is not a very happy one; and, in so far as one can use it at all, one must accept that both mission and service have spiritual and temporal aspects.

## Relief and Development

Let us look first at how the notion of the Church's service of people has developed. The Church continues to offer a caring service to the world today. But now we have to make distinctions that were scarcely thought of a generation ago. The basic reason is that the notion of human development has come to the fore. Consequently, we can now no longer be content with just a general notion of providing services for needy people; we have to make a fairly clear distinction between relief and development. In practice, relief may at times shade into development; but they differ in their aims. To provide relief services is to try to deal with the effects of evil. To work for development, by contrast, is to attempt to overcome the evil itself, rather than just its effects. Relief services are still required in two situations:

(a) emergencies, where some disaster such as an earthquake leaves people in urgent need of aid; and

(b) situations of chronic need where there is no possibility of people being able to care for themselves — for instance, where people are very severely handicapped or seriously and incurably ill.

Needless to say, it is preferable, wherever possible, to care for people by helping in their development rather than simply providing immediate relief. That is a crucial point which is taken for granted by those who have reflected seriously on how best to help others. But it is a point that is very frequently forgotten — not least by many compassionate Christians who do not stop to think before rushing in to offer help. Once a relief service is provided, the recipients easily become dependent on it. Those who are providing the service may then feel trapped — unable to break out of the relationship of dependence, though they realise that it is bad for both parties.

This danger of creating dependency is not avoided simply by committing oneself to development rather than relief. In fact many of the projects which go under the heading of development scarcely merit that title at all — because they still create dependency. They are attempts by well-meaning people to bring development to others. But there is really no such things as development 'for others'. It is of the nature of genuine human development that it be self-development — of the individual, the community, or the nation. The basic

206

aim of anybody who wants to engage in development work must be to facilitate people in helping themselves.

But that is not sufficient. We have to make a further distinction — between on the one hand what I would call 'worthy projects' and on the other hand an approach to development that seeks to tackle the basic causes of poverty and powerlessness. Almost everywhere in the Third World (as well as in deprived areas of the wealthy countries) there are very many worthy projects, designed to help people to help themselves. Among the more common ones are projects to teach poor women dressmaking or cookery or dyeing. Many of the Third World projects designed to help people in the spheres of agriculture, community health and youth work have a basic weakness. They may be 'worthy projects' in so far as they impart skills to people or meet some basic needs. But they do not really get to the heart of the problems. Only a relatively small number of programmes or projects can be called 'authentic development'. They are the ones that tackle the causes of poverty by setting out to overcome structural injustice and to build a just and humane society.

As I noted earlier in this chapter there are negative and positive aspects to the process by which the world moves towards being transformed into the Kingdom. The negative aspect is liberation; the positive aspect I called 'humanisation'. Any programme which seeks to promote authentic human development needs to take both of these aspects seriously; and neither can be postponed. It might seem logical to begin by overcoming structural evils and only when this negative work is complete to start on the positive aspect. But the two are inseparable in practice. For instance, the evil of lack of participation in decision-making can be overcome only by a process which gives people the opportunity of shaping their own history. The real challenge for those who want to overcome structural injustice is to find ways in which the process of liberation from evil is at the same time a process of building alternative just structures. This applies not only in the political sphere but also in economics, in the cultural sphere, and in the life of the Church.

The 'psycho-social' approach, which I described in Chapter 10, takes into account both the positive and the negative aspects of authentic human development. Its basic aim is to help people — above all the poor — to become the primary agents of their own development. The activities involved cannot be labelled either 'spiritual' or 'temporal'. They include economic, political, educational, and religious matters — all as part of an integrated vision of human liberation and growth. The notion of social justice is one of the key concepts in this vision; and it is at once spiritual and temporal, secular and transcendent. The vision itself includes a particular understanding of the role of the Church; and part of that understanding is the belief that the Church is called to be at the service of the world. The aim of the Church is to promote the Kingdom, rather than just to look after its own sectional interests.

### Frontier Mission

I have been describing how in recent years the notion of the Church's caring service has become more sophisticated. Now it is time to look at what has happened during the same period to the notion of 'mission'. The very first point to note is that we can no longer assume so easily that 'mission' is to be understood almost exclusively in geographical terms. Indeed we now use the word 'mission' to refer above all to the task of the Church wherever it exists — as they say: 'The Church is mission'. But having accepted that, I think it is helpful to try to locate what I would call the 'frontier mission' of the Church today. I use this phrase to describe the situations where the Church meets those aspects of the world to which it is sent but in which it is not yet effectively present.

One such frontier exists wherever there are cultures that have had little contact with Christianity. There are still ethnic groups in need of 'first evangelisation'; so there is still need for the work of foreign missionaries. But before going on to describe what that work involves today, I must add that we should not assume that it is only *culturally*-defined groups that stand on the Church's frontier. It seems clear that there are also *social* groups in many areas who are in need of primary evangelisation — e.g. the working class in some countries. First steps in the process of evangelisation would include finding ways of living in solidarity with such culturally or socially defined groups. This can go hand-in-hand with a careful study of the life of the group so as to identify the needs that the people themselves experience most vividly, while trying to see if these offer points of insertion for the Gospel.

The process of evangelisation is to be carried out both by word and by witness. The witness is interpreted by the word, while the authenticity of the word is made evident by the witness. It would be foolish to say that the word is more important than the witness or the witness than the word. Neither can a general rule be laid down that one must always begin with one or the other: that depends on circumstances. The aim will be, not to impose something alien on the group, but to enable people to experience the liberating power of faith in Christ in their own situation. Theologians speak of 'inculturation' and of enabling people to 'incarnate' the faith in their own culture. More recently the word 'contextualisation' is being employed to describe what is involved. Used in this technical sense it suggests that all aspects of the situation (the context) are to be taken seriously – not just the culture but also the situation of impoverishment and powerlessness in which so many people live.

The work of first evangelisation shades off into the task of being of service within the newly established local Church. There is little point in trying to locate some boundary-line between the two, since in fact the founding and service of the Church is implicit from the very beginning in the process of evangelisation. Once the emerging Christian community begins to have a clear identity as a 'Young Church', a good deal of the work of evangelisation is strictly ecclesiastical in character. There are the pastoral activities of public prayer and religious education. These traditional pastoral activities are now supplemented by – and partly subsumed under – newer forms of pastoral action: for instance, the building up of basic Christian communities or prayer groups, and specialised ministry to youth, to workers, to married couples. The ecclesiastical part of evangelisation also includes the formation of Christian leaders.

Another important part of the process of evangelisation is what I would call 'the witness apostolates'. Many groups of Church people live out their faith by the witness of a life of contemplative prayer, or by sharing the life of the poor, or by educating young or not-so-young people, or taking care of the handicapped, the homeless, the old, or the sick. These activities all have a value in their own right. But when they are undertaken formally in the name of the Church, they have the further purpose of enabling the Church itself to give witness publicly to Kingdom values. That is why I am calling them 'witness apostolates'.

The older and the newer forms of pastoral activity, and the witness apostolates, are not, of course, confined to the frontier mission of the Church; they are part of the general on-going mission of the Church wherever it exists. But these evangelising actions have a particular significance on the cultural or social frontiers of the Church; and quite often it is on the frontier that new approaches are pioneered. In the past, we tended to think of the 'foreign missions' as a one-way movement: the areas that were already at least partly Christianised were seen as sharing the faith with the non-Christian part of the world. Nowadays there is a strong reaction against this way of thinking. One expression of this is the phrase 'mission in six continents' — implying that the geographical concept of mission no longer applies, since the Church is equally in a state of mission everywhere. Another expression is 'reverse mission'; and in my opinion this is preferable. It suggests that while the older Churches continue to offer help to the young Churches, there is also a notable flow in the opposite direction. The new life, and new forms of Church activity, which are generated in the more recently established Churches have a feedback effect on the older Churches. One thinks, above all, of the model of Church which gives top priority to basic Christian communities; and other examples are the commitment of the Church to human liberation and various efforts to adapt liturgy to local culture. When I speak of the frontier mission of the Church, I am not simply thinking of a movement from the centre to the periphery. I include also the activity of 'reverse mission' from the frontier back to those older zones and aspects of Church life which are in danger of becoming stiff in the joints.

The 'frontier mission' of the Church today includes many other important activities which were scarcely taken into account in the older concept of mission. Ecumenism is one obvious case; the most obvious frontier for each Christian

Church ought to be the point where it meets other Churches. Then there is the wider ecumenism, where Christianity meets the other religions and philosophies of life. The Church needs people who are specialists to work on this frontier. Their mission is one of dialogue – of sharing the riches of the Christian faith and of helping the Church to be open to the values and beliefs of other religious traditions.

The account given so far of the Church's frontier mission has been concerned with activities that are obviously ecclesiastical in character – they have to do with the building up of the Church. But there is another, and perhaps even more crucial, aspect of the work of evangelisation, where the focus is rather different. The Christian community has a 'prophetic' role to play in the world. As we saw in earlier chapters, a crucial part of the Church's mission is to witness to the Kingdom and to anticipate it in its own life. This too is part of the Church's 'frontier mission'; it takes place on the frontier where the Church meets the secular world. This sphere of activity includes the work of the Church for the promotion of peace, of human rights, and of respect for people's culture; it takes in the commitment of the Church to working for a just economic order, for political systems that enable people to participate in decision-making, and for a style of life and development that respects the environment. In all of these matters the prophetic role of the Christian community is twofold: evils are to be denounced and the Kingdom is to be announced. I believe that in practice the best way to help the Church to exercise its prophetic role, in its positive and negative aspects, is to become involved in a training programme using some form of psycho-social approach. For this can help people to locate the basic causes of poverty and powerlessness. Equally importantly, it helps to break down the barriers of elitism and clericalism and gives real power to 'ordinary' people.

## Section Three
## Kingdom and Church

The question may be asked why this kind of 'prophetic' action for justice and authentic human development should be mentioned here as part of the 'frontier mission' of the

Church. Have I not already dealt with it as a central part of the 'caring service' of the Church? The reply is that such action for humanisation and liberation is a crucial part both of 'mission' and of 'service'. It may be recalled that when I was describing the outlook of a generation ago I noted that in the work of a foreign missionary — say, a teacher or nurse — there could be a conjunction of the current notions of 'mission' and of 'service'; much the same applies today in the case of missionaries working for human development. But now there is a much stronger theological basis for the conjunction of 'frontier mission' and 'caring service'.

This is an important point but a rather subtle one; I think I can best explain it by referring to actual cases. I have two friends who are both deeply committed to overcoming structural injustice. Both have an understanding of justice which is inspired by the Christian faith. But they have two slightly different viewpoints — each of which I consider to be valid. Patrick wants the Church to be an agent of justice in the world. He is deeply saddened whenever he finds Church leaders compromising on issues of justice or failing to take strong action. He sees the great potential of the Church and is willing to spend a lot of time and energy in animating and training Church people to work for justice. Mary is equally committed to working for justice; and her conception of justice is equally Christian. But she devotes her energies perhaps more directly than Patrick to the people around her, without thinking too much about the role of the official Church.

I want to describe these two outlooks in theological terms in order to differentiate between them. I would say that Mary's purpose is to build the Kingdom — even if she herself does not use that kind of language, but prefers simply to say she is working for justice. She is so concerned about the Kingdom that she is eager to promote it through all appropriate means — whether they be tenants' associations or peace movements or Church agencies. But she herself is a Church person, sustained in her work by the support of the Christian community. So her work is a fine example of the 'caring service' of the Church. The subjects of her care are the poor among whom she works; for them she wants a world that embodies the Kingdom values of justice and humanity. That is the main focus of her interest.

Patrick's interest, by contrast, has two focal points — his ultimate goal which is identical to that of Mary, and an intermediate goal which is that the Church should be an effective agent and witness of these Kingdom values. Patrick's work for justice, like that of Mary, is a promotion of the Kingdom and an instance of the 'caring service' of the Church. But Patrick devotes so much energy to ensuring that the Church itself be an agent and witness of justice that his outlook and motivation have a particular ecclesiastical dimension. He is concerned both that the work be done and that the Church be fully committed to it. That is why I say that his work for justice represents not only an instance of the 'caring service' of the Church but also a clear and conscious commitment to what I have been calling its 'frontier mission'. For his purpose is analogous to that of missionaries working in other cultures. Their aim is not merely to promote the Kingdom but also to establish the Church as an agent of the Kingdom and a witness to its values. Similarly, Patrick's aim is not merely to promote justice but to make the Church present as an agent of justice in an unjust world.

## Development agencies and missionaries

I have spent time teasing out the slight differences of approach between Mary and Patrick because they represent two outlooks which are common today among committed Christians. In fact an understanding of the two approaches throws a good deal of light on the relationship between missionaries and development agencies. One of the most significant features of Church life within the past generation has been the emergence of strong Church agencies founded to promote human development in the Third World. The Church authorities who gave a mandate to Misereor in Germany, Trócaire in Ireland, and similar agencies all over the world, based the definition of the role of these agencies on a distinction between 'evangelisation' and 'development'; and this in turn was a slightly more sophisticated version of the older distinction between 'the spiritual' and 'the temporal'. The distinction served a very useful purpose at the time: it helped the Church to accept its responsibility for the more secular aspects of human development. It retains a certain usefulness today in so far as

213

it makes clear that the aim of these agencies is not to build up the Church in the Third World but to support authentic human development no matter who controls the project. But it should be clear from everything that I have been saying in this book that it is far too facile to say that missionaries are concerned above all with 'evangelisation' (meaning 'spiritual' matters) while the mandate of the new agencies is 'development' (meaning secular affairs).

I think it is much closer to the truth to say that the outlook and purpose of Church development agencies is similar to that of Mary, as described above. The outlook of Patrick, on the other hand, represents that of many committed missionaries. Clearly the two have a great deal in common; and there is a basis for very close cooperation between them. Nevertheless, each has to respect the validity of the other's slightly different approach. What it means in practice is that in the effort to promote justice and human development the missionary may at times give a higher priority to working within the institutional Church. The development agency may consider at times that the project which deserves most support is one that has little or no institutional links with the local Church. It is easy to envisage how such a difference of priorities could occur in a country like India or Pakistan where Christians are a small minority: the most effective agents for the promotion of justice could well have no contact with Christianity. More controversially, this difference in priorities could also happen in a situation where the local institutional Church is tied to an unjust regime. The development agency might consider that projects sponsored by such a Church should not be supported. Missionaries might feel a commitment to continue working within such a Church in order to transform it.

## Convergence

One major conclusion that emerges from what I have been saying is that it is important not to be misled by over-simplified interpretations of the key words which are bandied about so freely. 'Development' and 'liberation' can be contrasted with 'evangelisation' if each of these terms is restricted or distorted in meaning. 'Development' may be taken to refer to merely temporal, secular progress — especially when it does nothing to challenge the existing structural injustices in society. 'Liberation' may be understood to extend merely to the political and economic sphere, while excluding all transcendent or 'spiritual' aspects. Meanwhile the word 'evangelisation' may be limited in various ways:

— it may be taken to refer mainly to a verbal proclamation of the Gospel;

— if it is extended to include witness as well as word, it may still be understood in a narrowly 'religious' way that restricts it mainly to 'spiritual' affairs;

— even if it is accepted that evangelisation impinges on secular life, it may still be assumed that it should not challenge the existing social, political and economic systems.

If the meaning of the terms is restricted in any of these ways and the two terms are then opposed to each other, one can see why Church leaders would insist on the priority of evangelisation. But if the different terms are properly defined then there will be a convergence between development and liberation on the one hand and evangelisation on the other. Such a convergence can be envisaged if one thinks of a development and liberation that extend to every aspect of the human person and the world — a process that begins in this world but finds its completion in that unimaginable culmination of human history which we call the Kingdom.

One may understand the word 'evangelisation' in a very broad sense so that it more or less coincides with the notion of development-liberation just outlined. But it seems preferable to restrict the scope of the word by taking account of its literal meaning — the bringing of 'the Gospel', 'the Good News', to all who are open to it, especially the poor. Then 'evangelisation' will refer especially to the ways in which the life and words of Christ — and his death and resurrection — illuminate the deepest meaning of human liberation and growth. Evangelisation will not then be opposed to development but will rather be the Christian *interpretation* of that process. To interpret life in this way, one does not stand back from it as an observer. Rather one has to find meaning in life by immersing oneself in the struggle to make the world human. I believe that in our world today the most powerful instrument of human liberation is the interpretation of life offered

215

by Christ and the Judaeo-Christian tradition. I find it unhelpful, then, if somebody sets evangelisation over against development-liberation and asks me which should have priority. For when each of the terms is properly understood there is no reason why we should have to choose between what they stand for. Rather than having to opt for one over the other, the enlightened Christian will be fully committed to *both*. What the Christian faith inspires us to work for is an integral human development — the fullness of life. It is the Gospel that gives the essential key to understanding what that involves. For the Gospel is the Good News of human liberation from evil of every kind, in a Kingdom that is already coming into existence by a divine power that uses us as its agents.

# 13

# Prayer in two moods —
# Freedom and Desperation

In the first chapter of this book I suggested that a balanced spirituality must be based on a conversion that has three dimensions — religious, moral, and political. Then I went on to point out the distortions that can occur when one of these three dimensions is lacking. In most of the following chapters I have tried to spell out in some detail what it means to be 'politically converted'. This is not because I believe that it is more important than the other two aspects of conversion. It is simply that many Christians find it hard to relate spirituality to the public sphere; so it seems particularly important to explain the relationship of spirituality to justice — and that is the subject of this book.

However, I am not writing simply about the spirituality *of* justice, but about spirituality *and* justice. As I pointed out in the introduction, I would like to help people to have a more integrated vision, a sense of how the different aspects of spirituality fit together and support each other. In various parts of the book I have tried to convey this sense of integration. In the first two chapters I did it in rather broad general terms. In Chapter 8 I went into more detail, trying to show how personal and interpersonal values relate to the more 'public' values which were the subject of the previous chapter. In Chapter 10, I gave an account of the psycho-social method, which sets out to help people to be more effectively converted in the personal and interpersonal spheres as well as in the public sphere. However, the main body of the book so far has been concerned with political conversion. So I feel it is now time for me to return more explicitly and thoroughly to other aspects of conversion.

The topic I want to deal with in these two final chapters

is prayer — specifically, prayer of petition. In the present chapter I hope to discuss the religious moods in which this kind of prayer can be authentically made. In the following chapter I intend to offer some reflections on the theological basis for prayer of petition, by examining the concept of providence. Prayer of petition is not a subject which is commonly related to justice. Indeed one might say that the two topics stand at opposite ends of the religious spectrum. I have seen hardly any religious or theological literature which seeks to relate the two. So I feel it is particularly important for me to attempt to link them.

In spite of all this, I have been tempted to omit these two final chapters. For I am afraid that I may fail to communicate to others what is, I suppose, a rather personal vision. I have a strong sense that the Christian commitment to working for justice and liberation needs to be combined with a rather childlike readiness to turn in petition to God. People who do not have a simple and spontaneous trust in God are likely to take themselves and their own efforts too seriously. Their dedication to human liberation is liable to be too earnest, too blinkered, perhaps too self-righteous. Hence the importance of childlike prayer of petition. On the other hand, like many others who believe that God has called us to work for justice and human liberation, I am constantly dismayed that so many Christians use prayer as a substitute for action.

What saddens me most is the awareness that people on both sides seem to see petition and action as alternatives rather than as complementary to each other. It is very hard to find anybody who has a passionate commitment to both. The witness of even one such person could inspire both those who rely on prayer of petition and those who see little point in it to reconsider their attitudes, and see if something is missing. In writing here about prayer of petition I am hoping that I may encourage readers to broaden their outlook and seek a better integration of different aspects of Christian spirituality. All through this book I have been working towards such an integration. In this chapter, however, the starting point is different. This may at first give rise to a sense of discontinuity. But I hope the connection with the previous chapters will become more obvious as I go on — and especially when I treat of what I am calling 'the prayer of desperation'. But before I come to that I must first consider the prayer that is made in freedom of spirit.

### How Jesus prayed

The example of Jesus shows us how we can pray in freedom to the Father. The Gospels make it clear that he never hesitated to heal the sick or to free those who were troubled or oppressed in spirit. The only indication that there were limits to what he could ask for is in the account of his visit to Nazareth. It is suggested that the failure of the people to believe in him left him unable to perform many marvels there (Mk 6:5-6). So the limits were set not by Jesus himself but by the people he wished to help.

There are times when Jesus seems quite exasperated that his friends do not share his own utter trust in the Father: 'How little faith you have. Why did you doubt?'; 'Why are you so frightened?'; 'How long do I have to put up with you?' (Mt 8:26; 14:31; 17:17). When his friends found themselves unable to heal one troubled boy, Jesus attributed their failure to a lack of the kind of faith that is prepared to ask to have the mountains moved (Mt 17:19-20). Indeed it would appear that what Jesus meant by 'faith' was precisely the kind of trust that enables one to ask for just anything.

There is a unique quality to the faith of Jesus: he takes it entirely for granted that, whatever he asks, God is prepared to give. There was harmony between the deepest desires of Jesus and what he knew to be God's will. So much so that Jesus was able to know the will of the Father by getting in touch with his own deepest desires. When he found himself touched by compassion for a sick or oppressed person, he took it for granted that this compassion was shared by the Father. When he experienced the urge to heal or feed the needy people around him, he did not doubt for a moment that this was what God wanted him to do.

This turns upside down the usual way in which we think about God's will. It means that Jesus did not normally have a sense of being pulled in two directions — the one in which God's will called him and the one in which his own desires would have led him. Even in his Agony, the issue for Jesus was not really whether he would do his own will or God's will; it was whether he could brace himself to complete the mission he had set himself, and which was his own deepest desire: 'Now my soul is troubled. What shall I say: Father, save me from this hour? But it was for this very reason that I have come to this hour.' (Jn 12:27; cf. Lk 12:50).

God, as known and revealed to us by Jesus, is one who wants above all to help us discover and fulfil the deepest call of our own hearts. We are not being asked to relinquish what is dearest to us but only to *discover* it. If we can really believe this, if we can approach the Father as Jesus did, then we will be healed of the awful split that mars so much of our religious experience — a split between duty and desire, between obligations imposed from outside and the call of the heart. From Jesus we learn to trust the compassion and the intuition which God has given us. In him there is no trace at all of 'the original, generic sin' which lies at the root of all other sin — namely, 'radical distrust of our Creator' (Sebastian Moore, *The Inner Loneliness*, DLT, London, 1982, pp. 82-3).

So great was the freedom of Jesus before his Father that there was no need for him to make an explicit petition on each occasion that he wished to heal or help somebody. For he was vividly aware that the Father was answering every prayer of his heart: 'My Father has given me all things' (Mt 11:27). He was speaking from his own experience when he told his followers, 'your Father knows what you need even before you ask him' (Mt 6:8). So we find that the Gospels generally present Jesus as performing his cures and other marvels on his own authority, so to speak, rather than making an explicit petition to the Father. But, in St John's Gospel, there is one special occasion when Jesus made it clear that he saw all his marvels as the response of his Father to his prayers of petition. John attributes the following words to him, just before he called Lazarus back to life: 'Father I thank you for hearing my prayer. I knew indeed that you always hear me. But I speak for the sake of those who stand around . . .' (Jn 11:41).

Quite a lot of good Christians are reluctant to make prayers of petition. Some of them feel that it is a bit childish to be constantly asking God for favours. In support of this view they recall that Jesus is reported as saying that our Father already knows what we need before ever we ask (Mt

6:8). But the real issue is not whether the Father needs to hear our requests but whether *we* need to make them. The reason for making a prayer of petition is simply to make explicit the attitude of petition that should permeate the whole life of the Christian. If we do not do so, there is a danger that we will develop a sense of independence, of reliance on our own power more than on God's.

Anybody who wishes to live according to the overall example and teaching of Jesus will adopt an attitude of petition, of reliance on the Father. At times the petition will be made explicitly — either in public or in private. At other times the follower of Jesus will simply want to stand before God with open hands — in an attitude of supplication but without formulating any specific request. There may even be times when one's faith is so strong, and one has such a vivid sense of identification with Christ — and with the Father as revealed by Christ — that one can simply 'command' that something take place.

Jesus adopted this mode of 'command' in almost all of his healing. Peter adopted the same tone when, in the name of Jesus, he healed the cripple at the gate of the Temple (Acts 3:6). Even at the present time some well-known healers adopt this 'commanding mode' when they perform cures. But that does not mean that they are no longer making a prayer of petition. The petitionary aspect has not been eliminated. But it can remain implicit precisely because the whole life of the person has become a petition — and because the healer is so utterly convinced that the 'command' is in accord with what God wants for this person.

### The Prayer of Freedom

The Gospels tell us that Jesus assured his followers that whatever they ask in prayer will be given to them, if only they have sufficient faith. Faith makes everything possible — even the moving of mountains (Mt 17:20; 21:21-22). Jesus wants his followers to be persistent in making their requests. That is the point of his parable about the friend who came late at night to look for bread (Lk 11:5-8). The message is spelled out very clearly in these words of Jesus: 'Ask and you will receive; seek and you will find; knock and the door will be opened to you' (Lk 11:9).

221

Do we really take these words seriously? Faced with the exaggerated enthusiasm of faith healers, a lot of scholars in the main Churches tend to play them down — they seem to be afraid that people will take them too literally. I have heard preachers put so much emphasis on how important it is to accept the will of God that they were, in effect, explaining away the promise of Jesus that our prayer will always be heard. I think this is a great mistake. For it can deprive people of the challenge of making almost impossible requests — and the excitement of having their prayers answered.

On the basis of my own experience I venture to claim that these passages of the New Testament can be taken seriously and literally. I have often found that, when I am in the proper mood, I can ask the Lord for anything and the prayer will be answered. It may be some trivial matter — like finding a mislaid letter or recalling sombody's name. But it is no longer trivial once it has become the occasion for prayer. It now offers me the chance to stand before God in weakness and in total trust. More importantly, it gives God the opportunity to show his endless interest in me, and his care for every detail of my life.

But, as I said, I have to be in the right mood. What this means is that I have to be free myself, and I have to be willing to leave God free. These are not two different things. Leaving God free and being free myself are just two aspects of the basic stance I have to adopt when making a genuine prayer of petition. For, of course, God is always free, whether I agree or not. The only issue is whether I am prepared to accept that he remains free; it means accepting that he can say either 'yes' or 'no' to my request.

To leave God free means having the freedom in myself to accept the answer 'no'. If I am not free, if I think that at all costs I must obtain what I want, then I will try to force God's hand, to compel him to say 'yes' to my petition. That would not be prayer at all. Efforts to manipulate God into doing what I want are magic rather than prayer. God could not allow such magic to succeed, for to do so would be teaching me the wrong lesson about what prayer is. The irony, then, is that God can say 'yes' to my prayers only when I am willing to accept that he might say 'no'. My prayer has to be a prayer of freedom. Then it can always be answered.

It would be a very different situation, of course, if I really were in a desperate plight. Suppose I were being tortured to force me to betray my faith — or my friend. Then surely I would be entitled to 'demand' that God hear my plea for help. I shall have more to say later about such a 'prayer of desperation'. But for the moment I want to stay with my more normal situation. I may be very upset because, say, the weather prevents me keeping an appointment. It seems desperately important that I get there; for otherwise all my plans will be upset. How do I face this crisis in prayer? Do I *demand* that God enable me to keep the appointment — refusing to accept that it might turn out to be a good thing that I miss it? If so, I am not praying in freedom. In fact, strictly speaking, I am not in the mood of prayer at all. And for that very reason I cannot expect to have my demand answered.

I am not really saying that God will baldly refuse this kind of petition. My experience has been that his answer is, 'no — or at least not yet'. The 'not yet' is very important. It means that even though I have been praying in a very imperfect way, God still wants to help me, wants even to grant this particular request. But he has postponed the answer, in order to lead me into freedom.

Quite often I turn to God when I am harassed by something like the loss of the key of my house. But I don't get the instant response to my prayer that comes when I pray in freedom. In such situations I generally sense, deep down below the level of my worry and upset, that God is reminding me that true prayer is made in freedom. He is bringing home to me that my situation is not as desperate as I imagine. Rather, the loss of my key is a call to me to be more flexible, more free. It upsets my previous plans — but it opens up all kinds of interesting new possibilities. If my key is not found, I may have to ask the neighbours for a bed for the night. That might be very good for me — and for them. It gives them the chance to do me a favour and it could lead to a lasting friendship. In any case it makes me less aloof, more open to dependence on the kindness of others.

There is no need to list all the other interesting opportunities opened up for me by the loss of my key. The crucial point is that it is not, as I had thought, something to be avoided at all costs. Rather it is a challenge. It calls me, as I've said, to relinquish my plans, to be open to new possibilities. Furthermore — and more profoundly — it challenges me to let go of the frustration and anxiety which have invaded me. It is this anxiety which deprives me of freedom and convinces me that my situation is desperate. As soon as I shake myself out of the anxiety, I can stand before God in freedom. I am then in the right mood to make a request. When that happens, I can almost feel God's pleasure in being able to say 'yes' to my prayer of freedom.

God refuses to be the 'answer-man', the magical slot-machine that produces the answer once the right button is pressed. He will freely grant a request made in freedom. But he refuses to be manipulated. That is because he does not want to encourage me to pray in a magical way. It is also because, if he did so, he would be pandering to my anxiety, nourishing a part of me that is less than fully human. By saying 'not yet' instead of an unconditional 'yes', God is teaching me to overcome the anxiety and frustration which diminish me as a human person.

What I have been saying about the prayer of freedom may be summed up in this paradox: God may say 'no', so long as I demand that he must say 'yes'; but once I stop imagining that I desperately need what I am asking for, then God is only too delighted to grant my request.

### Discernment

Two of the parables of Jesus encourage us to be persistent in making our petitions to God: the man who disturbed his friend at night to ask for bread (Lk 11:5-8); and the widow who pestered the unjust judge to vindicate her (Lk 18:1-5). But in each case the presupposition is that the need was genuine, otherwise the request would be a trivial or misguided one. Persistence in prayer of petition is fully justified so long as we can be sure that we are asking for what we really need. We need help to distinguish between selfish stubbornness and patient persistence in prayer. It may take us time to know what we really ought to pray for. To bring out this point let me recall an experience I had some time ago.

The sister of a good friend of mine suffered a severe brain haemorrhage and she lay unconscious in hospital for six months. I sometimes went with the family to visit her. As we prayed together at her bedside, I learned a lot about prayer of petition. The whole purpose of the medical technology and the staff was to treat the sickness of the patients. But the very singlemindedness of the effort seemed to leave little room for the patient as a person, or for the troubled family. It was quite difficult to pray in that modern aseptic hospital. The scientific equipment intimidated me, made me feel that prayer was irrelevant. My faith in God's providence was really put to the test. To pray for this dying woman in these circumstances was to make an act of almost blind faith in a personal God who cares for us as persons. I had a particular difficulty in praying in this case. The hospital staff had told me that the patient's chances of regaining consciousness were very small. And even if she did so, it was most likely that her mind would be impaired. So I hardly knew what to pray for.

The situation of the patient's family was quite different. Her daughter, for instance, had been quite shattered by the sudden collapse of her mother; and she was quite unable to face the possibility that her mother might die. Day after day she prayed in desperation, utterly convinced that the only possible answer to her prayer was her mother's full recovery. Where I found it hard to believe that God could say 'yes' to our prayer, she could not believe that God might say 'no'. As the weeks went by with no change in the condition of the sick woman I saw a gradual change in the attitude of her daughter. After six months she was no longer demanding that God cure her mother; she had come to see that this might well be the best time for her to die. So, when her mother eventually died, she was more or less ready to let her go. The regular prayer, combined with the passage of time, had led her into resignation. That might seem a rather meagre outcome for so much praying. But I believe it was as much an answer to prayer as a recovery would have been. For no recovery is final. Everybody has to face death eventually; and only God can know when is the best time.

I have recalled this incident to bring out the importance of discerning what we ought to pray for. In a way, it is a dangerous thing to make a prayer of petition, for I cannot easily know beforehand what will turn out to be good for me. I have already suggested that God wants to grant us the deepest desire of our hearts. But we need some way to discover those profound desires. This need for discernment throws light on an interesting text in St Luke's Gospel. It is one of the passages in which Jesus assures his followers that God will not refuse their requests. But the ending is unexpected: he says the Father will give the Holy Spirit to those who ask (Lk 11:13). One would have expected him to say that the Father will grant their requests for 'good things' — as he is reported as saying in the corresponding text in Matthew's Gospel (7:7-11). But instead he suddenly promises that the Holy Spirit will be given to them. The implication is that the Spirit is the best of all the 'good things' that could be given.

The Holy Spirit is indeed the greatest of gifts. For it is the Spirit that enables us to pray 'in the name of Jesus' — which means allowing ourselves to be moulded by his values and attitudes. When we 'abide in' Jesus and make our petitions 'in his name', we are assured that they will be granted (Jn 14: 12-14; 15:7, 16). The Spirit knows what is in our hearts better than we know ourselves — and can ensure that we are truly asking for our heart's deepest desire. St Paul assures us that the Spirit prays with us and in us — and even instead of us, when we are unable to pray properly (Rom 8:26). But how am I to think of God's Spirit working in me in a manner that respects my freedom? Above all, the Spirit does this by setting me free of the anxiety that distorts my vision of what I really need, the worry that deludes me into feeling that some minor matter is a life and death issue. Discernment is above all a matter of allowing the Spirit to put us in touch with our deepest centre.

*The Prayer of Desperation*

What I have been describing so far is a type of petition that is made with some freedom of spirit. No matter how persistent the request may be, there is implicit in it a certain conditional element. It is as though I were saying to God: 'Please do me this favour — if you don't mind.' The petition is rather like a request I might make of a friend, prefaced by the words, 'if it is not too much trouble'. But that is not the only mood in which we can pray the prayer of petition. There is another type of petition, one that contrasts sharply with this prayer of freedom. I call it 'the prayer of desperation'.

There is little or no freedom in the prayer of desperation. It is rather the cry of one who is in urgent need. The person who prays in this mode is one who has been deprived of the freedom of spirit that ought to characterise our relationship with God. It is important to note this element of deprivation – generally an unjust deprivation. The one who prays the prayer of desperation is somebody who is prevented from being fully human. This means that, ideally, nobody should ever have to pray in this way; for all our prayer should be made in freedom.

In a sense, then, the prayer of desperation is an inhuman and wrong type of prayer. It is the expression of a situation which should never exist. In practice, however, many people live in situations that are far from ideal. They find themselves in positions in which they cannot be fully human. They cannot pray the prayer of freedom; the best they can do is cry out to God in desperation. If I find my very humanity threatened, I react in shock and outrage. My whole being protests: 'This should not be happening.' When I cry out for rescue to God there is no room for a request that permits the answer 'no'.

If I believe in a just and caring God and I nevertheless find myself in such a desperate situation, I am entitled to be scandalised. Why should a good God allow such an outrage to occur? So not merely can I look for help but I can even rail against God, as the psalmist often does:

Will the Lord always reject me? . . .
Has he stopped loving me?
Is his promise no longer good?
Has God forgotten to be merciful?
Has anger taken the place of his compassion?
Then I said, 'What hurts me most is this –
that God is no longer powerful.'

(Ps 77:7-10)

But now, God, you have rejected us and let us be defeated . . .
You allowed us to be slaughtered like sheep . . .
You sold your own people for a small price . . .
Our neighbours see what you did to us,

227

And they mock us and make fun of us.
. . . We have not been disloyal to you;
. . . Yet you left us helpless . . .
Wake up, Lord! Why are you asleep?
Get up! Don't reject us for ever!
Why are you hiding from us? . . .

(Ps 44)

The psalms, then, teach us to be ready to pray the prayer
of desperation when it is called for — and that is a very
important lesson. It would be all too easy to sink under the
weight of the oppression, to lose heart. Crying out is already
the first step in changing things, in breaking the silence of
oppression. If I cry out against *God*, that is much more: it
is an initial act of faith, for it expresses my conviction that
there exists a God who should not allow this situation. But
the psalms teach us even more than this about the prayer of
desperation. They are not static. There is a movement, a
change of mood, even in those psalms that express broken-
ness and apparent despair. The very uttering of a cry of protest seems to lead the psalmist out of the sense of desperation,
into greater freedom.

Perhaps the best example of this kind of movement is
that which occurs in psalm 22. It begins with a cry of hopelessness and protest against God:

My God, my God, why have you abandoned me?
I have cried desperately for help, but it still does not
come . . .

Then there is a moment of relief as the psalmist recalls
how God was merciful to his people in the past: 'Our ancestors
put their trust in you . . . and you saved them; you did not
let them down.' But the writer immediately contrasts this
with his own desperate plight:

I am no longer human but only a worm
Despised and scorned by all.
All who see me mock me . . .
They say: 'You trusted in the Lord
Why does he not save you?'

Next, the psalmist recalls how he himself was helped by God

228

in the past: 'When I was a child you kept me safe.' This leads on to another plea for help:

> Do not stay away from me
> Trouble is near,
> And there is no one to help me.

The author then gives a vivid description of his suffering — bones out of joint, throat dry as dust, tongue stuck to the roof of his mouth, surrounded by enemies like a pack of dogs. This culminates in a renewed cry for help: 'Save my life from these dogs, rescue me from the lions.'

Suddenly the mood changes. The psalmist has now come to believe that his prayer will be heard. So the concluding section of his prayer is a promise to make known how God came to his help:

> I will tell the people what you have done
> I will praise you in their meeting.
> ... He does not neglect the poor or ignore their suffering ...
> All nations will remember the Lord. . .
> People not yet born will be told:
> 'The Lord saved his people!'

The movement in the psalm follows a pattern that is psychological rather than logical. It reflects the swings of mood of its author. But the overall pattern is quite obvious: there is a flow from desperation to hope, from oppression and constriction to freedom. No wonder, then, that Christ chose this psalm for his prayer on the Cross. One may assume that he also prayed it in Gethsemane on the previous evening. Certainly it reflects perfectly the pattern of his prayer there. The starting-point of the agony of Jesus in the Garden is a cry of desperation in which he admits that he finds his situation unbearable: 'My soul is sorrowful even to death.' (Mt 26:38). So he begs the Father to take away the cup of suffering. It may well have been hours before Jesus reached the second half of this sentence — 'nevertheless, not my will but yours be done.' (Mt 26:39).

In this Agony prayer of Jesus we see an ideal example of what prayer is, and what it does for the person. Christ found himself in a situation so awful that it was destroying his humanity: he was 'troubled' and 'sorrowful even to death'; 'his sweat came like drops of blood' (Mt 26:37-38; Lk 22:44). His prayer enabled him to triumph over this intolerable situation. It is an inadequate account of the Agony to present it simply as a struggle by Jesus to submit to the will of God and to do his duty. What was happening was a struggle for his own humanity, which was nearly submerged by the ordeal he faced. The hours of prayer restored his threatened humanity, his peace of soul, his freedom. His prayer left him free to be faithful to his values and his mission. He was now once again able to stand before God in full freedom of spirit. The words, 'not my will but yours be done' represent the transition from the prayer of desperation to the prayer of freedom.

*Who is desperate?*

Christ facing death for his beliefs and commitments is the classic instance of the person who must pray the prayer of desperation. But people in a much less noble situation than this may also find themselves desperate. In our own time millions of people have been turned into refugees — homeless, Stateless, deprived of human dignity, and at times literally starving. Other millions live a life that is hardly human. They include the people struggling to survive as migrant workers or unable to find work — the kind of people who are forced to flee from rural misery to urban squalor; people who are relatively lucky if they can find a shack or a make-shift tent on the fringes of great cities run by 'respectable' people. Many individuals and groups are marginalised by being deprived of their dignity and security — and other fundamental human rights.

The desperation of such people would be bad enough if they were themselves responsible for their plight. But it is made even more intolerable by the fact that they are mostly the helpless victims of forces they do not understand and can do little to change. The amazing thing is that many people in such awful circumstances continue to have hope. Their hopes are often misguided and may be quite ineffectual from a practical point of view. But they retain their humanity so long as they are able to hope. Their hope puts them in touch with a God who can give them redress. So they turn to God with desperate urgency.

230

From my limited contact with such people I have come to believe that some of them are even able to pray in a certain freedom of spirit. It is a triumph of the human spirit — and of God's grace — when any such poor and oppressed person succeeds in passing from the prayer of desperation to the prayer of freedom; but it does not change the fact that the situation remains objectively intolerable and utterly unacceptable.

Faced with the fact that so many people in this world of ours are forced to pray the prayer of desperation, I must question myself radically about my own prayer of freedom. Is it perhaps a prayer not of genuine freedom but of complacency, of sinful complicity? Does my freedom arise from a situation that drives others to desperation? If I am in any way responsible for the indignities of poverty and marginalisation inflicted on others, how can I stand freely before God? For I know that this is the God of the poor, the God who has seen the suffering of his people and is determined to come to their rescue (Exod 3: 7-8). The answer of God to the desperate cry of his oppressed people may be one that shatters the complacency of those of us who have the leisure to read or write about the prayer of freedom . . .

The obvious and most immediate reason why a great many people are in a desperate plight is the fact that our world contains so much persecution, oppression, and poverty. But having insisted on that, I want now to go on to note that the prayer of desperation is not confined to such obvious victims. Economic and political factors are not the only causes of desperation.

There are people who suffer from a depression so severe that life seems utterly meaningless and every moment is an ordeal. Perhaps it is true that such depression is caused by the person's anger turned inward; so the victim may be in some sense responsible for this terrible suffering. But even if that is true it does not lessen the desperate plight of the person — if anything, it makes it worse. The 'enemies' that surround and oppress a man or woman in this state are not external ones; but there can be no doubt that anybody who is severely depressed is being prevented from living a fully human life. It is difficult to see how such a person can make any prayer other than the prayer of desperation. The psalm prayed by

Jesus on the Cross could be very appropriate for a person who is in this state.

The depressed person is severely tempted to yield entirely to despair; to resist this temptation one must engage in a desperate struggle. In a complex and moving poem called 'Carrion Comfort', Gerard Manley Hopkins expresses something of the agony and the struggle:

> Not, I'll not, carrion comfort, Despair, not feast on thee;
> Not untwist — slack they may be — these last strands of man
> In me or, most weary, cry 'I can no more'. I can;
> Can something, hope, wish day come, not choose not to
> be . . .

At the end of the poem he appears to have come through the ordeal. He reflects on the struggle and sees it as,

> . . . That night, that year
> Of now done darkness I wretch lay wrestling with (my
> God!) my God.

This suggests that the prayer of desperation, when prayed by somebody weighed down by depression, may lead that person into a certain freedom of spirit.

There are many other causes of desperation. A couple whose marriage is breaking up may endure intense suffering. So too may a person who has been bereaved. The pain arising from sickness or injury may be so severe that the person finds it intolerable. Again, we all carry with us the traumas of our own personal history, from the moment of conception up to the recent past. This legacy may be one of desperate pain or anxiety. Furthermore, everybody has to die ultimately; and that means that each one of us has to face that desperate situation. Even the anticipation of death may generate intolerable anxiety or hopelessness.

Clearly, then, one is not protected from the state of desperation simply by being wealthy or powerful. To be human is to face the prospect of desperation, at least at times. And, if I am in a deeply reflective mood, the very awareness that I will be desperate at some time in the future must already evoke a certain sense of desperation in me at present.

The person who faces a desperate situation — whether its cause be politico-economic, or interpersonal, or purely personal — needs the support of a truly understanding friend. Indeed, anybody who has no real friends is already in a desperate situation; so the person who is left alone in facing oppression, dire poverty, severe pain, or the prospect of death, is doubly desperate. A touching incident in the Gospels brings out this point. The occasion was the anointing of the feet of Jesus by Mary of Bethany. Mary sensed the imminent death of Jesus and the anguish with which he faced this ordeal alone.

> In a gesture of the utmost tenderness she reached out to him, to heal the healer. Jesus recognised what she was doing: 'She has done a beautiful thing to me. . . . She has anointed my body beforehand for burying.' . . . Jesus had himself become poor, not least in sharing our human need to be supported and loved by others. In his mortality, he shared in the ultimate poverty of all human beings. . . . Mary's response to the poverty of Jesus shows what the Christian's response must be to the poor who are always with us, and to the poverty that is within us all.
> (Dermot Connolly, 'Mary of Bethany', in *The Ambassador* 4/3, 1983, pp. 26-7)

It may be added that those who are sensitive to the plight of the poor and oppressed are often the people who are most aware of the 'poverty' that is inherent in all of human life; and they are perhaps better able to cope with the desperation to which it can give rise. That was the experience of Jesus and of many of his followers, right up to the present day.

*Convergence*

At the beginning of this chapter I emphasised the difference between the prayer of freedom and the prayer of desperation. Later on I noted that it is of the nature of the latter to lead us back towards the prayer of freedom. Now I have added that it is of the very nature of the human situation to evoke a certain desperation. For this reason, any fully human prayer, no matter how much it is marked by freedom of spirit, must also contain a note of desperation. So there is a paradoxical quality in prayer. In describing it one needs to do a kind of juggling, in order to take account of its different aspects. But the complexity arises for the one who is doing theology, rather than for the person who is praying. The actual experience of praying is not one of complexity but of increasing simplicity.

In everyday living there are two different starting-points for prayer — the situation of desperation and the situation of freedom of spirit. But as one's prayer deepens it becomes clearer that there is a convergence. The person who begins to pray in desperation discovers a certain freedom; and prayer enables the person to become more free. Meanwhile the one who starts to pray in apparent freedom of spirit gradually finds that the human situation is inherently desperate. This means that, as one comes to appreciate more fully the fundamental nature of the prayer of petition, prayer becomes less determined by the external situation. At that point, the prayer of freedom and the prayer of desperation are no longer two totally different kinds of prayer but rather two facets or dimensions of all prayer.

The Christian attitude is one of standing before God with open hands with a sense of need and an attitude of constant petition. In this on-going prayer there may be an oscillation from freedom to desperation and back again. Sometimes when I turn to God I am so 'scattered' that I hardly know what my true feelings are. The best way forward then is to express my immediate feelings in the hope that in doing so I will become aware of those that are deeper and more authentic. So, when something goes wrong for me, I often find it very helpful to express my annoyance to God. I may begin to cry out against God, as the psalmist sometimes does, using the kind of words that are appropriate for a prayer of real desperation; 'What kind of God are you that you allow this to happen? How much longer will I have to put up with it?' Expressing my feelings in this way has a ventilating and freeing effect. Almost as soon as I begin to complain to God, I start to laugh at myself — at first ruefully and then with greater freedom of spirit. I realise that things are not really as desperate as I had imagined. Or, more accurately, I come to realise the true grounds for desperation: not the immediate situation but the fact that I allow myself to be so upset by a minor set-back.

At first I found it very hard to complain like this to God. It seemed a very risky thing to do; and in any case I had been taught to believe that annoyance was bad — and annoyance with God would almost be blasphemy. But now I am convinced that God wants me to say just how I feel. If I cry out in indignation to God, it nourishes my sense of familiarity with him. If I express shock that God would let me down, this strengthens my conviction that he is on my side.

Furthermore, having the freedom to be so open and 'easy' with God has an effect on my relations with other people. Once I get into the mood of freedom in which prayer of petition should be made, a certain lightness of touch comes into other parts of my life. Anxiety diminishes. It no longer seems so desperately important that people conform to my ideals and plans. I am more willing to allow others to be truly free — just as I have learned to allow God to be free. I find myself ready to take the risk of asking my friends for some favour; I am less afraid of becoming indebted to others. To be proudly independent is no longer my highest ideal; for prayer has taught me to accept gifts.

I hope that what I have been saying in this chapter brings out the point that prayer of petition helps a person to be more human. That is because it enables one to be more genuinely converted. Firstly, it plays a crucial role in religious conversion. That is what I have been trying to indicate during the main part of this chapter. Secondly, it can affect our relationships with others, helping us to be morally converted. That is the point I have been making in the last paragraph. But what about the third aspect of conversion — the political dimension? Some people feel that prayer of petition is used as a substitute for authentic commitment to justice and human liberation; it can encourage one to rely on God for things that we ought to do ourselves. This raises an issue which I hope to take up in the second half of the next and final chapter. But before considering that specific point, I want to examine the wider question of 'prayer and providence'.

# 14

# Prayer and Providence

I shall begin this chapter by taking up a major religious and theological issue which arises out of what I said about prayer of petition in the last chapter. The presupposition in that chapter was that it makes sense for us to ask God for favours because he can and does grant them. But now I want to ask: in what sense does God really answer our prayers? In other words, does prayer of petition really 'work'? I shall try to answer that question in the first half of this chapter. That will lead on to the topic which I shall consider in the second part of the chapter: how best to pray with people — especially the poor — in a manner that enriches their sense of God's active care for them and challenges a fatalistic conception of providence.

*Does prayer really 'work'?*

It may seem a bit late to be asking at this stage whether prayer really works. For I have already claimed that those who pray in freedom of spirit will not be refused whatever they ask. I have also suggested that people who are in utter desperation are in some sense entitled to 'demand' that God should save them, in order to show that evil does not triumph over good. I went on to suggest that one way in which the prayer of desperation can 'work' is by leading the one who prays into greater freedom of spirit. Nevertheless we may still validly raise the question whether prayer of petition is effective in bringing about what we ask for. And I want to begin the answer by making the controversial claim that in a certain sense prayer makes no difference.

An ancient Chinese saying is: 'Act as if the gods existed'. This does not necessarily imply that the gods do not exist;

but it suggests that whether they exist or not makes no practical difference. In a somewhat similar way I would want to say that God and prayer make no difference – at least in the sense of having some measurable, provable effect. I think that if prayer of petition could be shown to 'work' in the way that medicine works, then God would be 'pinned down' and would no longer be transcendent, beyond our grasp. The only God I am interested in is one that remains beyond human control. Of course it would be great (in some ways) if God were more tangible. But, as Sebastian Moore points out: 'The heart wants a God that the mind cannot grasp, and if the mind could grasp him the heart would lose interest' (*The Inner Loneliness*, 41).

We hear a good deal about 'the silence of God'. The truth is not that God is silent but that he/she refuses to be confined to my vocabulary. God, in order to be God, has to communicate at a different level from anything in the world:

. . . For God is not all
In one place, complete
Till Hope comes in and takes it on his shoulder . . .
. . . God is in the bits and pieces of Everyday . . .
(Patrick Kavanagh, 'The Great Hunger')

I need a God who is transcendent; yet I need to be in touch with that God – or, more importantly, I need to feel touched by that God. Which means that this transcendent God must also be immanent in my world. Is that a contradiction? Yes, if being immanent means that God can be located 'here at this point' as distinct from somewhere else. But transcendence and immanence are compatible if God is in touch with me not exclusively through some one or two means but through everything in the world. The transcendent God is present 'not all in one place complete' but in all 'the bits and pieces of Everyday'.

Furthermore, I want my relationship with God to be more like the way I relate to another person, a close friend, rather than how I relate to a quarry or to a slot-machine. If I want sand I dig it out of a quarry; if I want bubble-gum I put a coin in the slot. But if I want help, I go to a friend. The slot-machine may fail, but it does not say 'no'. The friend is entitled to say 'sorry, I must refuse your request'. If I do not

237

allow for such a refusal, then I am not treating that person as a friend at all but simply as a kind of machine, to be manipulated for my purposes. The relationship of friendship allows the other to be free. In somewhat the same way an authentic relationship with God presupposes freedom on both sides. That means that the results of prayer are not predictable; they cannot even be specified in the strict sense. Perhaps the point may be put like this: I want to find God reliable not in the way I may rely on a machine, but dependable as a staunch and resourceful friend is dependable — only infinitely more so.

I have been suggesting that the only kind of God that makes sense must have two characteristics:
(1) transcendence — but of a kind that still allows me to be touched by God;
(2) the reliability of a friend — as distinct from the predictability of a machine.

The notion of providence must be understood in the light of these characteristics of God; and of course the question about whether prayer of petition 'works' has to be answered in terms of a concept of providence.

*Does God intervene?*

Theologians often get caught up in what might be called 'the physics of providence'. By that I mean that they concern themselves with the question whether the idea of God 'intervening' — or interfering — in our world is compatible with the laws of science as we now understand them. They ask: is there room for miracles? Or is there room for answers to daily prayer — for favours which are not quite miraculous but are somehow beyond the effects that science would predict?

It seems to me that to approach the issue in this way is to ask the wrong kind of question. It leaves one trapped:
— On the one hand you may say that God does *not* 'intervene' in our world. This seems to leave us with an absent God, a God who is unable to help us. It deprives prayer of petition of its obvious meaning — leaving it with, at most, some psychological function, such as giving comfort or helping auto-suggestion.
— The other alternative that is offered is to say that God *does*

intervene to bend the laws of nature. This raises a double difficulty. Firstly, it casts doubt on God's transcendence — for it seems to imply that the action of God is somehow comparable to the action of other forces that are part of our world. Secondly, it raises a serious difficulty about the whole notion of 'laws of nature'. The word 'laws' in this context means predictable regularities in the spheres covered by such sciences as physics, chemistry, and biology. A miracle might be understood as a rare exception to such 'laws'. But what is one to make of the belief that God grants a vast number of 'favours' in answer to our daily prayers of petition? Are such answers to prayer to be seen as 'interventions' by God? If so, are they contraventions of the 'laws' of nature or exceptions of some kind? Would not such frequent 'interference' by God in the order of the world make nonsense of science, which presupposes that we can find a predictable pattern in nature?

I have another objection to this whole approach to the question of providence, an approach that focuses attention mainly on whether or not God 'intervenes' in our world. It is like trying to prove that somebody is really my friend by making a statistical analysis of the number of times the friend has performed the favours I asked for. This ignores the fact that a refusal of my request may also be an act of friendship. But, more importantly, it misses the central point: that the awareness of friendship has priority over the awareness of receiving favours. In fact I interpret the actions of the other person as favours precisely because I know that this person is my friend. Many actions could be interpreted in different ways — as favours or as signs of hostility, but I give my friend the benefit of the doubt. On the other hand, if I receive a favour from somebody whom I do not know to be a friend, it raises a question for me: is this really an initial act of friendship or am I perhaps being manipulated or 'bribed'?

In somewhat the same way, my belief in the love, the care, the providence, of God is in some sense *prior* to the receiving of any particular favours from God. I know, of course, that many people have come to believe in God's care for them as a result of some dramatic answer to prayer. But, no matter how one may have come to believe in providence, once that faith is there, it is not dependent here and now on receiving the answer 'yes' to all one's requests. On the contrary, it is my belief in providence that enables me to interpret each event that takes place as an instance of God's care, and an answer to my expressed or unspoken petition.

There is no such thing as a purely disinterested observer of the pattern of my life. But if there were such a person he or she would find many aspects of it open to different interpretations. Fundamentally, my sense of providence is a gift I have been given that enables me to interpret the ambiguities of life in a positive sense. There are times when everything goes well for me, and all my petitions are granted. This I experience as a palpable sign of God's constant care. Such favours nourish my sense of providence. But there are dark times too, when everything I attempt goes wrong and my prayer of petition seems to fall on deaf ears. Do I consider this to be evidence against a belief in providence? Not at all. There is no question of measuring the 'successes' in my prayer of petition against the 'failures', so as to decide on the basis of the evidence whether I should continue to believe in God's providential care. On the contrary, there are no real 'failures'. My sense of providence leads me to presume that the darkness and 'failures' and God's apparent silence all have a purpose.

There is a beautiful passage in the Bible which I have found particularly helpful in this connection. It is in the book of Judith. The town of Bethulia has been under siege and the situation is desperate. Eventually the leader proposes that if God does not hear the people's prayer within five days then they should surrender. But Judith protests:

> Who are you, to put God to the test, . . . to set yourselves above him? If you cannot sound the depths of the human heart . . . how can you fathom the God who made all things, or sound his mind or unravel his purposes? . . . Although it may not be his will to help us within the next five days, he has the power to protect us for as many days as he pleases. . . . But you have no right to demand guarantees where the designs of God are concerned. For God is not to be coerced as the human person is, nor is he, like a human, to be cajoled. Rather, as we wait patiently for him to save, let us plead with him to help us. He will hear our voice if such is his good pleasure. . . . So let us give thanks

to the Lord our God who ... is now testing us. ... This is not vengeance ... but a warning from the Lord to those who are near his heart. (Judith 8:11-27)

This passage sums up almost everything I have been saying about prayer. Judith insists that we cannot force the hand of God: he must be left free. She mentions several possible reasons why God has not yet answered the desperate prayer of the people:

— It might have been a punishment for idolatry; but in the present case she rules out that possibility (vv. 18-20).

— She suggests that it is a warning from God to his friends (v. 27).

— It may be seen as an ordeal sent to test the faith of the people as their ancestors were tested (vv. 25-7).

But, though Judith mentions these possible interpretations of God's slowness in responding, the really crucial thing is that she does not claim to know God's mind. In fact her whole point is that one cannot hope to fathom God's purposes; all one can do is turn to God in total trust. Her own belief in God's providence is so firm that she stakes her life on it. Though utterly trusting, her faith is not totally unquestioning. She sees the situation as one that calls for discernment. While accepting that she cannot comprehend God's purpose she feels impelled to search for some practical meaning or message in God's silence: — is it perhaps a punishment? a warning? a test of faith? a sign of God's friendship? We find, then, an interesting combination of total confidence with careful discernment. Belief in providence enables me to search for and find a meaning in life. The meaning I find is a provisional and tentative one that is constantly in need of being deepened and corrected. Nevertheless it is sufficient to assure me that my life so far has not been pointless; and my sense of providence gives me a sense of purpose in facing the future.

The conclusion that emerges from what I have been saying about prayer and providence is this: when my daily prayers of petition are answered, I am entitled to accept such answers as 'favours' from God, instances of providence at work in the world. But, however convincing I may find them, they cannot be cited as a proof, in the strict sense, that God hears our prayers. Those who do not share my faith may say I have simply been lucky. They are quite entitled to interpret these events as just coincidences, for that is what they are. Providence, as I understand it, means that I find sense or pattern in particular events or in series of events, which are merely coincidental from the point of view of the 'laws' of nature or science. I experience them as marks of God's care, signs of his friendship, responses to my prayer. They strengthen my conviction that God is immanent in our world — but they leave intact both the laws of science and the transcendence of God.

I have been dealing with the question of what I have called 'the physics of providence', i.e. the question of whether God has to 'intervene' in this world if our prayers are to be answered. I have noted that the word 'intervene' is misleading:
— it suggests that any involvement by God would have to come from outside our world;
— it also suggests that the action of God would be comparable to the action of any of the causes that operate within the world.
My conception of providence allows me to hold that God is present and active all the time in our lives and our history — but in a unique way. God is not a manipulator. If I pray that I will not have a car crash or that the pain of somebody's cancer will be relieved, I am not asking that God push or pull the driving wheel of the car or the nerves of the sick person's body. If I pray to God that I may pass an examination, I am not expecting that some subtle pressure will be brought to bear by God on the mind of the examiner. I am not asking that there be any exception to scientific laws or the natural order. What I am asking for is that the conjunction of events will form a particular pattern.

Those who think of the universe as a gigantic clockwork mechanism will still insist that every event that happens is rigidly determined; and that the pattern is no more than the sum of all the events. But science no longer presupposes such a mechanistic view of the world. There is a lot of randomness in the world and plenty of room for coincidences. Science can 'explain' the occurrence of such things as metal fatigue or human exhaustion. But scientific explanations include, implicitly or explicitly, the proviso, 'all other things being equal'. In other words, the scientific explanation of a given event focuses attention on certain factors that led up to it (generally those which are frequently present). But the scientist does not take account of factors that are thought of as random or not intrinsic to the situation.

The car in which I am travelling may meet another car at a dangerous bend; alternatively, the meeting may occur at another point on the road. In the former case there would be an accident but not in the latter. The avoidance of this accident does not require a contravention of the laws of physics. And the scientific 'explanation' of an accident concentrates on such measurable and repeatable factors as metal fatigue or human exhaustion; but it does not normally take account of all the random factors that led to the meeting of the two cars at that particular part of the road (e.g. the decision of one of the drivers to stop en route for a meal, or the fact that one of the cars was delayed because of an earlier accident). Similarly, there are very many healings which can take place without any bending of the laws of physics, chemistry, or biology; all that is required is a certain conjunction of events. What I am praying for may be quite an unusual pattern. One way of expressing it might be to say I am praying for a coincidence. The Lord of Providence is the master of coincidence.

*Psychic Energy*

I have no doubt that prayer can at times have most extraordinary effects. Quite a lot of people have been cured mysteriously when they were praying or being 'prayed over'. In my own experience, there are times when I 'know' that a prayer of mine will be effective; for instance, when I pray that I may find something I have mislaid I very often experience a sense of composure during which I can immediately put my hand on the missing object. Prayer can also give one an ability to discern the core of another person's problem. Even more frequently it enables one to speak intuitively without any rational discernment; and in speaking like this one often says the very thing that the other person needed to hear. All these are effects of prayer that seem to come from getting in touch with some generally untapped source of inner life or psychic power in us. We know very little about such powers and how to use them. They are not easily amenable to study by the usual scientific methods — though some attempts have been made to do so. I do not think they can be accounted for entirely in conventional psychological terms e.g. by speaking of hysterical or psychosomatic illness cured by the power of suggestion. Obviously, psychosomatic factors are involved; but prayer can at times put us in contact with some source of energy that is cosmic in scope. There are even some grounds for claiming that prayer can 'cause' things to happen in the physical world, where psychosomatic explanations are inappropriate (e.g. changes in the weather).

I have not mentioned such effects of prayer until now because I believe it is important to deal first of all with the question of providence. I have noticed that people who concentrate attention on the psychological or psychic effects of prayer seem very often to reduce prayer to a kind of technique for getting what they want. They seem to empty it of its deepest religious content. For instance they may understand prayer as a way of relaxing; or as a means of 'visualising' the kind of cure we are looking for, and in this way of 'encouraging' the body to heal itself. Such visualisation certainly seems to work, at least for some people. But when prayer is seen as a technique — whether it be to heal myself or others or simply as a way of calming myself down and coping with stress — then the central core of prayer has been left out. One will be thinking solely in terms of some form of 'worldly' causality, however mysterious. This means that one is not facing up to the central theological issue of whether there can be such a thing as a divine providential causality. And if I see prayer in this way I will be aiming to harness some spiritual power rather than committing myself in trust into the hands of the living God.

But, having tried to take seriously both the religious and the causal aspects of providence, I can now afford to emphasise the psychological and psychic effects of prayer, without the danger of explaining away its most important elements. From a religious point of view the psychic effects of prayer are secondary — perhaps even a side-effect. Nevertheless, they can be very important. Needless to say, the operation of this worldly causality is in no way in conflict with divine causality. Indeed it is only to be expected that God would answer our prayer by making use of 'worldly' causality. Furthermore, the person who gets in touch with this kind of psychic energy is not very likely to have a purely mechanistic view of the world. The one who is sensitive to spiritual energies is opened up in some way to God.

But there are dangers here, too. Sensitivity to psychic or spiritual energy is a two-edged sword. While one would normally expect it to make the person more deeply religious, it is also possible that it will be abused in the interests of exercising power over others. There are some people in whom there seems to be a strange mixture of the good and the bad aspects. They may, for instance, be exercising a healing ministry which is genuinely religious; but this may co-exist with a kind of spiritual arrogance or domination that must be seen as a distortion of the Christian faith.

When faith-healers seek to cure somebody they often build up tremendous psychological pressures both in themselves and in the persons they want to heal. They do this partly by their commanding presence and urgent style of prayer. But in addition they often suggest that what people require in order to be healed is simply a belief that they will be healed — or are already healed; they say or imply that it is only weakness of faith that prevents the cure taking place at once. I am inclined to believe that extreme pressure of this kind can sometimes cause the sick person to get in touch with some inner reserve of energy which may bring about the desired cure. But in many cases this does not happen; then not only do the patients remain unhealed but they have to carry the added burden of being told that they are lacking in faith.

This kind of prayer, whether it 'works' or not, is, in my opinion, not a good thing from a religious point of view. It smacks too much of putting pressure on God; and it also seems somehow disrespectful to the sick person, since it subjects him or her to extreme pressure. The 'successes' of faith-healing of this kind do not prove that it is the proper way to pray. The one who prays like this is stirring up in the patient a desperate need to be healed. In effect, such 'healers' are turning what ought to be a prayer of freedom into a prayer of desperation. The person who is driven by a sense of desperation may find an extraordinary way out: a remarkable recovery may take place. But this still does not justify the means used.

Desperation can be a spur to superhuman achievements.

This applies not merely in such personal matters as healing, but also in the political field. Some of the greatest feats of bravery and endurance in human history were carried out by people who found themselves in desperate straits. When people in such situations cry out to God in the prayer of desperation, the answer from God may not always be the removal of the evil. The desperate person may instead discover inner resources of energy, courage, and peace which enable him or her to triumph over the evil. That too is an answer to prayer — the kind of answer given to Jesus in his Agony.

But it is one thing to find oneself in desperate straits and quite a different thing to stir up a sense of desperation about some situation where it is uncalled for. Those who act in this way may succeed in gaining remarkable results — whether in curing sickness or simply in carrying out some task on which they have set their hearts. But they do this at the cost of manipulating themselves and introducing a kind of dishonesty into their lives. Furthermore, it is dangerous to use desperation as a weapon or tool. Its good effects are unpredictable; and it always has one bad effect — it deprives the person of that freedom of spirit which is so fundamental to truly human living.

Does this mean that we should not attempt to tap that inner source of energy which the desperate person can sometimes touch? Not at all. I think it can be touched in a better and safer way — a way that is the very opposite of the way of desperation. It is the way of freedom. People who have attained a high degree of inner freedom often find that they are 'tuned into' a hidden source of life and energy which produces remarkable effects. These are the powers of healing and discernment I mentioned at the beginning of this section. They can be brought into play without any great effort or strain. Indeed they often function best when the person is not trying to 'harness' them at all. This may be because they spring from a level of the personality which is not easily amenable to conscious control. But it also has a religious significance: they come in response to a 'prayer of freedom' and so they are more likely to come in the form of a free favour than as the result of something one has worked for.

246

*Praying with people*

Christians often ask their ministers or leaders or friends to pray for them — for healing or some other favour. I would like here to consider how best one may respond to such requests, in the light of what I have been saying about providence. The first thing to be said is that such requests should not be refused or played down. Secondly it is not enough for me to promise to pray for the person and then go off and do it on my own. In Africa I have learned that when people ask me to pray *for* them they normally want me to pray *with* them, to lead them in prayer; and that is a lesson that can be applied in other places besides Africa.

If I do agree to lead somebody in prayer, I am undertaking a particular kind of ministry: I am performing a service, trying to meet the other person's need rather than my own. So I have to take time to understand that need, and have some sense of the roots of the person's anxiety. I must 'be with' the person in this time of need. And that presence must be evident both in the way I listen and in the way I pray. Suppose I am filled with a vivid sense of the presence of God just at the time when somebody comes to me in deep darkness of spirit; it would be both insensitive and futile for me to try at once to get the other to share my religious experience by beginning to pray out of the 'place' I am at. Rather I have to exercise what I would call 'ministerial solidarity'. This means somehow getting inside the feelings and mood of the other — and using that as the starting-point for the prayer.

In practice it is quite likely that those who ask me to pray for and with them are suffering from some serious anxiety or trouble. In that case the appropriate thing for me to do is to lead the person in a 'prayer of desperation'. This enables the person to have the comfort of feeling that somebody else knows what they are enduring. It also helps the person to identify with the prayer that is being said and to be led along by it. Passages from the psalms are particularly helpful, since they express the desperation of the person in a language that is not only very vivid but is also poetic and allegorical. This means that it can 'carry' a variety of different meanings — even things that the person would not dare to say openly. Certain parts of the psalms express disappointment and even anger against God. By using some of these passages one is encouraging people to admit to themselves that that is how they feel; they can allow their real feelings of hurt and frustration to be openly experienced and expressed.

'Ministerial solidarity' means more than just sharing other people's present pain and frustration. It aims to lead them out of desperation and into freedom of spirit. There can be no readymade formula for a prayer of this kind. The pattern of the prayer will have to be tailored to the response of those involved. If I try to push on too quickly to the desired outcome, I may leave people behind; or, worse still, I may create in them a kind of false consciousness — 'forcing' them to have the feelings and attitudes I am proposing. It is preferable to stop short of an ideal conclusion unless that expresses their real feelings.

There is an interesting psychology in many of the psalms. They do not move directly from desperation to peace of mind. Instead, the psalmist begins to praise God. This is a first step towards freedom of spirit: it takes one's mind off the immediate situation and gives a wider perspective in which the present situation may seem less desperate. It can be very helpful to follow this pattern in prayer with people who are deeply troubled. It helps one to avoid manipulating their feelings while at the same time inviting them to look beyond their present desperation.

Some years ago a book called *From Prison to Praise* was very popular in pentecostal and charismatic circles. The author maintained that the one certain way of obtaining any request was to praise God. The *simpliste* style of the book irritated me at the time; it sounded as though praising God were some kind of magic formula. But now I am inclined to think that the author had hit on a very important point. If I am able to praise God authentically (and not just in words) then I am no longer totally fixated on my own desperate situation; I have attained a real freedom of spirit — and therefore (as explained in the previous chapter) God can answer my request.

The kind of authors who write about praying with people almost always belong to the charismatic or pentecostal school of thought. This is a great pity. It means in practice that praying with people is associated almost exclusively with a kind of spirituality that focuses most attention on the personal aspects of the Christian faith. For it must be acknowledged

248

that the pentecostal tradition has generally been inclined to promote a rather individualistic kind of piety. It has not concerned itself in any very constructive way with political matters or the issues of the wider society.

There is no reason at all why prayer for people should be confined in this way to one tradition and to one area of life. I have suggested in the previous chapter that the primary instances of desperation are those millions of people who are poor, oppressed, and marginalised. These, above all, are the people who can benefit from prayer. There are very good grounds, then, for praying in solidarity with such people — and for being willing to lead them in the prayer of desperation.

*Praying with the poor*
A crucial question arises at this point: what should I ask for when I pray with people who are oppressed or desperately poor? Should I encourage them to pray to God to take away their troubles? That is the kind of prayer that really annoys many of those who are committed to the struggle for justice. Their main objections to it can be summed up in two closely related points:
— They see it as an escapist form of prayer. For it can give people the illusion that they are doing something to change their situation when in fact they are making no practical effort to deal with the source of their problems.
— The second objection to this kind of prayer is that it encourages a passivity that is rooted in fatalism: if the prayer is not answered, people will think that God approves of the evils they have to endure.

These are very cogent objections. So it seems to me that anybody who prays with the poor ought to do so in a way that does not encourage escapism or fatalism; indeed the prayer itself should help people to overcome these temptations. The only proviso is that this should not be done in an arrogant way. The need to be sensitive to 'where people are at' is particularly important in the case of very poor or marginalised people, who feel that nobody respects them. This means that one may have to begin with a form of prayer in which one begs God to take away the trouble. But in the course of the prayer one can endeavour to raise the consciousness of the person or group.

249

The poor can be helped to see that their suffering is not part of God's plan, nor is it the result of the order of nature; it arises mainly from the injustice of individuals or society. Of course, most people who are crushed by poverty are well aware that they are being mistreated and exploited. But quite commonly that awareness is not allowed to surface in their *prayer*. An escapist and fatalistic type of religion creates in the poor a kind of self-deception or false consciousness, one that smothers the sense of injustice that they feel. Authentic prayer does not therefore have to set out to stir up anger and a sense of injustice in people. The task is simply to facilitate them in getting in touch with their real feelings and expressing them honestly to God. Prayer is not to be reduced to political education; but what is in question here is, rather, a religious education. The poor are to be helped to understand the nature and concerns of the true God.

Perhaps no religious concept has been so abused as that of providence. A false conception of God's will has been invoked to justify colonial conquest, racism, the gross exploitation of the poor by the rich, and shameless abuses of political and even ecclesiastical power. The clearest examples can be found in the history of Latin America over the past few hundred years. There is one important point to note about the distorted notion of providence that was brought to that continent — and indeed to the rest of the Third World as well. It was not simply that a fatalistic piety was given to the poor and oppressed — one that taught them to accept their sufferings as the will of God. There was also the other side of the coin: the colonial soldiers were taught to believe that they were the agents of God in their conquest. A passive version of providence marked the religion of the poor while a very active version of it legitimated the oppressive actions of the oppressors. The main aim of a liberating religion must be to correct these distortions.

In Chapter 3 of this book I gave an account of the God that was glorified by Mary in her song of praise (Lk 1:46-55). This is a God who is actively involved in rescuing the poor from those who oppress them. To proclaim one's faith in such a God is to challenge the distorted notion of providence which I have outlined above. Any religion or theology which encourages people to work for justice and liberation must have an explicit or implicit teaching on providence. But many Third World theologians seem to be rather reluctant to speak very explicitly about providence. I suspect that this is partly because they have not fully freed themselves from the inadequacies of recent Western theology. But another reason may be that they fear that the concept 'providence' cannot be rescued from the distortions of the past; it remains too tied up with fatalistic attitudes. I believe, however, that the notion of providence, and even the word itself, are too important to be abandoned. It is better to mount a direct challenge to the wrong teaching of the past. The Bible provides an abundance of material for a positive and active concept of providence, one that underpins our efforts to promote human liberation.

In the Old Testament the Exodus story is the primary instance of active involvement by God in the liberation of his people. It is frequently recalled by the psalmist when he finds himself crushed by enemies and turning in desperation to God:

> In the day of distress I cry out to the Lord;
> I groan and am discouraged.
> . . . Will the Lord reject me for ever?
> . . . But then, Lord, I remember your great deeds
> You led your people like a shepherd
> With Moses and Aaron as their leaders.

> (Ps 77)

We have every reason to follow the same pattern in our prayer with those who are oppressed today.

The Bible offers many instances of prayers of desperation said by people setting out on an apparently hopeless task of resistance to oppression. These can be both a source of inspiration and a model for our own prayer. Among the more striking examples are the prayers of two brave women — Judith and Esther (Judith 13:5-7; Esther 4:19: 'O God, whose strength prevails over all, listen to the voice of the desperate . . .'); and the final prayer of Samson (Judges 16:28). Other notable prayers of desperation are to be found in the two books of the Maccabees (1 Macc 3:51-3; 2 Macc 13:10-12) and in the Book of Daniel (3:40).

The presupposition of all these prayers is that God is

251

actively involved in directing the course of human history — and that his saving power is exerted on behalf of the poor and the weak. It is important to note, however, that God's answer to the prayer of the desperate is hardly ever a direct miraculous intervention. Rather, the prayer is answered by a strengthening of the person's own courage and determination. One of the best correctives for a fatalistic or escapist conception of providence is familiarity with these biblical stories and prayers. If we model our prayers of petition for people on these prayers, and our prayers of thanksgiving on Mary's song of praise (Lk 1:46-55), then we will be inculcating a correct understanding of divine providence. It will inspire people to take responsibility for their lives and to work to overcome evil in society.

Once the poor become active in the struggle for justice, it could be very useful to borrow some of the charismatic techniques of prayer. For instance, when a few people are about to lead a protest march, the group could impose hands on them, and pray over them for courage and protection. There are times, too, when it would be opportune to pray for healing of various kinds. For example, when 'the security forces' use violence against protesters, people are likely to suffer not merely from bodily injuries but also from deep resentment. Such resentment gnaws at the human spirit and deprives people of inner freedom; so it is good to pray that they be healed of it.

In praying with those who are poor and desperate one might well use a version of the Lord's Prayer, expanded to apply to their situation: 'Our Father. . . . May your Kingdom come, and may we be active in promoting it — a Kingdom of peace and love, founded on true justice. . . . Give us this day our daily bread, and strengthen us in our efforts to build a world where we all have the opportunity to earn our bread through meaningful work, where nobody has to go hungry, and no group lives in luxury while others starve. Forgive us our trespasses — our failure to believe in your Kingdom and your call to us to bring it about, our sinful apathy in the face of injustice, our failure to work together, our dissipation of energy in fruitless resentment rather than courageous challenge. Lead us not into temptation: do not test us beyond our strength by leaving us in our desperate situation. But

252

deliver us from evil: lead us out of bondage as you led your
people in the past out of slavery and into the Promised Land;
raise up leaders for us as you called Moses and Deborah,
Judith and David; inspire and strengthen them to lead us into
freedom.'

## Facing Death, Facing Life

Of course the greatest and most moving prayer of desperation is the prayer of Jesus in his Agony. There may well come
a time when the poor and those who struggle with them for
justice have to pray as Christ prayed at that time. It is the
prayer of one who knows that, from a practical point of view,
he has failed; the only way forward for him is to be true to
his call to the bitter end. He prayed for the courage to face
death with the single-mindedness he had displayed throughout his life.

There are some people today whose commitment to justice
puts them in a position here and now where the Agony prayer
of Jesus is the best model for their prayer. However, there is
a danger here. We may fail to distinguish clearly between two
situations of desperation. On the one hand there is the
'normal' desperate situation of people who live in poverty
and oppression. On the other hand there is the ultimate
desperation of the one who faces death in rejection and
failure, as Jesus did. If we confuse the two, we may make the
mistake of trying to decide how we want to die before we
have determined how we want to live. I believe that Christians
have often made this mistake in the past. We have tried to
develop a spirituality of death and failure without first paying
sufficient attention to a spirituality of struggle against failure.
This causes a serious 'short-circuit' in our understanding of
the Christian faith; and it helps to explain our failure to
develop an adequate spirituality of liberation.

We learn from Jesus the importance of discerning one's
purpose and mission in life before trying to face the problems
of failure and death. The Gospels tell us that before beginning
his public life he went out into the wilderness to be tempted
(Mt 4:1-11). This was his time of discernment, the time when
he articulated the values he stood for, and planned his
strategy; for instance, he resisted the easy options of seeking
glory and power. In the years that followed he tried his best

not merely to live by his values but to succeed in his mission. His initial success as an itinerant preacher and healer did not last; there were few who shared his vision; and those in power saw him as a threat. As opposition mounted, he changed his strategy, concentrating more attention on his immediate followers. But it became clear that he was not going to be a 'success' in the obvious sense. So he turned his face to Jerusalem and the ultimate test. The night before he was put to death he faced that challenge alone. As his enemies exerted their full power to overcome him, he sought desperately for the courage to face death with the same integrity as he had shown in discerning his mission in life. That was his Agony prayer. It does not make sense in isolation but only as the culmination of his life.

Like Jesus, I must first decide how I want to live; then in due time I may, like him, have to make a clear choice about how I shall face death. At present, the only really authentic decision I can make about my death is the one that is implicit in my choice of what I stand for in life. From the life of Christ I learn that it is crucial to discern how best to devote my life to bringing Good News to the poor, and liberty to those who are oppressed in any way. If this discernment leads to a life of commitment modelled on that of Christ, I may face the future with confidence. I can be assured that when I eventually have to face the ultimate desperation of death then I, like Jesus, will be given the grace to be consistent to the end.

At the end of the last chapter I made the claim that prayer of petition can make us more human by nourishing our conversion in its religious and moral aspects. I left over the question whether it helps or hinders conversion in its public or 'political' aspect. I hope that what I have been saying in this chapter provides an answer to that question. I have tried to show that, at its best, prayer of petition is not a distraction from political conversion but rather a powerful means of promoting it. Properly used, it nourishes an authentic sense of providence in those who seek to overcome poverty and injustice. It challenges apathy and fatalism, and gives the poor a new confidence in themselves and a strong sense of mission. It leads them to see themselves as chosen instruments of God, called to follow Jesus in bringing about God's Kingdom of justice and peace. Each of them can say with Christ:

The Spirit of the Lord is upon me;
he has chosen me to bring good news to the poor,
to proclaim liberty to the captives,
and recovery of sight to the blind,
to set free the oppressed
and to announce that the time has come
when the Lord will save his people.

And, like Christ, they can add: 'This passage of scripture is coming true today as you listen to it.' (Lk 4: 18-20)

# Index

258

economic power in, 53, 155
exploitation of, 53-4, 59, 65
and liberation, 149
poverty in, 53-4, 65-6
Third World theology, 37, 46-7,
164-6
and commitment to liberation,
39, 40-1
as a proclamation of personal
faith, 37-40
see also black theology; feminist
theology; liberation theology
trade
and debt, 135
and self-sufficiency, 134, 137
Trócaire, 193, 194

unemployment, 114-15
United Nations Confernce on Trade
and Development, 134
unity of human race, 104-7

values of the Kingdom of God, 96-8,
102, 103
in personal sphere, 119-29
in public sphere, 104-18
Vatican and episcopal authority, 162
Vatican II, 199, 200
voluntary simplicity, 140-1
spirituality of, 142-5

Welfare State, 67
Wenger, Susanne, 122
Western theology
and colonialism, 44
and the conscience, 32
see also theologians
women theologians in the Third
World, 172-3
work as a Kingdom value, 114-15
World Council of Churches, 111, 117

Yahweh, God as, 87-8